WOMEN IN EDUCATIONAL ADMINISTRATION

CHAROL SHAKESHAFT

SAGE PUBLICATIONS
The Publishers of Professional Social Science
Newbury Park Beverly Hills London New Delhi

For information address:

SAGE Publications, Inc.
2111 West Hillcrest Drive
Newbury Park, California 91320

SAGE Publications Inc.
275 South Beverly Drive
Beverly Hills
California 90212

SAGE Publications Ltd.
28 Banner Street
London EC1Y 8QE
England

SAGE PUBLICATIONS India Pvt. Ltd.
M-32 Market
Greater Kailash I
New Delhi 110 048 India

Printed in the United States of America

Library of Congress Cataloging-in-Publication Data

Main entry under title:

Shakeshaft, Charol.
Women in educational administration.

Includes bibliographies and index.
1. Women school administrators. 2. Sexual division of labor. I. Title.
LB2831.6.S53 1986 371.2'0088042 86-6634
ISBN 0-8039-2664-2

Contents

Acknowledgments

What follows in this book is what I think I know now about women in school administration. However, I am aware that if I am doing things right, what I think I know will change as I continue to try to understand the implications of gender for women in organizations.

Portions of this book have appeared in other shapes in "A Female Organizational Culture" (*Educational Horizons,* Spring 1986); in "Androcentric Bias in the *Educational Administration Quarterly*" (with Majorie Hanson; *Educational Administration Quarterly,* Winter 1986); in "Strategies for Overcoming Barriers to Women Administrators" (*Handbook for Achieving Sex Equity Through Education,* Sue Klein, Ed., Johns Hopkins University Press, 1985); and in "Research on Theories, Concepts, and Models of Organizational Behavior: The Influence of Gender" (with Irene Nowell; *Issues in Education,* Winter 1984).

There are many people who have helped me to concentrate my thinking about women in school administration, and I would like to thank them for their guidance and encouragement. The National Academy of Education, through its Spencer Fellowship Program for junior scholars, recognized the importance of the research by naming me a Spencer Fellow alternate. Several scholars and friends took the time to read and comment upon various forms of this manuscript and for their advice and feedback I would like to thank Donna Barnes, Sari Knopp Biklen, Ley Browder, Selma Greenberg, Maxine Greene, Daniel Griffiths, Nona Lyons, James F. McNamara, Robert Neidich, Irene Nowell, Robert Owens, Mary Anne Raywid, Toni Rea, Patricia Schmuck, Timothy Smith, Philip West, and Donald Willower.

Assistance from others came before there was a manuscript to read. Janet Wagner helped me locate hard-to-find and little-known studies and historical documents. Joan Formisano, Johanna Schwencke, and Valentine Titus were research assistants without whom it would have taken me much longer to locate the literature on women administrators. Johanna Schwencke noted that I was technologically barren and helped to bring me into the 1980s. Irene Nowell and I worked very closely on many of the ideas contained in this book, and I am particularly grateful for her work, some of which is represented in Chapter 5. Patricia Schmuck encouraged me as far back as my doctoral work, and she was joined by others—Sari Biklen, Pat Campbell, Dolores Grayson, Jean Greggs, Margie Hanson, Susan Klein, Marcia Linn, Eleanor Rofheart, Liora Schmelkin, Frances Smith, Gail Smith, Gerald Smith, Roberta Trachtman, Julia Van de Water, and Sandy Walsh—who kept me focused. The students in my classes, particularly the "Women in Administration" class, and the women administrators who allowed me to share their conversations provided not only data but inspiration as I came to understand the continuing courage and persistence they demonstrate by living their lives.

And finally, I was fortunate enough to be part of a nurturing female environment that sustainedd me. At Hofstra University, I function in a School of Education whose faculty is predominantly female. My dean, Lois Beilin, provides me with daily proof that women can and do administer from a female perspective. My colleagues Donna Barnes, Selma Greenberg, Mary Anne Raywid, and Liora Schmelkin offer me a supportive refuge when I need it. Loretta Mears gave me editorial, bibliographic, and political advice, in addition to both comfort and encouragement. Throughout the long process, the anticipation of the arrival of my daughter, Emma Shakeshaft, served as the motivator I needed to finish. But it was Sarah Meyland who offered the day-to-day support that afforded me the time to think, read, and work on this project, and I thank her the most.

Introduction

"A wild patience has taken me this far" might well be an appropriate motto for the women who have become school administrators during the last century. A phrase from an Adrienne Rich poem (1981), "wild patience," evokes an image of dedication, persistence, energy, and expectation constrained by a world that neither values nor rewards the women who live these contradictions. Societal memory records a time when all teachers were women and most administrators were too. But has memory reconstructed history? Were women always administrators? If so, what happened to them? Who were these women and who are they now?

Answers to these questions aren't easy to find. The traditional literature in school administration largely ignores women. It tells us little about their past or present lives, nor do we hear of their struggles. This book was written as a response to that vast quantity of literature published on administration and administrators that purports to be comprehensive—a more honest description of it might be research and writing on the behavior and characteristics of male administrators. Generalizing to all administrators from male behavior would not be problematic if there were no differences between women and men in administration or if women never served as principals or superintendents. However, we know that women school administrators have always existed and that there is a rich literature indicating that men and women in educational administration have neither a shared history nor identical experiences.

Because the bulk of the literature on women is not found in easily accessible sources but rather in dissertations, ERIC documents, and unpublished papers and because it has not been incorporated into the traditional writing of the field (Nagle, Gardner, Levine, & Wolf, 1982; Schmuck, Butman, & Person, 1982; Tietze, Shakeshaft, & Davis 1981), there is a need to assemble the research on women in school administration. My purpose has been to collect and synthesize this literature in one place in an attempt to document the experiences of women administrators so that we may begin to expand the theory and lore of the field to include them.

The following pages represent a first step that asks us to reconsider what we know about organizational behavior. It asks us first to learn of the world of women in schools and then to speculate upon what would happen if we took that world into account when we developed theory and practice in school administration.

Although there are a number of recent books focusing on the topic of women in management in the business world, there are very few books available on the topic of women in educational administration. Some excellent publications have focused on the woman administrator (Biklen & Brannigan, 1980; Ortiz, 1982; Schmuck, Charters, & Carlson, 1981), but missing from this literature is a comprehensive synthesis of current research on women in positions of formal educational leadership. Further, no book addresses the inadequacy of organizational theory, lore, and advice for women. Nowhere has anyone presented a large-scale analysis of the ways in which theories and advice based upon male samples and male experience may not be appropriate for women.

To help us think about a reconceptualization of the theory of the field, an attempt has been made in this book to bring together as much as possible of what we know about women in educational administration. I have drawn upon three kinds of data. The first is a synthesis of research literature—dissertations, journal articles, ERIC documents, and unpublished papers—on women in educational administration. These studies were located using formal and informal bibliographic procedures. Both hand and computer searches were undertaken. The major strategy for identifying dissertations was to systematically check *Dissertation Abstracts International* from 1970 to 1985. Titles of articles and dissertations were sought in the indexes to dissertations and journal articles under the following headings: educational administration, female, feminine, feminism, feminist, sex, sexism, sex-role, sex role, sexuality, woman, and women. Any study that related to women administrators in any educational setting and at any level was selected for synthesis. Further, research outside the educational milieu that studied women in management was included.

Five models for synthesis have been used in this work on over 200 dissertations and 600 research articles. The overall model of integration follows that of Maccoby and Jacklin (1974) in their book *The Psychology of Sex Differences*. Particular methods of synthesis of findings include listing of factors, taking a vote, averaging the statistics, and meta-analysis, each used when appropriate for the data available.

It has been the dissertation, more than any other source, that has provided research on women in administration. Dissertation literature is perhaps an appropriate genre for the integration of studies because, by its very nature, it indicates the trends of a discipline. In the ideal it reflects the newest directions and current interests within a field. Additionally, a study by Campbell and Newell lends support to the idea that much of the cutting edge of educational administration research is found in the dissertation for the reason that "professors of educational administration engage in many activities, but they appear to have little time for, or inclination toward research" (1973, p. 139). For these reasons, dissertation research would appear to be an important area in which to undertake a synthesis on women in administration. Nevertheless, dissertation literature has its limitations (Shakeshaft & Saffer, 1984) and thus restricts what we know and how we know it. It is somewhat reassuring that the findings of the dissertation literature are supported by the published work in educational administration and management. However, it is fair to say that the literature on women in educational administration could profit from increased methodological and conceptual rigor, an observation often made of the research in the field in general.

The second source of data presented consists of research that I have been doing over the past seven years on women in administration. Some of the work has been published or presented at scholarly meetings previously, but most is discussed here for the first time. This work includes mail surveys, observational, and interview studies—all of which try to discover how women view their worlds. The strongest of this data are the interviews of over 100 women administrators and administrators-to-be that were conducted between 1979 and 1985. These voices have helped me to understand the world of women in schools more clearly as well as to ask questions of the theory and lore of the field that would not have presented themselves had I not heard the women speak.

The third source of evidence comes from my personal experience in directing a program for women in educational administration from 1980 to 1986 (Shakeshaft, Gilligan, & Pierce, 1984). This project has given me valuable insights into what works and doesn't work for women administrators as well as providing me with further accounts from the women themselves.

This is not a book on how to make it in administration, neither is it a book instructing women to be more like men. If anything, it is a book that asks us to question the assumptions of the so-called "self-help" tracts that have first analyzed how men manage and then urged women to do the same. I am saying something quite different in this book. The effective woman does not copy the effective man, neither does she find that what works for him necessarily works for her. This book attempts first to pull together in one place much of what we have learned from research about the woman school administrator and then to use that information to challenge administrative theory and advice to be reconceptualized to include both women and men. It also suggests that schools might profit if all administrators—men as well as women—borrowed from the strategies and practices more traditionally associated with women. By focusing on women administrators, by addressing facts conventionally ignored or taken for granted, I hope to provide a background that will allow us to reappraise organizational theory so that we can eventually come to a larger understanding of human life in organizations. As Rosaldo and Lamphere (1974, p. vi) have noted, we must "integrate an interest in women into a general theory of society and culture."

The literature synthesized in this book progresses through six stages essential in the evolution of a paradigmatic shift, stages similar to those involved in curriculum change reported by Schuster and Van Dyne (1984). Table i.1 presents these stages and the research questions they represent in the literature on women and school administration.

The first stage documents the lack of women in positions of administration, providing the reader with information about where women are and aren't in the school hierarchy. This stage is guided by such questions as: "How many women are in school administration?," and "What kinds of positions do they hold?" The second

TABLE i.1

Stages of Research on Women in Administration

Stage	*Questions*	*Approach*	*Outcome*
1. Absence of women documented.	How many women are in school administration? What positions do they hold?	Surveys that count.	Documentation of numbers by administrative position.
2. Search for women who have been or are administrators.	What are the characteristics of the women who are in school administration? What is the history of women in school administration?	Surveys of women administrators. Historical research that uncovers "great" women.	Demographic and attitudinal descriptions of women administrators. Stories of former administrators.
3. Women as disadvantaged or subordinate.	Why so few women leaders in schools?	Surveys of attitudes toward and of women. Surveys of experiences of women. Experimental and quasi-experimental studies of discrimination.	Identification of barriers to women's advancement in administration.
4. Women studied on their own terms.	How do women describe their experiences and lives?	Survey/interview/observational studies of women.	A view of the world from a female perspective.
5. Women as challenge to theory.	How must theory change to include women's experience?	Analysis of theories/methods as appropriate for women.	Reality that theories don't work for women.
6. Transformation of theory.	What are theories of human behavior in organizations?	A range of approaches.	Reconceptualization of theory to include experiences of both men and women.

stage identifies "famous" or "exceptional" women in the history of school administration, adding to the existing data in the conventional paradigm. The work here answers in the affirmative the question, "Is there a history of great women in school leadership?" It examines whether women have done the same things that men have done and if women's achievements meet male standards. Stage 3 investigates women's place in schools from the framework of women as disadvantaged or subordinate, and the question asked is, "Why are there so few women leaders?" At Stage 4, women are finally studied on their own terms and the female world is documented. The data gathered from the female perspective in Stage 4 leads to a Stage 5 challenge of existing theories in educational administration. At this point, we are asking: "How must theory change to include women's experience?" Finally, Stage 6 transforms theory so that we can understand women's and men's experiences together. At this level, we will, hopefully, be able to produce an inclusive vision of human experience based on differences and diversity, rather than on sameness and generalizations.

Part I of this book discusses the history of women in administration and the status of women in the field today. Specifically, it tries to illustrate women's place in school administration. This section makes it clear that women's history in schools is different from men's and that the "typical" woman school administrator varies in important respects from her male counterpart. Part I is reflective of Stage 1 and 2 research.

Part II focuses on the barriers that have kept women out of school administration. This is a departure from the literature on white men, because they have not been closed out of administrative positions on the basis of their sex, and thus have not generated a literature on discrimination. Strategies for overcoming the barriers to women that have been documented as successful are also discussed in Part II. This section of the book uses Stage 3 research to document barriers and change strategies.

The final section examines the working world of women administrators and shows how women's day-to-day experiences create a female culture that differs from the world males occupy in schools. This section begins an examination of current theory in educational administration, demonstrating how it fails to take into account the experiences of women, and speculates upon ways that such a distortion does damage both to women and to school life in general. Part III is built upon the research of Stages 4 and 5 and brings us to the most recent thinking. It lays the groundwork for research at Stage 6, which will build inclusive theory and practice that takes into consideration the diversity of the experiences of females and males.

REFERENCES

Biklen, S. K., & Brannigan, M. B. (1980). *Women and educational leadership.* Lexington, MA: D. C. Heath.

Campbell, R. F., & Newell, L. J. (1973). *A study of professors of educational administration.* Columbus, OH: University Council for Educational Administration.

Maccoby, E. E., & Jacklin, C. N. (1974). *The psychology of sex differences.* Stanford, CA: Stanford University Press.

Nagle, L., Gardner, D. W., Levine, M., & Wolf, S. (1982, March). *Sexist bias in instructional supervision textbooks.* Paper presented at the annual meeting of the American Educational Research Association, New York.

Ortiz, F. I. (1982). *Career patterns in education: Women, men and minorities in public school administration.* New York: Praeger.

Rich, A. (1981). *A wild patience has taken me this far.* New York: Norton.

Rosaldo, M. Z. & Lamphere, L. (Eds.). (1974). *Women, culture and society.* Stanford, CA: Stanford University Press.

Schmuck, P. A., Butman, L., & Person, L. R. (1982, March). *Analyzing sex bias in Planning and Changing.* Paper presented at the annual meeting of the American Educational Research Association, New York.

Schmuck, P. A., Charters, W. W., Jr., & Carlson, R. O. (Eds.). (1981). *Educational policy and management.* New York: Academic Press.

Schuster, M., & Van Dyne, S. (1984). Placing women in the liberal arts: Stages of curriculum transformation. *Harvard Educational Review, 54*(4), 413-428.

Shakeshaft, C., Gilligan, A., & Pierce, D. (1984). Preparing women to be school administrators. *Phi Delta Kappan, 66*(17), 67-68.

Shakeshaft, C., & Saffer, S. (1984, April). *Does dissertation research have anything to do with scholarship?* Paper presented at the annual meeting of the American Educational Research Association, New Orleans.

Tietze, I. N., Shakeshaft, C., & Davis, B. N. (1981, April). *Sexism in texts in educational administration.* Paper presented at the annual meeting of the American Educational Research Association, Los Angeles.

Part I

Where Are the Women Managers?

Were women once the majority of principals? Have things changed drastically over the past century? These are questions that are often asked about women in school administration. There is a belief, both spoken and written, that women were once in charge of the majority of schools but that this has changed in recent years. Is this true?

This section provides a brief history of women's role in school management as well as focusing on where women are in the mid-1980s in the school hierarchy. Very little has been written that helps us to understand women's contributions to the formal leadership of schools. Courses in the history of education seldom highlight women, whether as teachers or administrators (Lather, 1981; Sadker & Sadker, 1985). Thus, most educators have little awareness of the legacy of strong women leaders within the field. Whereas this section provides only a brief summary, it attempts to give a historical foundation for understanding how women became teachers while men became administrators.

In looking at what kind of woman administers schools today, Chapter 2 presents a description of the woman administrator as well as models of career paths. These data demonstrate that the woman in administration is much different than the man in terms of personal characteristics, motivation, background experiences, and career path. Part 1 suggests that the history of educational management as well as the literature on the sociology of administrators is one-sided in its focus. Women have different histories and different stories than do men, and this section provides a glimpse of those differences.

REFERENCES

Lather, P. (1981). Reeducating educators: Sex equity in teacher education. *Educational Horizons, 60*(1), 36-40.

Sadker, D., & Sadker, M. (1985). The treatment of sex equity in teacher education. In S. S. Klein (Ed.), *Handbook for achieving sex equity through education* (pp. 145-161). Baltimore: Johns Hopkins.

. 1 .

Women School Administrators
Too Few for Too Long

Women are destined to rule the schools of every city. I look for a majority of big cities to follow the lead of Chicago in choosing a woman for superintendent. In the near future we will have more women than men in executive charge of the vast educational system. It is woman's natural field, and she is no longer satisfied to do the greatest part of the work and yet be denied leadership. As the first woman to be placed in control of the schools of a big city, it will be my aim to prove that no mistake has been made and to show critics and friends alike that a woman is better qualified for this work than a man. (Ella Flagg Young, quoted in 1909 in *The Western Journal of Education* article, "The Highest Salaried Woman in the World," after her appointment as the first woman superintendent of the Chicago public schools)

Women . . . are quietly making history by taking their places as top level leaders in the educational institutions of this country. . . . In spite of the fact that progress has been made over recent years, there are still some glaring inequities which cry out for remedy . . . less than 1 percent of school superintendents are female. But I'm not worried. I know we will learn whatever we need to learn to open the doors of the nation's executive suites and to ride through them with confidence and competence. . . . I am convinced that we will institute a whole new form of management, a feminine form that is rooted in solid human values, that nurtures everyone connected with it, that accomplishes practical results with no loss of idealism. (Ruth B. Love, 1980, prior to appointment as the second woman superintendent of the Chicago public schools)

Nearly three-quarters of a century passed between the appointment of the first woman superintendent of the Chicago school system and the appointment of the second. Much happened in those 75 years in the field of education, but women did not achieve the magnificent destiny predicted by Ella Flagg Young in 1909. The administrative prospects for women in both eras were nearly identical.

The probability that a woman will be appointed to an administrative position in the schools is as slim for Love's colleagues in the 1980s as for Young's at the beginning of the century. Although the two women lived in worlds technologically and socially different, both Ella Flagg Young and Ruth B. Love were anomalies in a time when their presence in the position of the superintendent was seen as a sign that things were looking up for women.

If the history that followed Flagg's appointment is used as a guide, proponents of women in school administration today have little cause for optimism. Although determining how many women are administrators is a difficult task, a reading of the numbers appears to tell us that women's presence in school administration is increasing at an evolutionary pace.

A golden age of women in administration is often alluded to in writing that points out that women are overwhelmingly underrepresented in the formal management of schools. It is not uncommon to hear or read that as early as the mid-1920s women held a majority of administrative positions in the schools. Statistics do not support these claims.

This chapter will outline the historical background of women's work in schools in an effort to set the stage for the current explanations for women's lack of advancement into administration. The reality that women have never dominated school administration will be documented, followed by a brief history of women's place in educational employment between the mid-nineteenth century and the late twentieth century. Finally, a discussion of the social and historical forces that coalesced between 1905 and the 1980s to slow women's advancement in administration in the twentieth century will be presented.

NEVER THE MAJORITY

A look at the number of women in school administration since 1905 uncovers consistant male dominance in all positions except in

TABLE 1.1
Eighty Years of Women as Workers in Public Schools: 1905-1985

Percentage	*1905*	*1928*	*1950*	*1972-73*	*1982-83*	*1984-85*
Female elementary school teachers	97.9	89.2	91.0	84.0	83.0	83.5
Female elementary principals	61.7	55.0	38.0	19.6	23.0	16.9
Female secondary teachers	64.2	63.7	56.2	46.0	48.9	50.1
Female secondary principals	5.7	7.9	6.0	1.4	3.2	3.5
Female district superintendents	UK	1.6	2.1	0.1	1.8	3.0
Female school board members	UK	11.0	12.0	12.0	28.3	38.3

the early days of the elementary school principalship. Using the scattered sources available, we can see from Table 1.1 that after a bubble in the 1920s, women's representation as workers in schools has diminished. Although it would appear that slight gains are being made, they don't yet warrant optimism.

Although the bulk of teachers since 1905 have been women, they have primarily clustered in the elementary schools. Over the past 80 years, the only administrative position in which women have been dominant is the elementary principalship. Women have never been the majority of secondary principals or district superintendents. Since 1905 there has been a decrease in the percentage of women elementary and secondary teachers and elementary principals. Between 1905 and 1985, as Table 1.1 demonstrates, women's representation in the work force in schools has decreased at all levels except for the school board and the superintendency.

The figures in Table 1.1 must be viewed with caution as they have been collected sporadically and are not always representative of national samples. Furthermore, definitions of what constitutes a teacher and an administrator vary both geographically and over time, posing problems of comparability. Finally, information by sex is just not available for all years, resulting in a display that includes figures at uneven intervals.

This latter observation gives us some clues as to how gender has been viewed, in an official capacity, in a nation that compiles statistics on the most minute facets of everyday life. It is not only difficult, but in some cases impossible, to find the number and percentage of women administrators or teachers for a particular year or geographic location. Although numbers are available, they have often not been compiled by sex. Hansot and Tyack report that the National Education Association (NEA) and other agencies that collected such information ceased breaking down their tables by sex by 1930. They go on to observe:

> Amid proliferation of other kinds of statistical reporting in an age enamored of numbers—reports so detailed that one could give the precise salary of staff in every community across the country and exact information on all sorts of other variables—data by sex became strangely inaccessible. A conspiracy of silence could hardly have been unintentional. (Hansot & Tyack, 1981, p. 13)

This "conspiracy of silence" has made it difficult to determine women's representation in school administration. For instance, the National Center for Education Statistics, a bureau charged with such tasks, compiles statistics on educational workers infrequently and then only breaks them down by gender in certain categories. Further, they do not separate elementary and secondary school principals into two distinct categories, a practice that confuses the issue of female representation.

Accurate records of sex differentials in school administration are important for a number of reasons. Incomplete information on representation of women in school administration makes it easier for the belief that things are better for women to flourish; conversely, by not being able to cite figures on the number of women in formal leadership positions in schools, it becomes more difficult to identify, and thus remedy, the condition of underutilization of women in schools.

A further problem with available statistics is that prior to the 1970s, the number of minority workers in schools was seldom reported. Thus, a historical account of the ebb and flow of women in administration either details the experiences of white women only or obfuscates the lives of women of color by subsuming them within statistics and reports of women in general.

When historical information on minority participation in the school work force is available, it is generally data on black educators. Statistics on members of other minority groups are rare, if available at all.

Although information on black teachers and administrators is slight, we do know that black women are more likely to have been employed as administrators in the rural South and Southwest. Initially, racially segregated schools were staffed by white teachers and administrators, but as rules changed, black schools provided jobs for black women teachers and administrators. "In the late nineteenth century, many southern school boards yielded to pressure to hire black teachers for black schools. The enrollment of black girls in the St. Louis schools went up after the reversal in 1877 of a policy against hiring black teachers in the city's black schools" (Clifford, 1982, p. 252).

Thus, black women gained positions in teaching and administration. By 1920, 2% of the black women who worked outside the home were employed as educators, the seventh ranking field of work for all black women at the time (Clifford, 1982, p. 252). Like their white counterparts, black women were more likely to be teachers than administrators, a trend that has held constant throughout the twentieth century. By 1978, 8.1% of all administrative positions were held by minority men whereas only 3.4% were occupied by minority women, who were most likely to be found in the positions of consultant and supervisor of instruction (Haven, Adkinson, & Bagley, 1980, p.4). Thus, an estimate of black women's representation in school administration between 1905 and 1985 presents a picture even more bleak than that of white women.

In 1985, whether looking at statistics on black or white women, a comparison of the number of female teachers and the number of female managers illustrates women's underrepresentation in the formal leadership of schools. Women are 83.5% of the elementary teachers but only 16.9% of elementary principals; they are 50% of the secondary teachers but 3.5% of secondary principals; and they are two thirds of all school personnel, but only 3% of the superintendents (Table 1.1).

This imbalance is all the more disquieting when one considers that the woman teacher or administrator is, by and large, more able than the male teacher or administrator. A number of researchers

(Brown, 1981; Fishel & Pottker, 1977; Frasher & Frasher, 1979; Shakeshaft, 1981; Tibbetts, 1980) have pointed out that in studies comparing the effectiveness of male and female teachers and administrators on selected criteria (teaching evaluations, teacher exam scores, college grade point averages, warmth, administrative functioning, in basket/out basket exercises), when there is a difference, females are rated higher than males.

These findings shouldn't come as a surprise as teaching has been a profession to which the most able women turned if they were to work outside the home. Because women had few professional options, many of the brightest women chose teaching. Men had more professional opportunities than did women, and traditionally the most able men sought professions that offered both higher salaries and higher status than teaching. Teaching has been a profession comprised of strong, gifted women whereas the majority of men who entered teaching were either unable to procure other work or were on their way to another profession. Consequently, studies that contrast male and female teachers and administrators are not examining similar groups, but rather comparing the more capable educators (women) with the less capable ones (men).

Although there are indications that the best and brightest of women—like the best and brightest of men—are not becoming educators today, historically it must be remembered there has been both a gender and a talent imbalance in the ranks of administration so that schools have operated under a minority rule both in terms of sheer numbers and ability.

How can this be? Why the "higher you go, the fewer you see" syndrome for women in educational administration? A look at both the historical record and recent studies in the social sciences gives us some answers.

WOMAN'S NATURAL PROFESSION

The history of women in school administration is intertwined with the history of women in teaching. To understand the former, one must know the latter. Although teaching has been identified in the twentieth century as a female profession, teachers have not always been women. Records indicate that until the late eighteenth century, all teaching was done by men. "The injunction of St. Paul, 'I permit not a woman to teach,' was enforced" (Woody, 1966, p. 129). However, by the close of the Colonial period, the practice of utilizing women to train boys and girls, ages 4-7, developed. The teacher-housewife would assemble the local children in her home where she taught the little ones their letters. These women became known as "school dames" and later, their establishments were known as "dame schools." Such women were the "lowest on the teaching ladder . . . often the spouse of the local minister seeking extra income" (Bonn, 1974, p. 29). They were paid " 1/5 of what schoolmasters were paid, and were permitted to teach only the very young and only in the hot summer. Because they had received no formal education for teaching they were not considered as qualified or as important as men teachers, yet often they did the same work" (Stern, 1973, p. 47).

Between 1820 and 1830, growth in industry and business provided more lucrative job opportunities for male teachers while the numbers of immigrants greatly increased the school-age population but not the tax base. It was the opening of these new employment opportunities for men, increased industrialization and urbanization, and population growth in the United States that led both to a need for more teachers and to a shortage of male teachers.

School boards searching for male teachers found a dearth of men with the desired class background. There were males from lower-socioeconomic classes who might have been available to enter the profession, but they were not the kind of men that school boards sought to hire. School boards wanted literate, middle-class men—men for whom there were other opportunities at much higher pay and status.

The few middle-class men who were available tended to be young men who dabbled in teaching, using it as a stepping-stone to another career. They were men with short-term commitments who were satisfied with the minimal pay as it required little personal or professional cost to them. At the same time, school teaching provided visibility to men who sought careers in law, commerce, or the ministry. Young men, working for money to attend college, often taught for a short time as did men beginning as farmers who used the winter as a time to earn extra money. Teaching asked very little of these men—in rural areas minimal preparation was required, and it only took a few months out of the year to accomplish the duties of the teacher.

Interestingly, as teaching became more professional, demanding certification and longer terms (but no more money), even these men dropped out because what they had to put into the job was more than they could take away from it. Between 1840 and 1860, the percentage of male teachers in Massachusetts dropped from 60% to 14% and school boards were faced with a labor shortage (Reich, 1974).

As the following passage from an 1838 issue of the *Connecticut Common School Journal* indicates, women were chosen to meet this labor shortage:

> How shall we get good teachers for our district schools, and enough of them? While we should encourage our young men to enter upon this patriotic, and I had almost said, missionary field of duty, and present much higher inducements to engage them to do so, I believe . . . that there is but little hope of attaining *the full supply* . . . from that sex. This will always be difficult, so long as there are so many other avenues open in our country to the accumulation of property, and the attaining of distinction. We must . . . look more to the other sex for aid in this emergency . . . (Galludet, 1838, p. 10)

Although women were first sought for teaching because men were unavailable, women's entrance into teaching had been promoted and rationalized already by the work of such leaders as Catharine Beecher and Emma Willard. These women had set the stage for women to become teachers by popularizing the concept of women's true sphere. Believing that teaching was a proper sphere for a woman and that it prepared her for the work of marriage and motherhood, these women led crusades to bring women into teaching. Beecher's primary ambition was to recruit educated and trained women in the East to act as "missionary" teachers in the West and South, serving both to provide knowledge and spread middle-class values. In recruiting women for this endeavor and in raising money to support her work, Beecher employed three distinct tactics. The first was to secure the support of leading community women, the second was to enjoin the cooperation of religious organizations, and the third was to have a man deliver her speeches.

The latter tactic illuminates her position on women's proper sphere. Like Emma Willard, she believed that women and men belonged in different worlds. In addition to marriage, she advocated only three fields of work for women: domestic service, nursing, and education. Beecher crusaded fervently against the employment of women in mills and factories, believing that men were "designed by God" for this type of work and that women did not belong in these spheres. On the other hand, teaching was "woman's natural profession" and women were described as the solitary possessors of the nurturant, receptive qualities necessary to be both a teacher and a mother (Sklar, 1973).

Thus, women were seen as natural teachers—using their nurturant "maternal" abilities in a natural extension from home to schoolroom and back again. Women were also cheap. In 1838 in Connecticut, for example, men earned $14.50 per month whereas women were paid $5.75. In that same year in Massachusetts, men took home $23.10 a month whereas women had to make do on $6.49 (Melder, 1972, p. 22). From the beginning, women teachers were treated less favorably than were men teachers—whether it was measured by pay or by status. In common schools, men were the masters or principals whereas women were the assistant teachers; in high schools, males were called "Professor" and females were addressed as "Miss." Women were identified by their sex, whereas men were acknowledged for the roles they played. A pertinent example can be found in the 1805 catalogue of the Bradford Academy, which described its 75 teachers in training as "twenty-nine Students and forty-six Females" (Clifford, 1982, p. 237.)

Despite low pay and status, women flocked to teaching. During the pre-Civil War era in Massachusetts, when the average woman teacher earned but one-fourth of what her male counterpart was earning, 20% of all women became teachers at some point in their lives (Bernard & Vinovskis, 1977).

A number of reasons have been offered to explain why women would engage in a profession that wasn't very kind to them. The most compelling reason that women chose to teach seems to be that it was better than the alternative of complete dependence on their families. Solomon (1985) points out that demographic and social changes in the country resulted in more unmarried women than available men. Teaching made it possible for women to support themselves, thus reducing the financial burden on their parents.

Further, industrialization meant that traditional domestic responsibilities for which daughters had been responsible lessened, providing them with the time to work outside the home. The need for women to work combined with Beecher's notion that teaching was not only woman's natural profession but also a benefit to society coalesced to make it both posssible and desirable for them to become teachers.

> Taking a school [job] offered a respectable and sometimes pleasant alternative to young women who needed to work and found few alternatives except textile mills or domestic service. Teaching permitted educated women, who found most professional roles closed to them, an outlet for their skills. (Melder, 1972, p. 25)

Most of the foregoing discussion has centered on white women teachers. We know little of early minority women teachers and what we do know tends to be about black women. Collier-Thomas points out that "black women had no real status in the teaching profession until the late nineteenth century" (1982, p. 175). However, this does not mean that black women teachers were not educators early on. Despite the odds, they taught.

Slave owners usually forbade education for slaves as they feared uprising and rebellion. In addition to strong unwritten rules in the South against teaching black people to read and write, formal laws were passed that made it a crime. South Carolina, for instance, passed a law in 1740 that punished those who taught slaves to read. Similar laws were passed up to the beginning of the Civil War throughout other southern states (Weinberg, 1977).

When black people did receive an education, research suggests that free black men were more likely than free black women to be taught to read and write (Vinovskis & Bernard, 1978), but there is little information on the literacy rates of male and female black slaves. We do know that prior to the Civil War, despite the threat of punishment and death, some black women slaves learned to read and write, becoming teachers and passing these skills on to others. For instance, Milla Granson, a black woman slave in Natchez, Louisiana, held school between midnight and 2:00 a.m. for seven years and taught many black pupils their lessons (Lerner, 1972).

In Georgia, black slave Susie King Taylor wrote about the secret school she attended in which the teacher was a free black woman:

> I was born under the slave law in Georgia in 1848. . . . My brother and I being the two eldest, we were sent to a friend of my grandmother, a Mrs. Woodhouse, a widow, to learn to read and write. She was a free woman and lived . . . about half a mile from my house.
>
> We went every day with our books wrapped in paper to prevent the police or white persons from seeing them. We went in, one at a time, through the gate into the yard to the kitchen, which was the school room. She had 25 or 30 children whom she taught, assisted by her daughter, Mary Jane. The neighbors would see us going in some time, but they supposed we were there learning trades, as it was the custom to give children a trade of some kind. After school we left the same way we entered, one by one and we would go to a square about a block from the school and wait for each other. (cited in Lerner, 1972, pp. 27-28)

Teaching and learning was also a dangerous activity for black women in the North. In Connecticut in 1833, Prudence Crandall, a white Quaker teacher, was arrested for opening a school for black girls that would train them to be teachers. Crandall's problems had begun in 1832 when she admitted a black woman who "wanted to get a little more learning, enough if possible to teach colored children" (Fuller, 1971, p. 16). In response, the parents of the white students removed their daughters from school. Those white students who had not already withdrawn were asked to do so by Crandall to make room for 19 black women to be trained as teachers. This caused the townspeople to pass a law making it illegal to teach black students from other states. This law was used as the basis for Crandall's arrest. Further, local residents attempted to burn down the school as well as to physically harm Crandall and her pupils (Fuller, 1971).

A similar problem was encountered by Myrtilla Miner in 1851 when she tried to open a school for black students in Washington, DC Although mobs attacked the school several times, setting it on fire and threatening the students and Miner, her school not only endured for 10 years, but was accused of "educating colored children beyond their station in life" (Green, 1967, p. 51; O'Connor/Miner, 1885/1969).

Not all black teachers-to-be faced such overt hostility. For instance, Charlotte Forten was sent by her parents from segregated Philadelphia to nonsegregated Salem, Massachusetts, to live with an abolitionist family and get an education. In 1855 she entered a teacher training school and in 1856, upon graduation, was offered a teaching position in Salem:

> Amazing, wonderful news I have heard today! It has completely astounded me. . . . I have received the offer of a situation as teacher in one of the public schools of this city—of this conservative, aristocratic old city of Salem!!! Wonderful indeed it is! . . . Again and again I ask myself—*Can* it be true? It seems impossible. I shall commence tomorrow. (Billington, 1953/1981, p. 82)

Education became more accessible to black women after the Civil War when schooling for freed slaves in the South was attempted by the federal government and northern philanthropic agencies. This need for teachers provided opportunities for black women as over 9000 teachers, more than half of them women and many of them black women, journeyed to the South during Reconstruction to teach black people (Jones, 1979). Charlotte Forten was among these who moved from Salem, Massachusetts, to the Georgia Sea Islands to teach in a newly formed school. Although Forten was protected from hostile crowds of white people by Union troops who helped her succeed in her mission to teach black people, other black women teachers were less fortunate. Julia Hayden, 17 years old, was murdered in Tennessee for teaching black people. Not only teachers, but black people who boarded teachers from the North, were killed. For instance, in Mississippi, a black man, Charles Caldwell, was murdered by a mob for harboring a white woman who had come South to teach. She stayed, rearing Caldwell's daughter, and many of her pupils went on to become teachers themselves (Kerber, 1983).

Despite the hostilities facing black women teachers in all parts of the United States, their numbers continued to grow throughout the nineteenth century. An article published in 1904 (Hunton), claimed that more than 25,000 black women teachers had been educated, whereas another writer (Jones, 1905) pointed out that over 4000 black women had graduated from normal schools and universities by 1905. After 1890, black women teachers outnumbered black men teachers, and by 1910 two-thirds of black teachers were women (Collier-Thomas, 1982, p. 175).

In the period from 1830 through 1900, women—both white and black—became more identified with teaching, so that by 1880,

57.2% of the teachers in the United States were women and by 1900, 70.1% were women (Woody, 1929/1966, p. 499). Not only were the majority of teachers women by the twentieth century, but women were assuming leadership positions within the field of education. Margaret Haley was the leader of the Chicago Teachers Federation, the most militant association of teachers and a charter member of the American Federation of Teachers (Reid, 1982). In 1910, Ella Flagg Young was president of the NEA (Smith, 1979) and Grace Strachan (1910) was leading the fight in New York City for equal pay for male and female teachers. And yet, as schools began to evolve into hierarchical organizations, the majority of positions of formal leadership were occupied by men.

THE MAKING OF ADMINISTRATORS

In the early days of public schooling in the United States, the teacher did everything, including administration. However, as schooling became more complex and as bureaucratization was imposed upon schools, the functions of administrator and teacher became more distinct.

In 1890 in "Middletown," the superintendent was "the only person in the system who did not teach," but by 1929 there was between the teacher and the superintendent "a galaxy of principals, assistant principals, supervisors of special subjects, directors of vocational education and home economics, deans, attendance officers, and clerks, who do no teaching but are concerned in one way or another with keeping the system going" (Lynd & Lynd, 1929, p. 210). By 1918, teaching and administration were two separate professions; special requirements to become an administrator had been instituted in several states, and departments of educational administration were begun in universities (Callahan, 1962). Separation of work in schools into administration and teaching categories had serious implications for women. Cubberly (1929) notes that the subject of school administration did not begin to attract attention until 1875. At that time there were only 29 school superintendents.

> With the still more rapid growth of cities since about 1880, and the still more rapid expansion of our city school systems since about 1900, even further specialization of functions and delegations of authority has become a necessity. (Cubberley, 1929, p. 161)

As schools were reorganized from one-room centers of teaching to cost-efficient models of business, it was no longer thought appropriate for teachers to carry out all duties. Instead, a hierarchy of roles was to be instituted so that the work of schooling could be done more efficiently.

Typical was the reorganization of the Quincy Grammar School in 1870 to a graded school that followed the principles of scientific management; a manager oversaw a number of teachers who instructed several hundred students. For schools to be transformed from fairly autonomous organizations with loosely coupled classes headed by strong school men and women into bureaucracies under the role of one administrator, superordinates and subordinates had to be manufactured. Male teachers were put in charge and women were looked to as the ideal subordinate.

> Their minds are less withdrawn from their employment, by the active scenes of life; and they are less intent on scheming for future honors or emoluments. As a class, they never look forward, as young men almost invariably do, to a period of legal emancipation from parental control, when they are to break away from the domestic circle and go abroad into the world, to build up a fortune for themselves. (Mann, 1841, p. 45)

Supporters of bureaucratization argued that "women should be teachers while men should be retained as principals and superintendents" (Tyack & Strober, 1981, p. 141), and the graded school became the vehicle that carried out this two-tiered system, as the Quincy School Committee noted in the 1870s:

> One man could be placed in charge of an entire graded school of 500 students. Under his direction could be placed a number of female assistants. Females "are not only adapted, but carefully trained, to fill such positions as well as or better than men, excepting the master's place, which sometimes requires a man's force; and the competition is so great, that their services command less than half the wages of male teachers." (cited in Katz, 1973, p. 73)

Scientific management and, specifically, bureaucratization, then, helped keep women out of administrative roles because of the belief in male dominance that made it easier for both males and females to view women as natural followers and men as their leaders.

> Hierarchical organization of schools and the male chauvinism of the larger society fit as hand to glove. The system required subordination; women were generally subordinate to men; the employment of women as teachers thus augmented the authority of the largely male administrative leadership. (Tyack, 1974, p. 60)

In addition to partriarchal views, a female style of administration, taught and fostered by such organizations as the national Congress of Mothers (now known as the Parent Teachers' Association) was seen as inconsistent with the efficient functioning of schools. Women in these organizations had learned—both formally in classes and informally through experience—leadership skills that promoted democratic and egalitarian styles of decisionmaking. These styles of administration were at odds with the authoritarian approaches to school leadership currently in vogue, comfortable styles for males with backgrounds in both business and the military (Burstyn, 1980).

Bureaucratization and the emphasis on businesslike procedures chipped away at the autonomy of teachers, most of whom were women, and often interfered with the educational goals of schools (Callahan, 1962). An 1889 account by Boston teacher Mary Dogherty of being observed by her principal illustrates both the subservience demanded of women as well as the emphasis on uniformity:

> It was with that first class that I became aware that a teacher was subservient to a higher authority.... The genial principal came in one day to see how things were going ... and announced that he would hear the little girls read. . . . Our principal was a stickler for the proprieties and ... the proper way to read in the public school in 1899 was to say, "Page 35, Chapter 4", and holding the book in the right hand, with the toes pointing at an angle of forty-five degrees, the head held straight and high, the eyes looking directly ahead, the pupil would lift up his [sic] voice. (cited in Hoffman, 1981, p. 265)

The demand for a division of labor resulting in an assembly line approach, which forced unquestioning acceptance by teachers, most of whom were women, was resented. Teachers, and particularly women teachers, began to fight back. Ella Flagg Young noted:

> There has been a tendency toward factory-evolution and factory-management, and the teachers, like children who stand at machines, are told just what to do. The teachers, instead of being the great moving force, educating and developing the powers of the human mind in such a way that they shall contribute to the power and the efficiency of this democracy, tend to become mere workers at the treadmill, but they are doing all thru [sic] this country that which shows that it is difficult to crush the human mind and the love of freedom in the hearts and lives of people who are qualified to teach school. As a result they are organizing federations to get together and discuss those questions which are vital in the life of the children and in the life of the teachers. (Young, 1916, p. 357)

Despite resistance, bureaucracy reigned and with it male dominance of administrative positions. Beliefs about women's place sometimes found their way into laws restricting women in school administration. Until 1858 in New Hampshire, men and women needed different qualifications to become school administrators. As late as 1875, the circuit court in Iowa ruled that Elizabeth Cook could not be Warren County superintendent despite the fact that she was elected by the citizens of the county (Beale, 1936, p. 495).

Hansot and Tyack note that since the 1880s, men have consistently held administrative positions in which "power, pay, and prestige were greatest" (1981, p. 8); positions in which they supervised other adult males as opposed to females and children; jobs that were linked with the nonschool world; and jobs that were defined as managerial rather than instructional. Although this imbalance has remained consistent, there have been some eras that have a richer women's participation in administration than others. It must also be remembered that a number of women prior to 1900 were administrators of the schools they founded (Giddings, 1984; Greene, 1984; Solomon, 1985), and that these women represent a significant proportion of female school administrators throughout the nineteenth century.

WOMEN MOVE INTO SCHOOL ADMINISTRATION

Between 1820 and 1900, then, a handful of women held administrative positions. Although some of these women managed public schools, the majority founded their own schools and served as the chief administrator (Giddings, 1984; Solomon, 1985). In the first decade of the twentieth century, a larger number of women began to win positions in school administration so that by 1909, when Ella Flagg Young made her optimistic predictions for women in school administration, she had reasons to believe them. The years leading up to Young's superintendency of Chicago—the first big city superintendency ever held by a woman—were ones in which women had begun to make an impact through political activism and social reform designed to bring women into school administration. As a result, the years 1900-1930 are sometimes referred to as a golden age for women in school administration (Hansot & Tyack, 1981). But even during this period, women achieved only modest success, arriving "in numbers only in the lower strata of the upper crust" (Connolly, 1919, p. 841), as Table 1.1 demonstrates.

Between 1900 and 1930, women primarily occupied elementary principalships and county and state superintendencies. By 1928, women held 55% of the elementary principalships, 25% of the county superintendencies, nearly 8% of the secondary school principalships, and 1.6% of the district superintendencies. These advances are not as significant as they might seem. Unlike the higher status and higher paying secondary principalships and district superintendencies held by men, elementary principalships and county and state superintendencies were low-paying, low-status, low-power positions.

In the beginning, county superintendencies oversaw a number of localities. As the populations of these towns grew, the school districts hired their own superintendents, usually replacing a female county superintendent with a male district superintendent who entered with more power and almost always with more pay. County superintendencies were seldom stepping-stones to positions with higher power, and elementary principals seldom moved up the hierarchy. Similarly, by 1928, women were only 8.4% of university or college presidents and 14.3% of heads of departments of education in higher education institutions (Educational News and Editorial Comment, 1928, p. 327).

Understanding the movement of black women into school administration up to 1930 is more difficult because not as much information that documents or compiles these experiences is available and the history of members of other minority groups is even more scarce. By the mid-1800s, some black women had begun their own schools and, thus, served as both the teacher and the administrator (Giddings, 1984; Green, 1967; Jones, 1980). In Georgia, for instance, Lucy Craft Laney graduated from Atlanta University in 1873 and began the Haines Normal and Industrial Institute, which offered a full liberal arts program. Some of the teachers who worked in Laney's school went on to found their own schools and become administrators in their own right; for instance, Janie Porter Barrett started a vocational school for girls in Virginia and Mary McLeod Bethune founded Bethune-Cookman College in Florida (Giddings, 1984; Kerber, 1983). These schools continued into the twentieth century and both employed and trained many women teachers and administrators.

An important vehicle for minority women to achieve positions of formal leadership was the Jeanes supervisory program begun in 1907 with a million dollar endowment from a Philadelphia Quaker, Anna T. Jeanes, for the

> maintenance and assistance of rural, community and country schools for the Southern Negroes and not for the use or benefit at large institutions, but for the purpose of rudimentary education . . . and to promote peace in the land. (Williams et al., 1979, p. 97)

This endowment became the core of the Southern Education Foundation and supported Jeanes's supervisors, mostly black women, who began working at "improving educational programs in segregated schools" (Williams et al., 1979, p. 15). The Jeanes supervisors were a force that helped increase the number of black women in school leadership by providing "unprecedented professional leadership . . . for black teachers and principals" (1979, p. 59).

Thus a number of factors coalesced to allow both black and white women to claim positions in educational administration in the first 30 years of this century. In particular, four of these—the feminist movement, the organization of women teachers, the right to vote in local elections, and economic advantages—all worked to women's benefit during this period.

Many women—both in and out of education—were part of a larger feminist movement that sought female power and leadership in many spheres, but particularly in that of the school. Margaret Gribskov (1980) writes of women reformers who saw school administration as an extension of women's natural sphere. In the beginning of this feminist movement, suffrage was but one of the goals of these female reformers. At the Seneca Falls convention of 1848, for instance, one of the resolutions unanimously adopted stated that women should have "equal participation with men in the various trades, professions, and commerce" (Anthony, Stanton, & Harper, 1881/1922, p. 73). Promoting women into spheres where men had always been, then, became a central part of the feminist movement.

Because doors were tightly shut in most professions, education was thought to be a good place to begin the assault as women were already a large part of the professional work force. Thus it was that women hoping to become school administrators had the backing of a diverse group of women—feminists, temperance activitists, members of women's clubs—who could put pressure both on local decision makers as well as cast their votes for women in school administration. Gribskov (1980) points out that the General Federation of Women's Clubs was one of the most influential forces in promoting equality for women and for supporting women professionals, including women in school administration. Not concerned just with suffrage (the Federation of Women's Clubs endorsed suffrage only in 1914), they worked hard to increase women's participation in management. These associations of women backed women candidates for school administration because they believed, as had Catharine Beecher 75 years earlier, that women would clean up the system, injecting a purity of purpose and a morality that men failed to possess.

In addition to the direct impact they had on increasing women in school administration, these groups helped swell the numbers of women in administration through indirect methods as well. For instance, they encouraged the increase in the number of women who attended college. More women in college meant more women trained to be teachers and, subsequently, to aspire to and achieve administrative positions.

Together with these strong women's groups outside of education, women candidates for administrative positions often had the support of female teacher organizations. Originally established to improve the working conditions for teachers, these organizations were begun in New York, Chicago, Atlanta, and Pittsburgh at the turn of the century. The associations battled centralization, which shifted power and autonomy from female teachers to newly appointed male administrators. From the beginning, these organizations were clearly identified with improving the condition of women and were seen by many as run by militant feminists. Grace Strachan headed the Interborough Association of Women Teachers in New York and worked to equalize male and female pay. Margaret Haley, an architect of the Chicago Teachers Federation, was called a "fiend in petticoats" (Tyack & Hansot, 1982, p. 186) because of her efforts to keep the NEA from becoming an organization of elite schoolmen who would forget the needs of the women teachers who supported it. In working both to organize women teachers and to promote women into administration, the Chicago Teachers Federation helped Ella Flagg Young win her superintendency in Chicago (Reid, 1982).

The impact of both the feminist movement and the teacher associations was strengthened in states where school directorships and county and state superintendencies were elected by popular vote. In these areas, schools were small and remote, and districts were managed by a head teacher or principal. The elected county superintendents oversaw these "middle managers" by traveling to all of the districts in her county, often over rough and hazardous roads and sometimes even by boat. Difficult as it was for the county superintendent to reach these schools, it was often more difficult to "supervise" the head teacher or principal once there. A great deal of personal power and skill was needed to manage such scattered personnel, and the county superintendency often proved to be an effective training ground for developing the political, social, and oratorical skills women needed to win state superintendency elections.

Although women's suffrage was not won until 1920, by 1910 women could vote in school elections in 24 states. In these states, primarily in the West and Midwest, the right to vote provided the support for women that women teacher associations provided in cities. Permitted to vote in school elections, members of women's groups and teacher organizations formed coalitions to ensure that women candidates would receive sufficient votes to win school elections. These women devoted considerable time and energy to electing women candidates and attending to local politics (Gribskov, 1980).

As a result, in states where women could vote, women won school elections. By 1922, women had been elected as state superintendents in 9 states and 857 women held county superintendencies, up from 276 in 1900 (Lathrop, 1922). Six years later, 900 county superintendents were female and, in states where women could vote, two-thirds of the county superintendents were women (Educational News and Editorial Comment, 1928). Edith Lathrop pointed out in a 1922 article that opportunities for women in administration were rich in the West, where county and state superintendents were elected, not appointed:

> There are more women state superintendents at the present time than ever before in the history of the country. . . . It is interesting to note, in this connection, that in these states this officer is elected by direct vote of the people. . . . The advancement of women in administrative positions is nowhere more evident, with the exception of grade school principalships, than in the county superintendency. . . . A large majority . . . of women county superintendents are found in the states west of the Mississippi River. . . . selected by a direct vote of the people. . . . The college girl who is ambitious for educational leadership, won by way of political competition, may well take Horace Greeley's advice to young men anxious for opportunity and a career: "Go West, young man, go West!" (Lathrop, 1922, pp. 418-419)

Although it is true that the primary reason women won elections was the support of women's political and social groups, it must also be pointed out that these were low-pay, low-status positions that few men sought. Like their teacher counterparts, women administrators sometimes attained their positions by default—either because no men were available or because women were a bargain as they were paid less than men. For instance, a 1905 study of 467 city school systems found that the average male elementary principal was paid $1542 whereas the average female elementary principal earned $970.00 (NEA, 1905, p. 23). Lathrop reported that in 1922, women still earned three-quarters of what men earned for the same work. Just as women teachers had been hired because they came cheaper than men teachers, so too, were economic considerations paramount in the appointment of some women administrators.

THE DECLINE OF WOMEN AS SCHOOL LEADERS

Gains made by women in administration during the first three decades of this century were not sustained after 1930. The number of female elementary principals, and county and state superintendents, began to decrease and the major power position in the school—the district superintendency—was still almost always held by a man. In 1932, there were "still 25 states with no woman serving as a superintendent" (Hansot & Tyack, 1981, p. 15).

Cuban (1976) reports that between 1870 and 1970 in the 25 largest cities, only six women served as superintendents. Three of these women served prior to 1900: in Los Angeles, C. B. Jones was superintendent from 1880-1881, in Portland, Ella Sabin served from 1888-1891, and in Seattle, Julia Kennedy was the superintendent between 1888 and 1889. Ella Flagg Young was Chicago's superintendent between 1909 and 1915, and Susan Dorsey served in Los Angeles from 1922 to 1929.

Women primarily held positions in the lower strata of school administration—supervisors of art, home economy, hygiene, kindergartens, music; staff positions as opposed to line positions; and the elementary principalship. A piece written in 1919 predicted the limits for women in administration:

> A place—usually in the supervisorship of primary work, or domestic work, or welfare work—is set apart for some women, *and the woman is selected by a board of men.* (Connolly, 1919, p. 843).

Several factors worked against women and resulted in their decline in administrative positions after 1928. Many of the barriers to women in the mid-twentieth century were indistinguishable from those of prior years. Century-old patterns of male dominance had solidified a number of beliefs about women that both men and women accepted and that limited women's access to school administration. Negative attitudes toward women continued to be a major barrier. Women were thought to be constitutionally incapable of discipline and order, primarily because of their size and supposed lack of strength.

Where administrators were not elected by popular vote, women seeking administrative positions still had to confront the ever-present bias of local school board members, most of whom were men. Then, as now, schoolmen tended to hire those most like themselves, white middle-aged Protestant males. Not surprisingly, they chose those with whom they felt most comfortable, and most members of school boards did not feel at ease with women. In a textbook for school administrators written by Elwood Cubberly in 1929, businessmen were listed as the best candidates for school boards. Those to be kept off boards included inexperienced young men, unsuccessful men, retired men, politicians, uneducated or ignorant men, saloon keepers, and all women (1929, p. 212).

Further, school boards claimed they didn't want to invest time and money in workers with short-term commitments, a description often given to women who were expected to leave teaching for marriage. Typically, men didn't stay in teaching much longer than did women, but curiously the undependable label was applied only to women, thus limiting their opportunities for administrative posts. Men moved in and out of teaching but they usually left for positions that offered higher pay or status or both—thus they were seen as professionals, even if transitory. Women, on the other hand, usually left for marriage. They were branded unprofessional, despite laws in many communities that forbade married women, but not married men, from continuing to teach.

Women's marital choices were directly related to their employment opportunities in education. In 1900, 90% of female teachers were unmarried (Hansot & Tyack, 1981, p. 23). The married women who taught or administered did so for the survival of the family. Laws were passed that kept the teaching force composed of single women. In 1903, the New York Board of Education adopted a bylaw barring married women from teaching:

> No woman principal, woman head of department, or woman member of the teaching or supervising staff shall marry while in the service. It shall be the duty of a District Superintendent to bring to the notice of the Board of Superintendents the marriage of any such person in his district, and such fact shall be reported to the Board of Education, which may direct charges to be preferred against such teacher by reason of such marriage. (Woody, 1929/1966, p. 509)

However, there were exceptions for some married women:

> No married woman shall be appointed to any teaching or supervising position in the New York Public Schools unless her husband is mentally or physically incapacitated to earn a living or has deserted her for a period of not less than one year. (Woody, 1929/1966, p. 509)

The position of the board was challenged and subjected to ridicule, as in the verse reprinted below, and in 1920 the regulation was repealed. However, not before it had kept many married women from teaching as well as serving as a rationale and model for school districts in other parts of the country to adopt similar regulations.

Song Satirizing New York Law on Married Teachers

CHORUS BY BOARD:
Now please don't waste
your time and ours
By pleas all based
On mental powers.
She seems to us
The proper stuff
Who has a hus-
band bad enough.
All other pleas appear to us
Excessively superfluous.

FIRST TEACHER:
My husband is not really bad-

BOARD:
How very sad, how very sad!

FIRST TEACHER:
He's good, but hear my one excuse-

BOARD:
Oh, what's the use, oh, what's the use?

FIRST TEACHER:
Last winter in a railroad wreck
He lost an arm and broke his neck.
He's doomed, but lingers day by day.

BOARD:
Her husband's doomed! Hurray! hurray!

SECOND TEACHER:
My husband's kind and healthy, too-

BOARD:
Well, then, of course, you will not do.

SECOND TEACHER:
Just hear me out. You'll find you're wrong.
It's true his body's good and strong;
But, ah, his wits are all astray.

BOARD:
Her husband's mad. Hip, hip hurray!

THIRD TEACHER:
My husband's wise and well—the creature!

BOARD:
Then you can never be a teacher.

THIRD TEACHER:
Wait. For I led him such a life
He could not stand me as a wife;
Last Michaelmas, he ran away.

BOARD:
Her husband hates her, Hip, hurray!

CHORUS BY BOARD:
Now we have found,
Without a doubt,
By process sound
And well thought out,
Each candidate
Is fit in truth
To educate
The mind of youth.
No teacher need apply to us
Whose married life's harmonious.
(From *Are Women People?* by Alice Duer Miller; found in Woody, 1929/1966, pp. 509-510.)

In 1928, 60% of urban districts still prohibited the hiring of married teachers and only half of those systems permitted teachers who married after becoming teachers to continue in their jobs (Peters, 1934). By 1942, a nationwide survey of school districts reported that 58% of school systems would not employ married women teachers (NEA, 1942).

These policies had a wide-ranging effect on the sex structuring of education, and in 1936 Helen Davis observed that education, "will be occupied on the whole by two kinds of women, those who refuse marriage except on their own terms and those who have not been able to find husbands, while the general run of able and so-called 'normal' women will be excluded because they prefer marriage" (Hansot & Tyack, 1981, pp. 23-24). Thus communities often made injustice legal by forcing women from teaching if they desired marriage and children.

Besides having to continue to fight public prejudice against them, women continued to have to deal with exclusionary practices. Men had the advantage of being able to interact with other men who held power and who were often in positions to hire. Clubs such as the Rotary were (and still are) limited to male members. Even school organizations kept women out; the NEA at first admitted only men, and until the 1970s Phi Delta Kappa was an all-male organization. Although the NEA had women presidents beginning with Ella Flagg Young in 1910, she describes her first meeting in 1867 as one in which women were only "permitted to sit in the gallery and listen to discussions carried on by the men" (Hansot & Tyack, 1982, p. 64).

Another bias that continued to work against women was the belief that males had a special gift for dealing with community issues and problems. The mores and beliefs at the time tended to separate women from men, thus hiring a female administrator who would have daily interactions with local businessmen was often unthinkable to hiring committees.

In addition to the barriers that kept women out of administration from the beginning, the 1930s brought additional obstacles to the movement of women into school administration. Gribskov (1980) points out that after women were granted the right to vote, many of the strong women's organizations that had rallied around women administrative candidates were disbanded. For instance, after women's suffrage was achieved, many women switched from the Federation of Women's Clubs, an organization with feminist goals, to the League of Women Voters, a group that was not identified with women's issues. Thus a strong force of support for women in administration vanished.

At about the time that suffrage was won, the growth of the teachers' unions began to slow, a decline that lasted approximately 40 years. Bureaucratization, against which early teacher leaders had organized, was fully implemented by 1920, and the other issues that the organizations were working to rectify—equal pay and tenure—also lost support as the economic depression spread.

Achieving equal pay for men and women educators has also affected the number of women school administrators. San Francisco passed the first equal pay law in 1894, after a fight led by a woman elementary school principal. By 1930, 10 states had equal pay laws; unfortunately, these were not always enforced and during the Depression they were often ignored (Kerber, 1983). Equal pay laws were just as likely to be used to hurt women educators as to help them. If the laws weren't being ignored, they were being used to justify hiring males over females. Schmuck (1979) points out that given a choice of a male or a female for the same pay, the woman lost the edge she once held when she was paid less. Many school boards believed, erroneously, that men had more financial obligations than did women (Davis & Samuelson, 1950) and thus used this as a rationale for hiring men. Several decades earlier, Grace Strachen had attacked the notion of paying a man more because he had a family to support: "Salary is for service, and should be measured by the service rendered" (1910, p. 118). Kalvelage (1978), in an analysis of hiring patterns, supports the argument that equal pay affected the number of women hired in school administration and points out that because state equal pay laws were instituted more males have been hired as elementary teachers and administrators.

The economic depression caused another set of conditions that led school boards and communities to cut back on the number of women teachers and administrators. In many localities, additional laws were passed that barred married women teachers and administrators from working, citing the financial needs of men, married or unmarried, for the jobs that women had previously held. Single women were also discriminated against in promotions. School boards legitimized their actions by arguing that men had families to support whereas single women supported only themselves. The economic reality was, of course, quite different. Single women were more often than not responsible for parents and siblings, and these responsibilities were most often equal to or greater than the obligations of their male counterparts (Gribskov, 1980).

Thus a number of factors combined to turn Ella Flagg Young's dream of a golden age for women in administration into a nightmare. After 1930, the number of women in administration progressively decreased except for during World War II, when male educators began serving in the armed forces. Ironically, communities reversed discriminatory hiring policies during World War II, and married women were welcomed into schools to teach and administer schools. Some systems even provided day care! However, the opportunities provided were brief. Women who served their country during World War II by taking on school jobs were rewarded by being dismissed when the men returned. Men who served their country in the armed forces were rewarded with the G.I. Bill, which provided funds for their educations—educations that trained them to be teachers and administrators.

At the conclusion of World War II, employment patterns returned to prewar conditions. Many men who returned to school on the G.I. Bill used education as men had done before them, becoming teachers in an effort to move across class lines. Once again, class differences between males and females surfaced in schools as lower-class men became teachers, joining the middle- and upper-middle-class women already there.

With the increase in the number of men receiving college educations, which prepared them to be teachers and administrators, women's role in educational administration declined after World War II. Fewer women than in previous years were trained as educators, and males appeared in surplus. In some communities, prohibitions against married female teachers were reinstated. The NEA reported that in 1948, the salaries of male elementary principals were substantially higher than those of women.

The 1950s saw a move to consolidate several small school systems into one large one. This practice almost always resulted in women administrators from small districts losing their positions to men in the new structure. Consolidation of white and black schools in the late 1950s and 1960s hurt minority administrators. School districts, which had formerly employed both a minority and a nonminority administrator to head segregated units, when forced to consolidate, kept the white supervisor and eliminated the minority administrator (Williams et al., 1979).

The 1950s were discouraging years for women educators; men were encouraged to become teachers and administrators, women were encouraged to remain at home. A number of strategies to encourage men to enter teaching after World War II were tried. Sensitivity to male egos was also heightened. For instance, R. H. Eckleberry found the frequent practice of referring to a teacher as she annoying and advised a change in an editorial in the *Educational Research Bulletin* entitled "Let's Say 'He' Instead of 'She'." Eckleberry (1945, p. 189) found the feminine pronoun inappropriate for two reasons:

> In the first place, good English usage requires the masculine pronoun when the reference is to an unidentified member of a group which includes persons of both sexes. . . . in the second place, because, by suggesting that teaching is women's work, it tends to discourage men from entering the profession.

The 1950 yearbook of the American Association of School Administrators urged superintendents to recruit men so that "more competent" staffs would exist in public schools:

> And while recruiting more men, let the profession look for the kind of men who see in teaching its great and vital challenges. . . . Let it make sure that teachers' salaries will enable men to live . . . treated with respect and dignity. . . . Then, teaching will become the kind of profession to which men of courage, ability, and vision will turn for the deep and abiding satisfactions which they do not too frequently find in it now. (1950, pp. 161-162)

Women weren't recruited for positions as teachers and administrators and when they did enter the profession it was not described as a "noble calling" but rather a semiprofession that would allow the duties of wife and mother to go undisturbed. The script that had been used by Beecher and Willard, nearly a century before, had been altered somewhat. Initially, women had been urged to enter teaching because it prepared them for marriage and motherhood; during the 1950s, teaching was presented as a good job for married women because it was a vocation that made it easy to combine motherhood, wifehood, and work. The summer vacations and the shorter in-school working day were seen as an ideal compromise.

The notion that teaching was compatible with the duties of wives and mothers had been created as a rationale for hiring married women teachers during World War II to fill the vacancies left by men who served in the military. During World War II, even maternity leaves were arranged (NEA, 1948). These leaves were not all that women might have liked, because they were unpaid and usually mandatory for pregnant women, but they did signify a change in attitudes toward married women and motherhood. Unfortunately, as the mood swung toward married women beginning in the 1940s, public sentiment against single women increased.

> The attractive woman who finds it easy to marry and establish a home is the kind of woman that the schools need and cannot secure or retain under regulations against marriage.... married women tend to have a saner view on sex, and are less likely to become "queer." (Chamberlain & Meece, 1937, p. 57)

Chamberlain's observations foreshadowed the changing view of the kind of woman appropriate to be a teacher. Where once *only* single women had been allowed to teach and be administrators, now they were described as deficient. In the 1940s, school boards wanted married women.

Both ideologies—as single woman or married partner—have limited women's participation in school administration by forcing them into extreme cultural stereotypes. The descriptions of single women include the woman administrator and teacher as a unidimensional person whose sole energy is targeted toward her work and who has no outside life, or the prissy unwanted schoolmarm no one wanted to marry, or a schoolmarm who out of her total devotion to her profession chose not to marry (suggesting that she could not handle both realms of life simultaneously). She may also have been a fuzzy-headed coed, attending college or becoming a teacher only until Prince Charming arrived. In the married version, she is a woman who works in schools only because it compliments her more important career, that of wife and mother. No matter which stereotype was in vogue from the colonial days through the 1950s, the lives of women administrators and teachers were seen as an appropriate sphere of control by school boards and society. Although men's credentials as teachers or administrators were never influenced by their marital or parental status, they too were subjected to public control of their behavior. Nevertheless, women teachers' contracts more often carried ridiculous and insulting provisions:

> I promise to abstain from all dancing, immodest dressing, and other conduct unbecoming a teacher and a lady . . . not to fall in love, to become engaged, or secretly married. . . . to sleep at least eight hours a night, to eat carefully, and to take every precaution to keep in the best of health. (Beale, 1936, pp. 395-396)

The preference for married women as teachers and administrators in the 1950s merely carried on a tradition of prescribing the personal choices of women acceptable to the teaching profession. The issue of lesbian administrators and teachers has seldom been discussed in the literature, although diaries of women teachers in the 1800s indicate that such relationships existed, many for the working lifetimes of the women involved (Hoffman, 1981). The most recent aversion to women, and particularly to single women teachers, probably reflects the homophobia of school boards and society in general. Thus married women are believed to be appropriate not only because they will be less committed to their work, and therefore less of a threat to men vying for school administrative positions, but also because of the misconception that they would be beyond the pale of homosexual life-styles. Interestingly, in the 1980s, divorced women may have become acceptable because they are believed to be able to devote themselves totally to the job. One hundred years after Catharine Beecher the message is the same!

The 1950s and 1960s witnessed a revival of the prejudices against women that had hindered their advancement into administration from the colonial period onward. In the late 1950s and early 1960s, women—married or single—began to be seen once again as the problem in education, instead of the solution. Since the beginning of women's participation in teaching and administration, there had been periodic bursts of protest against the effects so many women in such influential positions would have on society. Given the latent prejudices that American society held against professional women, it was inevitable that the increase in the number of women educators would be viewed with alarm. And indeed, the first outcries against "woman peril" sounded in the late nineteenth century, almost immediately after women began to predominate numerically. In 1908, G. Stanley Hall blamed many of the nation's troubles on female educators: "I think it is impossible not to connect a certain wildness of boys with the feminization of the schools" (Hall, 1908, p. 10239).). A few years later, Robert Rogers, a professor at MIT, asserted:

> For a half-century now, the largest part of our young people have been trained exclusively by women teachers. . . . Fifty years of this has produced a people incompetent to think politically and philosophically. . . . Our American thinking is feminine thinking, inculcated by women teachers, highly competent in detail, immediate in its applications, rigidly idealistic regardless of the working facts, and weak on critical examination. (Rogers, 1929, p. 24)

Probably the most influential and flagrant contemporary expression of this myth of woman peril was Patricia Cayo Sexton's polemic entitled "Schools are Emasculating Our Boys" (1973). Sexton charges that the preponderance of women in the school system has caused it to become "too much of a woman's world" (1973, pp. 138-139) with untold deleterious effect on generations of male students. According to Sexton, women teachers and administrators not only underrated "Johnny's" talents but they emasculated him. Under women, only girls could achieve in school because the successful student value system was feminine. Female teachers were suspect because they extended mother's protective role and utilized teaching methods correspondent only with feminine (frilly) values.

Sexton in her exegesis made overt the buried ambivalence of American society toward working women. This ambivalence was tolerated while society was preoccupied with the growth of the nation but it became intolerable in the post-World War II period. The onset of the Cold War intensified concurrently the importance of education and America's insecurity vis-a-vis the Soviet Union. Although women's influence in education had existed since the mid-1800s and had obviously produced generations of well-educated Americans, suddenly there arose the inordinate fear that America was ill prepared to meet the challenge of the Communists. In the Cold War era, the school was zealously focused on as the instrument for social change and the means by which the American warrior state could ready itself for the oncoming ideological and perhaps military conflict.

The Cold War raised the stakes of the educational process—survival, not success, was at issue. When American social status and political security were at stake, society could not tolerate a majority of female educators. Any failure to achieve, any lack of motivation in the ranks, was spotlighted. Who was to blame for the failure of some boys to achieve? Sexton and her disciples fixed the blame not on the males themselves, not on society, not on the educational process, but squarely upon the woman teacher and administrator, particularly those in the elementary schools.

In response to the deep chord rung anew by Sexton, many educators and the general public joined the chorus of voices raised in opposition to the woman teacher and administrator. All chimed in with support for the proposition that more men were needed to enter teaching and administration to overcome the handicap that boys suffered as a result of being taught by females. It was widely believed that a man could take charge more quickly and efficiently than a woman, that he could establish better contact with the children—particularly the boys—and that he specifically could be relied upon to maintain discipline.

Everyone welcomed *carte blanche* the avalanche of males eager to avoid the Vietnam war by entering teaching, a draftproof profession. The historical circumstances of the 1960s dovetailed neatly with the supposed psychological prerequisites of male teachers and administrators as role models, disciplinarians, and strong academicians. Carol Poll (1979), in a study of why males and females choose elementary education, found that many males entered teaching to avoid the draft during the 1960s and, not surprisingly, that their commitment to education was minimal. Typifying these men is Bob, who said, "I decided to go into teaching to stay out of the army. My last year at (college) I took six credits of ed each semester which was enough at that time to get a sub (substitute) license" (Poll, 1979, p. 6).

This push for males into school, first as teachers, had an enormous impact upon the administrative structure. Most of the men stayed in teaching for only short periods. Some left education for other fields, others taught a few years in impoverished school systems and then made their careers writing books criticizing schools, and some moved quickly into administration. These young men provided the bulk of administrators as school systems expanded and the call for administrators was greatest.

This movement of men into administration in the 1960s coupled with several factors discussed more fully in Chapter 3 served to keep the number of women administrators to a minimum through the 1980s. Although the Women's Liberation Movement, beginning in the 1960s, drew attention to the underrepresentation of women in traditional positions of leadership in the schools, very little movement occurred for women in school administration during the 1960s and 1970s. The percentage of women in school administration in the 1980s is less than the percentage of women in 1905. Women have seldom attained the most powerful and prestigious administrative positions in schools, and the gender structure of males as managers and females as workers has remained relatively stable for the past 100 years. Historical record, then, tells us that there never was a golden age for women administrators, only a promise unfulfilled.

REFERENCES

American Association of School Administrators. (1950). *Public relations for America's schools*. Washington, DC: Author.

American School Board Journal. (1985). *172*(1).

Anthony, S. B., Stanton, E. C., & Harper, I. H. (1922). *The history of woman suffrage* (Vol. I). New York: Fowler & Wells. (Original work published 1881)

Asher, S. R., & Gottman, J. M. (1973). Sex of teacher and student reading achievement. *Journal of Educational Psychology, 65*(2), 168-171.

Beale, H. K. (1936). *Are American teachers free? An analysis of restraints in American schools*. New York: Scribner.

Bernard, R. M., & Vinovskis, M. A. (1977). The female school teacher in antebellum Massachusetts. *Journal of Social History, 10*(3), 332-345.

Billington, R. A. (Ed.). (1981). *The journal of Charlotte Forten: A free Negro in the slave era*. New York: W. W. Norton. (Original work published 1953)

Bonn, M. (1974). An American paradox. *American Education, 10*(9), 24-28.

Brown, D. J. (1981). The financial penalty of the sex talent inversion in Canadian education. *Interchange 12*(1), 69-82.

Burstyn, J. N. (1980). Historical perspectives on women in educational leadership. In S. K. Biklen & M. B. Brannigan (Eds.), *Women and educational leadership* (pp. 65-75). Lexington, MA: D. C. Heath.

Butler, M. (1979). *Education: The critical filter* (Vol. 1). San Francisco: Women's Educational Equity Communications Network.

Callahan, R. E. (1962). *Education and the cult of efficiency*. Chicago: University of Chicago Press.

Carlson, R. O. (1972). *School superintendents: Careers and performance*. Columbus, OH: Merrill.

Chamberlain, L. M., & Meece, L. E. (1937, March). Women and men in the teaching profession. *Bulletin of the Bureau of School Service*, University of Kentucky, 9(3).

Clifford, G. J. (1982). "Marry, stitch, die, or do worse": Educating women for work. In H. Kantor & D. B. Tyack (Eds.), *Work, youth, and schooling: Historical perspectives on vocationalism in American education* (pp. 223-268). Stanford, CA: Stanford University Press.

Collier-Thomas, B. (1982). The impact of black women in education: An historical overview. *Journal of Negro Education, 51*(3), 173-180.

Connolly, L. (1919, March 8). Is there room at the top for women educators? *The Woman Citizen, 3*(41), 840-841.

Counts, G. S. (1927). *The social composition of boards of education: A study in the social control of public education.* Chicago: University of Chicago Press.

Cuban, L. (1976). *Urban school chiefs under fire.* Chicago: University of Chicago Press.

Cubberly, E. P. (1929). *Public school administration.* Boston: Houghton Mifflin.

Databank. (1982, March 10). *Education Week*, pp. 12-13.

Davis, H. (1936). *Women's professional problems in the field of education: A map of needed research* (Pi Lambda Theta Study). Unpublished manuscript.

Davis, H., & Samuelson, A. (1950). Women in education. *Journal of Social Issues* 6(3), 25-37.

Downey, G. W. (1985). Leadership. *Executive Educator, 7*(10), A8-A10.

Eckleberry, R. H. (1945). Let's say "He" instead of "She". *Educational Research Bulletin, XXIV*(7), 189.

Educational news and editorial comment: Women in educational administration. (1928). *School Review, 36*(5), 326-327.

Equal Employment Opportunity Commission. (1978). *Elementary-secondary Staff Information (EEO-5) Annual Surveys.* Washington, DC: U.S. Government Printing Office.

Fishel, A., & Pottker, J. (1974). Women in educational governance: A statistical portrait. *Educational Researcher, 3*(7), 4-7.

Fishel, A., & Pottker, J. (1977). Performance of women principals: A review of behavioral and attitudinal studies. In J. Pottker, & A. Fishel (Eds.), *Sex Bias in the Schools: Research evidence* (pp. 289-299). Cranbury, NJ: Associated University Presses.

Frasher, J. M., & Frasher, R. S. (1979). Educational administration: A feminine profession. *Educational Administration Quarterly, 15*(2), 1-13.

Fuller, E. (1971). *Prudence Crandall: An incident in racism in nineteenth century Connecticut.* Middletown, CT: Wesleyan University Press.

Galludet, T. H. (1838). Female teachers of common schools. *Connecticut Common School Journal, 1*(2), 9-10.

Giddings, P. (1984). *When and where I enter: The impact of black women on race and sex in America.* New York: William Morrow.

Green, C. M. (1967). *The secret city: A history of race relations in the nation's capital.* Princeton, NJ: Princeton University Press.

Greene, M. (1984). The impact of irrelevance: Women in the history of American education. In E. Fennema & M. J. Ayer (Eds.), *Women and education* (pp. 19-39). Berkeley, CA: McCutchan.

Gribskov, M. (1980). Feminism and the woman school administrator. In S. K. Biklen & M. B. Brannigan (Eds.), *Women and educational leadership* (pp. 77-91). Lexington, MA: D. C. Heath.

Hall, G. S. (1908, May). Feminization in school and home. *The World's Work*, 10237-10243.

Hansot, E., & Tyack, D. (1981). *The dream deferred: A golden age for women school administrators* (Policy Paper No. 81-C2). Stanford, CA: Stanford University, Institute for Research on Educational Finance and Government.

Haven, E. W., Adkinson, P. D., & Bagley, M. (1980). *Women in educational administration: The principalship*. Annandale, VA: JWK International Corporation.

The highest salaried woman in the world. (1909). *Western Journal of Education, 14*(10), 515-516.

Hoffman, N. (1981). *Woman's "true" profession: Voices from the history of teaching*. Old Westbury, NY: Feminist Press.

How do women rate? (1946). *Nation's Schools, 37*(3), 45.

Hunton, A. (1904) Negro womanhood defended. *Voice of the Negro, 1*(7), 280-282.

Jensen, R. (1973). Family, career, and reform: Women leaders of the Progressive era. In M. Gordon (Ed.), *The family in social-historical perspective*. New York: St. Martin's.

Jones, A. H. (1905). A century's progress for the American colored woman. *Voice of the Negro, 2*(9), 631-633.

Jones, J. (1979). Women who were more than men: Sex and status in freedmen's teaching. *History of Education Quarterly 19*(1), 47-59.

Jones, J. (1980). *Soldiers of light and love: Northern teachers and Georgia blacks, 1865-1873*. Chapel Hill: University of North Carolina Press.

Kalvelage, J. (1978). *The decline in female principals since 1928: Riddles and clues*. Eugene, Oregon: Sex Equity in Educational Leadership Project. (ERIC Document Reproduction Service No. ED 163 594)

Katz, M. (1973). The new departure in Quincy, 1873-81: The nature of 19th century educational reform. In M. Katz (Ed.), *Education in American history* (pp. 68-84). New York: Prague.

Kerber, L. A. (1983). *The impact of women on American education*. Newton, MA: Women's Educational Equity Act Publishing Center, U.S. Department of Education.

Lathrop, E. A. (1922). Teaching as a vocation for college women. *The Arrow, 38*(3), 415-425.

Lerner, G. (1972). *Black women in white America*. New York: Pantheon.

Love, R. B. (1980, February). *Women in school administration: The route to the top*. Paper presented at the meeting of the National Council of Administrative Women in Education, San Diego, CA.

Lynd, R. S., & Lynd, H. M. (1929). *Middletown: A study in American culture*. NY: Harcourt, Brace & Jovanovich.

Mann, H. (1841). *Fourth annual report to the board of education together with the Fourth annual report of the secretary of the board*. Boston: Dutton and Wentworth.

Melder, K. E. (1972, Fall). Woman's high calling: The teaching profession in America, 1830-60. *American Studies*, pp. 19-32.

National Education Association. (1905). *Report of the Committee on Salaries, Tenure, and Pensions of Public School Teachers in the United States to the National Council of Education*. Winona, MN: Author.

National Education Association. (1927). *Bulletin of the Department of Elementary School Principals*. Washington, DC: Department of Elementary School Principals, Author.

National Education Association. (1928). *The elementary school principalship*. Washington, DC: Department of Elementary School Principals, Author.

National Education Association. (1942) Marriage as related to eligibility. *NEA Research Bulletin, 20*(2), 60-62.

National Education Association. (1948). *The elementary school principalship—today and tomorrow*. Washington, DC: Department of Elementary School Principals, Author.

National Education Association. (1968). *The elementary school principalship in 1968: A research study*. Washington, DC: Department of Elementary School Principals, Author.

O'Connor, E. M. (1969). *Myrtilla Miner: A memoir*. New York: Arno. (Original work published 1884/5)

Office of Education. (1929a). *Statistics of city school systems, 1927-1928* (Bulletin No. 34). Washington, DC: U.S. Goverment Printing Office.

Office of Education. (1929b). *Statistics of public high schools, 1927-1928* (Bulletin No. 35). Washington, DC: U.S. Government Printing Office.

Office of Education. (1930). *Biennial survey of education, 1926-1928* (Bulletin No. 16). Washington, DC: U.S. Government Printing Office.

Pavan, B. N. (1985, October). *Certified but not hired: Women administrators in Pennsylvania*. Paper presented at the annual meeting of the American Education Association Special Interest Group: Research on Women in Education, Boston.

Pearson, J. B., & Fuller, E. (Eds.). (1969). *Education in the states: Historical development and outlook* (Vol. 4). Washington, DC: National Education Association.

Peters, D. W. (1934). *The status of the married woman teacher*. New York: Teachers College, Columbia University Press.

Poll, C. (1979, August). *It's a good job for a woman (and a man): Why males and females choose to be elementary school teachers*. Paper presented at the annual meeting of the American Sociological Association, Boston.

Reich, A. (1974). Teaching is a good profession . . . for a woman. In J. Stacey, S. Bereaud, & J. Daniels (Eds.), *And Jill came tumbling after: Sexism in American education* (pp. 337-343). New York: Dell.

Reid, R. L. (Ed.). (1982). *Battleground: The autobiography of Margaret A. Haley*. Urbana: University of Illinois Press.

Rogers, R. (1929). Is woman ruining the country? *Literary Digest, 102*(13), 24.

Schmuck, P. (1979). *Sex Equity in educational leadership: The Oregon story*. Eugene: University of Oregon, Center for Educational Policy and Management.

Sexton, P. C. (1973). The feminized male. In C. S. Stoll, (Ed.) *Sexism: Scientific debates*. Reading, MA: Addison-Wesley.

Shakeshaft, C. (1981). *Woman's "True" Profession Teaching Guide*. Old Westbury, NY: Feminist Press.

Sklar, K. (1973). *Catharine Beecher: A study in domesticity.* New Haven, CT: Yale University Press.

Smith, J. K. (1979). *Ella Flagg Young: Portrait of a leader.* Ames: Educational Studies Press and Iowa State University Research Foundation.

Solomon, B. M. (1985). *In the company of educated women: A history of women and higher education in America.* New Haven, CT: Yale University Press.

Stern, M. (1973). An insider's view of the teacher's union and women's rights. *Urban Review, 6*(5-6), 46-49.

Strachan, G. C. (1910). *Equal pay for equal work.* New York: B. F. Buck.

Tibbetts, S. L. (1980). The woman principal: Superior to the male? *Journal of the National Association for Women Deans, Administrators, and Counselors, 43*(4), 15-18.

Tyack, D. (1974). *The one best system: A history of American urban education.* Cambridge, MA: Harvard University Press.

Tyack, D., & Hansot, E. (1982). *Managers of virtue: Public school leadership in America, 1820-1980.* New York: Basic Books.

Tyack, D. B., & Strober, M. H. (1981). Jobs and gender: A history of the structuring of educational employment by sex. In P. A. Schmuck, W. W. Charters, Jr., & R. O. Carlson (Eds.), *Educational policy and management, sex differentials* (pp. 131-152). New York: Academic Press.

U.S. Commission of Education. (1911). *1910 Report.* Washington, DC: U.S. Government Printing Office.

Vinovskis, M. A., & Bernard, R. M. (1978). Beyond Catharine Beecher: Female education in the antebellum period. *Signs: A Journal of Women in Culture and Society, 3*(4), 856-869.

Weinberg, M. (1977). *A chance to learn: The history of race and education in the United States.* New York: Cambridge University Press.

Williams, M., Jackson, K., Kincy, M., Wheelter, S., Davis, R., Crawford, R., Forte, M., & Bell, E. (1979). *The Jeanes story: A chapter in the history of American education 1908-1968.* Atlanta, GA: Southern Education Foundation.

Women in educational administration. (1928, May). *School Review,* pp. 326-327.

Woody, T. (1966). *A history of women's education in the United States.* New York: Octagon Books. (Original work published 1929).

Young, E. F. (1916, July 1-8). A reply. *Addresses and Proceedings of the National Education Association,* 356-359.

· 2 ·

Profiles and Career Paths of Women in Administration

It is difficult to determine whether the women in administration today are similar to those women who pioneered administration in the early part of the century. Although biographies and remembrances of a handful of illustrious women administrators from 1900 to 1930 were written, there were few composite descriptions of women as a whole. Although Frances Donovan reports on female teachers in the United States in her 1938 book, *The Schoolma'am,* no similar composite exists for women administrators. Almost the reverse is true of women today. Aggregate descriptions of the women who have chosen to work in the male enclave of educational administration are abundant, although individual accounts are rare.

Few biographies of women administrators are written. Histories, case studies, and ethnographies almost always center on the male prinicipal or superintendent (see, for instance, Blumberg & Greenfield, 1980; Cuban, 1976; Martin & Willower, 1981; Willower & Fraser, 1980; Wolcott, 1973). Consequently, we know little of the individual lives of the women who occupy these positions.

Even in fiction, women administrators are ignored (Williams & Willower, 1983). This invisibility is perhaps preferable when one examines the rare instances where women teachers or administrators are portrayed, accounts that are seldom flattering:

> There was nothing elusive about Miss Dove's appearance. . . . Her hair was more shadowy than it had once been . . . twisted into a meagre little old-maid's knot. Her thin, unpainted mouth bore no sign of those universal emotions—humor, for instance, and love. . . . All in all, in bearing and clothing and bony structure, Miss Dove suggested that classic portrait of the eternal teacher. (Patten, 1954, pp. 19-20)

A more recent fictional account of an elementary school principal by her male superintendent describes her as "small and chunky with a handsome, big-featured face—big nose, big mouth, big eyes—and hair like a great lead-colored halo. Confronting her he was sometimes alarmed at what seemed to be her unfeminine strength of character" (Birmelin, 1984, p. 43).

To get a true picture of the woman administrator we must rely on a collection of studies, most of them mail surveys reported in dissertations, of women administrators as a group. We learn of the "average" woman administrator but little of the individual. From these studies we come to know something of the average female administrator, leading to the realization that she differs from her male counterpart in important ways.

This chapter presents a profile of the composite woman administrator and a description of her career path, illustrating that the literature on men is insufficient for understanding women in educational leadership.

PROFILE OF THE WOMAN ADMINISTRATOR

Personal Characteristics

Women in educational administration tend to be in their mid- to late 40s. Black women are somewhat younger than white women in similar positions and Hispanic women younger than women from all racial/ethnic groups (Ortiz & Venegas, 1978). For all women, the higher the position they hold, the older they are. Interestingly, K-12 administrators are older than are women administrators in higher educational institutions. A study by Ann Picker indicates that in some places women may be moving into administration earlier in their careers. She found that "younger women who enter administration are not waiting as long for administrative appointment as did their older female colleagues" (1980, p. 146).

Most women in administration are white, but studies of big cities find that percentages of majority to minority women are nearly equal.

Women in school administration come from rural areas (Brooks, 1976; Davis, 1978; Drust, 1977; Hankin, 1978; McCorkle, 1976; Paddock, 1978; Rideout, 1974; O.T. Robinson, 1978; Thomas, 1976) and are often (43.5%) firstborn or only children. If not an only child, the composite woman administrator was raised in a family with three or fewer siblings (Davis, 1978; Douglas, 1977; Drust, 1977; Hankin, 1978; McCorkle, 1976; Rideout, 1974; Tessler, 1976; Thomas, 1976; Walsh, 1975). There is considerable research that points out that firstborn women or only-child women are often higher achievers. For women, it is thought that as an only or firstborn child, the sex-role stereotyping that might later affect aspiration is not as strong as parents, particularly fathers, focus their hopes and dreams upon the only available child, even if she is female.

The average woman administrator was raised in a two-parent family. The modal level of education of the fathers of women administrators is more than an elementary education but less than a high school diploma. Fathers of female K-12 administrators tend to have less education than do fathers of female higher education administrators. The majority of all fathers are farmers, and in descending order of frequency, unskilled laborer, skilled laborer, educator, and businesss and professional men (Brooks, 1976; Davis, 1978; Douglas, 1977; Drust, 1977; Hankin, 1978; McCorkle, 1976; Paddock, 1978; Rideout, 1974; Scriven, 1974; Tessler, 1976; Thomas, 1976; Vance, 1978).

In the area of educational attainment it is not like father like daughter, but rather like mother like daughter. Women administrators achieve higher educational levels than their fathers. Mothers of women in administration were studied in 13 dissertations (Brooks, 1976; Davis, 1978; Douglas, 1977; Drust, 1977; Hankin, 1978; Martin, 1976; McCorkle, 1976; Paddock, 1978; Rideout, 1974; Scriven, 1974; Tessler, 1976; Thomas, 1976; Vance, 1978) and were found to have more formal education than their husbands. Whereas most of the mothers had either a high school or college education, the overwhelming majority of white women were homemakers.

Only black mothers tended to work outside the home and then, despite their educations, in unskilled labor positions.

Women administrators are more often married than not. Black women are more likely to be married than white women, and K-12 administrators are much more likely than higher education administrators to be married. A synthesis of 27 studies that explored women's marital status finds that 56% of all women administrators are married, with 63.5% of the black women and 61% of the K-12 women married. This is a slightly lower figure than the 1979 American Association of School Administrators' (AASA) study (Educational Research Service, 1981), which found 65% of women superintendents married. We know little of the life-styles of the 44% of women administrators who are unmarried. Although studies of the general population estimate that 15% of women are lesbians (Bell & Weinberg, 1978), no study has documented the number of women administrators who are woman identified. Neither do we have knowledge of heterosexual women living in committed relationships with men. Whereas the number of women openly identified with the latter two life-styles are no doubt small—given community pressures to conform to the myth of the happy family—closeted lesbians and unmarried heterosexual women living with men almost certainly constitute a large group of those women identified as single.

The majority of the husbands of women in educational administration are college graduates and a number have advanced degrees (Douglas, 1977; Drust, 1977; Hankin, 1978; Rideout, 1974; Smith, 1977; Thomas, 1976; Walsh, 1975). They tend to be employed in education, sales, and professional occupations. The AASA study reported that education was not the field of choice for the husbands of women superintendents—only 25% were educators. However, nearly 61% of working wives of male superintendents were employed in schools. For women at all administrative levels, Paddock (1978) found that in over half of the marriages, the husbands earned less than their wives.

Of women administrators, 65% are parents—a higher mean than are married. This is probably accounted for through divorce and death of a husband, although it is possible, but not probable given traditional community standards, that some of these mother may be never-married women (Baron, 1976; Brooks, 1976; Crosby, 1973;

Davis, 1978; Douglas, 1977; Drust, 1977; Fansher, 1978; Giggleman, 1978; Goerss, 1975; Hankin, 1978; Marable, 1974; Martin, 1976; Miller, 1976; Paddock, 1978; Rideout, 1974; W.C. Robinson, 1978; Smith, 1977; Tessler, 1976; Thomas, 1976; Vance, 1978).

The majority of women administrators are Protestant but a sizable minority identify with other religions (Goerss, 1975; Hankin, 1978; Paddock, 1978; Scriven, 1974; Vance, 1978). Half are registered as Democrats (Hankin, 1978; Paddock, 1978). Women administrators tend to belong primarily to educational organizations, but a number of other community groups claim their time, including the League of Women Voters, the American Association of University Women, and the National Organization for Women. More black women show strong participation in church work than women of other racial groups (Baron, 1976; Brooks, 1976; Martin, 1976; Paddock, 1978; Rideout, 1974; Thomas, 1976).

Educational Preparation

Amount of education is the area that has changed most for women in administration in the twentieth century. Doctoral programs in administration report that 50% or more of their students are women, and more aspiring women administrators report working for advanced degrees. A study of a graduate education program between 1976 and 1980 by Marshall (1984) documented that 71% of the Ph.D. and 63% of the Ed.D. aspirants were women.

Nevertheless, studies of those women who are currently in administration reflect conditions in which women were not only not encouraged to enter doctoral work, but were actively discouraged. Whereas half the doctoral candidates are women, of those who actually hold K-12 positions, most are likely to have completed only a master's degree, with only 17.6% holding a doctorate (Baron, 1976; Bock, 1976; Burton, 1976; Crosby, 1973; Davis, 1978; Douglas, 1977; Drust, 1977; Giggleman, 1978; Goerss, 1975; Hankin, 1978; Marable, 1974; Martin, 1976; McCamey, 1976; McCorkle, 1976; Miller, 1976; Nieboer, 1975; Paddock, 1978; Quinn, 1977; Rideout, 1974; O.T. Robinson, 1978; W.C. Robinson, 1978; Scriven, 1974; Taylor, 1977; Tessler, 1976; Thomas, 1976; Vance, 1978; Walsh, 1975). As undergraduates, about half of the women completed liberal arts' degrees and the other half hold a bachelor's in education. The woman administrator tends to return to school while a teacher or administrator, with the masters' degree completed in her early 30s and the doctorate in her 40s.

DIFFERENCES BETWEEN THE PROFILES OF WOMEN AND MEN IN ADMINISTRATION

The profile of the typical woman administrator differs from the profile of the typical man administrator in a number of ways. So different are they that one might ask, "Is there any similarity between the backgrounds of men and women in school administration?" Specifically, women in all levels of administration are older than men in similar positions, are less likely to be married, are more often members of minority and ethnic groups, more often come from more urban backgrounds, are politically more liberal, identify as non-Protestant more often, are more likely to have been a teacher for a longer period of time, and earn less for doing the same job as a man.

Women have moved into administration later in their lives for a combination of reasons, many of which will be examined more fully in Chapter 3. Although women administrators are older than men primarily because of sex discrimination, a number of other factors have contributed to women remaining as teachers longer than men. Literature on life stages of women indicate that career becomes a focus of midlife. Barnett and Baruch (1979) found that at midlife, self-esteem increased and women discovered self-worth. This, coupled for women with children with fewer demands as mother, means that middle age often marks the birth of new or renewed career commitment and focus. Paddock (1978) found that the demands of the role of homemaker and mother were listed as a major difficulty for women attempting to move from teacher to administrator. Over 40% of the women in her study took *sole* responsibility for housework, cooking, and child care in addition to their jobs as teachers. Only as these responsiblities lessened as their children grew up were these women able to add the additional tasks of school administration to their limited day.

Interestingly, some women find the job of school administrator much less demanding of time and energy than teaching. One secondary school principal of a large suburban high school commented on new leisure time that allowed her to read much more than she had ever been able to as a teacher: "I didn't realize how much easier it was to be an administrator than a teacher," she said. "I have so much more free time available to me." Her experience might indicate that the added commitment of time may be more imagined than real; perhaps school administration is just as compatible with childrearing as teaching is thought to be. On the other hand, the difference may lie not in the amount of work but in its location. Many of the duties of teachers such as grading papers and preparing class activities can be done at home. Most, but not all, of administrative duties need to be taken care of outside the home.

Fewer women principals than men are married (59.8% vs. 92%), a trend holding in the superintendency (Educational Research Service, 1981; Paddock, 1978). Of women superintendents, 65% are married, in contrast with 93% of men. Further, women are more likely to have been divorced or widowed than are men and, not surprisingly, women are more likely to be single parents than are men in administration.

Different from men is the race of women administrators. A higher proportion of female principals than male principals are minority people; 21% of women principals are members of ethnic and minority groups, compared to 4% of male principals (Paddock, 1981). However, because men predominate in the principalship, the number of minority male principals is greater than the number of minority female principals. Doughty found that of black administrators promoted prior to 1966, 29.3% were female, whereas only 24.3% of black administrators promoted after 1966 were women. She notes, "even though blacks, as a group, face significant discrimination in the administrative area, black women face more" (Doughty, 1980, p. 167).

More male administrators than females are from small town, rural backgrounds, more are Protestants, and more belong to and are active in the Republican party (Paddock, 1981). Women belong to more groups that have changing society as their goal than do men; not surprisingly, they belong more often to groups that are intent upon rectifying the discrimination faced by women in this society.

For instance, a study of superintendents found that the average male superintendent was slightly younger than the average female and that the oldest female superintendent was seven years older than the oldest male. Further, 93% of the men, but only 65% of the women, superintendents in this same study were married. The majority (60.5%) of the male superintendents had served in their positions six or more years, whereas only 20.8% of the women had served that long (Educational Research Service, 1981).

Studies of principals support these same differences between males and females. For instance, data from the National Association of Elementary School Principals show that since 1928, the average ages of women elementary principals have been higher than those of men (Pharis & Zachariya, 1979). At the secondary level, Paddock (1980) reports that the modal age of the female principal is 50, whereas for the male it is 44.

Similar to women in other administrative positions, women principals enter teaching earlier than do men but attain the principalship later. Carlson (1972) noted that men seek the principalship in their mid- to late 20s and research on women finds them pursuing such jobs in their 30s and later (Haven, Adkinson, & Bagley, 1980). The average woman principal spends 15 years as a teacher before seeking a principalship, whereas the average male spends 5 (Haven, Adkinson, & Bagley, 1980); minority women teach 12 to 20 years before becoming principals (Doughty, 1980). Studies of principals find that women earn less than men, even when the length of service, preparation, and other factors are equal (Smith, 1977).

Women belong to more professional organizations than do men. Pharis and Zachariya (1979) found that among elementary principals, women are more likely than men to belong to the National Association of Elementary School Principals, the AASA, the Association for Supervision and Curriculum Development, and the NEA.

The "average" woman administrator, then, is more likely to be older, of a different race, religion, and political party, to be unmarried, and from a more urban background than her male counterpart. She is more likely to hold liberal views, to be more supportive of women's rights, and to understand the issues of single parents and divorce more personally. This portrait of the woman administrator is vastly different from our profile of the male administrator and calls into question studies that have assumed the homogeneity of samples of administrators.

TABLE 2.1
Average Age of Elementary School Principals:
1928-1984

	1928	*1948*	*1958*	*1968*	*1978*	*1984*
Men	43	44	45	43	45	46
Women	49	50	52	56	49	47

CAREER PATHS OF WOMEN IN ADMINISTRATION

What Is a Career?

The typical woman administrator not only does not look like the typical male administrator, the path that she took to achieve her position differs as well. The literature on careers and career paths in administration doesn't fit the experiences of women administrators, primarily because the experiences we used to define career and to document career routes have come from men.

By focusing on male experience, definitions of career have been wrought that may not work for women. Biklen notes that:

> In spite of changes in the work force, of the opening of fields that were previously more resistant to women, of the addition of women in professional and upper management positions, the structure of career is based on the ways in which men have been able to live their lives, free from primary responsibility for the family. (1985, p. 2)

Traditionally, a career has been characterized as "a pre-established total pattern of organized professional activity, with upward movement through recognized preparatory stages, and advancement based on merit and bearing honor" (Bledstein, 1976, p. 172). Upward movement through the hierarchy and commitment to career demonstrated by lack of interruptions are essential components in traditional definitions of career. Because most teachers do not move through the traditional hierarchy and because many women teachers move in and out of the profession as their life circumstances change, many have labeled teaching as careerless or as a semicareer (Lortie, 1975). Carlson and Schmuck (1981, p. 117) write that a career in education involves a sequence of jobs: "Thus, being a third-grade teacher in the same school all of one's working life does not constitute a career in our definition." According to their definition, a definition that is consistent with the majority of the career literature on men, only administrators have careers. Teachers have jobs.

The research of Sari Biklen (1985) asks us to reconsider the definition of career, using the experiences of women as well as men in the reconceptualization. She argues that we have recorded what men do and then labeled it a career. If women do these same things, then they have careers. If not, they have jobs. In her study of elementary teachers, she analyzed the way women view careers and offered a definition that included both female and male experience. Biklen demonstrates that the way careers have been defined reflects an androcentric bias and limits our ability to illuminate the working lives of women in schools.

The purpose of questioning the concept of career is important as one comes to look at women's lives, particularly their lives in schools, as the literature of the field has tended to present the notion that career paths move along the bureaucratic structure. Many women make clear choices that they don't wish to follow the same paths as men, that they have reasons for choosing other routes. Because of these choices and because of sex discrimination in employment patterns in schools, women's career paths in education predominately exist at the teacher level. Growth and experience substitute for movement up the hierarchy. For many women, the climb to the top of the mountain is not even desirable—they would much rather gather around the valleys and rivers, "where life is really lived."

What Do the Career Paths of Women Administrators Look Like?

Even when we move from teaching to administration, we still don't find a replica of men's lives. Although very little research has been undertaken to understand the career paths of women in administration, that which exists is modeled upon male-generated assumptions of careers. The very notion of talking about career paths for women administrators is colored by the definition, generated from male experience, of career. Except for recent work such as Biklen's on teachers (1985), the careers of women in education have only been studied if the women were administrators, because, according to the traditional definition of career, only administrators have careers because teachers have jobs. It is important to stress that this chapter is not meant to reinforce or support this view of educational careers. Discussing women's administrative careers does not preclude seeing teaching as an equally valid and legitimate career path.

Women have attained positions of every type in the administrative hierarchy. They are superintendents of big city schools, they are education commissioners, they are presidents of universities, and principals of elementary schools. Some manage large systems with thousands of employees and budgets of millions. Others still preside over one-room schools. Wherever there are public schools, there are women holding positions of leadership. But despite all positions having been occupied at least once by a female, the majority of women are concentrated on the lower rungs of the ladder. They are most often found in central office staff positions, either as a specialist or a supervisor, or in the elementary principalship. They hold titles such as reading coordinator or English language arts director. Generally, their interactions are with children or female teachers. Black women are found primarily in staff positions or in positions that have to do with minority concerns.

Women in public schools have more chance of being top-level administrators in small districts or in elementary school districts. Natera (1977) found that in 1968, 100% of female superintendents in California were in elementary districts. Similarly, White (1976) notes that women superintendents in Texas are primarily in districts with from 100-1999 average daily attendence. Drust (1977) found women as principals in schools with fewer than 1000 pupils.

The minority woman principal is most often working in a school with 20% or more minority population, in a southern state. Whereas 15% of all principals are employed in the South, 30% of minority principals work there (Lovelady-Dawson, 1980).

Women begin their careers committed to education; nearly half major in education or in the humanities with an education specialization (Paddock, 1980). Most knew they wanted to be a teacher as early as the beginning of high school. After undergraduate school, women begin teaching. A few years later, many take a leave of absence from teaching to have and raise children. Whereas not all women have children, and not all of those who have children take a leave of absence, most who do take maternity leave do so in their 20s.

Leaves for child raising often serve a dual purpose for the women who take them as graduate training at the masters' level often comes during these years. Even if not on leave, most women begin graduate work in their late 20s or early 30s. The majority of these women specialize in education, although a few major in administration at this time.

In their 30s, women turn to administration, almost always at the urging of someone in their district. Studies indicate that it takes very little to turn a woman's attention to administration, but that it does take some overt act—however small—for most women to begin to think of becoming administrators. If the woman seeks a position on her own, rather than being tapped for it, and she doesn't get it, she'll try again only once or twice and then cease pursuing administration. Those who are tapped or who succeed in getting an administrative job in the first few tries generally move into one of two kinds of positions: the elementary principalship or a position as a subject matter specialist, particularly in reading, language, or fine arts. The typical woman in administration remains at this level; if she moves, the woman administrator will be promoted to a supervisory position in the central office, as director or coordinator of curriculum or some other districtwide program. And there the majority of women in administration stay.

For that minority of women who achieve the secondary principalship, an assistant or associate superintendency, or the superintendency, the career paths are somewhat different and more like those of males.

Gaertner (1981), Stockard (1984), and Ortiz (1982) have detailed specific career paths of all administrators, and particularly of women administrators, in their studies. For both the typical and atypical woman in administration, the three most common ways for women to enter school administration are through specialist positions, supervisory posts, and elementary principalships. The greatest number of women in administration hold central office positions—positions that tend to be staff rather than line jobs. Very often they get to these positions through specialist roles. Reading and fine arts are common specialist positions that Ortiz found women occupy. Usually, these are the first administrative jobs that women hold; often these jobs don't require administrative certification. Generally, a specialist, whether housed in a school building or in the central office, is in a position on the formal hierarchy above teachers but below principals.

Specialists undertake a variety of activities: teaching a special course to students, coordinating instruction of the specialty, developing curriculum guides and materials for the specialty, or administering local, state and/or federal programs. Thus specialists generally either engage in instruction or program administration. Ortiz (1982, p. 64) found that the specialist role provides a number of opportunities for women:

> First, there is at least partial departure from the classroom and instruction. Second, the role has changed in regard to the relationship of other teachers. Third, it is a post which provides increased visibility and schedule flexibility.

Therefore, a specialist position offers some real administrative experience coupled with visibility, which often leads to a promotion into a supervisory job.

The supervisory role is called by many names: coordinator, director, and assistant administrator. Usually, supervisors and principals are at the same level on the hierarchy, but supervisors are staff positions and principals are line. Briner and Iannaccone (1966, p. 193) point out the distinction between the line position of principal and the staff position of supervisor:

> Each . . . in working with a common subordinate (teacher) and a common superordinate (associate superintendent) was capable of exercising two bases of social power or sources of influence—(1) status as legal authority legitimated by general acceptance of impersonal rules, and (2) personal prestige derived from the quality of technical knowledge.

Briner and Iannaccone found that in addition to possessing different types of authority (legal vs. expert), principals and supervisors interacted with different players in the school district. Principals were more likely to work with assistant superintendents and other central office staff, whereas supervisors spent more time with subject specialists, principals, and teachers. Most of the supervisors spent time dealing with instructional matters. Ortiz (1982) found that supervisory positions rarely resulted in promotion to deputy, associate, or assistant superintendent positions, but that they did offer an opportunity for the establishment of a career as a central office staff member.

The third most common way that women enter administration is through the elementary principalship. Unfortunately, the elementary principalship, for both men and women, but primarily for women, is a dead-end job. Gross and Trask (1964, 1976) reported that once they take the job of elementary principal, women tend not to move. Meskin (1974, pp. 336-337) attributed this lack of movement to dedication to elementary school education:

> A career portrait of the female principal emerges. . . . The woman principal begins her working years strongly committed to the occupation of teaching. Her eye is rarely on career advancement, and she concentrates instead on knowing the ins and outs of her profession. When, often by a fluke, she is promoted to a principalship in later life, her long years as a basic service professional in an organization stands her in good stead. She shows greater ability and self-confidence in directing the instructional program than men do simply because of her deeper understanding of the art of teaching, and she also demonstrates a high degree of ability in administering the school, the milieu in which she worked so long. Because again she is not seeking promotion from her present rank, she commits herself wholeheartedly to the role of principal and is able to master the job in a highly competent fashion.

Women, then, move into and are moved into positions that have little opportunity or likelihood of helping them advance in the system. Haven, Adkinson, and Bagley (1980) report that from 1965 to 1977, the position that helped advance one into a secondary principalship changed. In 1965, 38% of secondary school principals had been elementary school principals prior to being selected for their current post; 48% had been guidance counselors. By 1977, the proportion of former guidance counselors who became secondary school principals was down to 18%, whereas 54% of secondary school principals were assistant principals of high schools with 35% having been athletic directors in middle, junior, and senior highs.

The position of guidance counselor was one that was very useful for women to use to move into administration. A six-year, longitudinal study by Greenfield and Beam (1980) illustrated how women used the counselor position to move into principalships.

The change in the route to becoming a secondary school principal very directly affected women's chances. Whereas women were moving into guidance counselor positions, it was no longer seen as a path to the principalship. Positions in which women had very little opportunity for being selected—assistant principalships and athletic directorships—on the other hand, were very likely to be the springboard into the principalship. Rosser (1980) points out that the emphasis on maintaining discipline as a component of the assistant principalship keeps women from being hired for those positions. The overwhelming amount of research that shows that women are better than men at maintaining discipline has done nothing to dispell this misperception from hiring committees:

> After ten years of teaching and five years of disciplining children as assistant principal, I felt I was the best qualified candidate for principal in my elementary school. I had a good working relationship with the staff and an excellent administrative record. I understood the needs of the community. I was stunned when I lost out to a former high school math teacher and football coach with two years of administrative experience. The superintendent told me he felt I wasn't tough enough to handle the discipline problems in the school. (Rosser, 1980, p. 32)

Athletic directors and coaches are thought to be able to discipline. There is no evidence to support these conclusions, but this belief has been used repeatedly to justify hiring a man and not a woman.

Black women, like white women, tend to be in the nonmovement positions of supervisor, consultant, elementary principal, and administrative assistant (Doughty, 1980). If the black woman is an elementary principal, she's most likely to be in a "so called tough, predominantly black school. Rarely can she be found in the high school principalship or the superintendency" (1980, p. 167).

WOMEN'S CAREER PATHS IN ADMINISTRATION ARE DIFFERENT THAN MEN'S

An examination of the literature reveals differences in male and female career paths. Men start their careers with less commitment to education and teaching. A majority of men have chosen teaching as a second option, rather than a first, whereas most women teachers know from an early age that being a teacher is what they wanted.

Men move more quickly than do women into graduate study where they tend to major in different specializations than do women. Paddock (1980) found that among secondary school principals, the majority of men (71%) held graduate degrees in educational administration whereas fewer than half of the women had such a major. Further, the men began work on their first graduate degree in their mid-20s, whereas women continued to go to school in their late 20s and early 30s.

Men achieve their first formal administrative position much sooner than women and in many positions come with less administrative experience (Paddock, 1980). Studies demonstrate that although male teachers are sponsored more than females for administrative positions, of those teachers who finally become administrators, women receive slightly more sponsorship (Picker, 1980) indicating that men need fewer doors opened for them to arrive at the same place as women. For both men and women, administrative careers are largely unplanned but women tend to plan less than men.

If men's work lives are interrupted at all, and they usually aren't, it is to satisfy military requirements or to attend universities to gain administrative certification or doctorates. By and large, men in administration have steady paths up the traditional hierarchy. From a teaching position, they move to an assistant principalship or a principalship; from a principalship, to an assistant superintendency, and then to a superintendent's job.

Women, on the other hand, often take leaves from their jobs to have and raise children. Paddock (1981) found that 49.1% of the women administrators in her study had not only taken maternity leaves but had taken leaves while administrators, something men rarely do. Although few men take paternity leaves, it may be that such an experience has an even more adverse effect on men than women. An incident in which a man who had taken a paternity leave and who wanted support from his university professors for an elementary school principalship is illustrative. The department chairperson told him to remove any references to the paternity leave from his resume and to never tell anyone. "It's better they think you were in prison or a mental hospital than that you took a paternity leave," the new father was told. Even with these deletions the chairperson was uneasy supporting the candidate, intimating that the man was homosexual. "What kind of man takes a paternity leave, anyway?"

Women, at least, are expected to care for children and subsequently take leave of their school careers to attend to homemaking and childrearing jobs. They stay in teaching much longer than do men and when they begin to move into administration they start with a specialist position and move to a supervisory one or on to an elementary school principalship. This is primarily where they stay. When they do move into secondary school principalships, assistant superintendencies, and the superintendency, they hold more administrative positions at more administrative levels than do men.

As can be seen in Figure 2.1, women hold staff positions and generally don't move into the line positions of secondary principal, assistant/associate superintendent, or superintendent. When they do, their career paths become more like those of men in similar positions (Paddock, 1981). Figure 2.1 also demonstrates that there are more entry positions for the typical male teacher to become an administrator.

Gaertner (1981) documented three mobility paths, two of which lead to the superintendency. In the first, the path is from specialist to administrator of instruction (also called supervisor) to assistant superintendent to superintendent. Ortiz (1982) and Gaertner (1981) found that the majority of administrators who complete this path are men and that women on this path usually stop at administrator of instruction.

A second mobility path finds even fewer women along the way. This route moves from assistant secondary principal to secondary principal to assistant/associate superintendent to superintendent. Women rarely achieve the superintendency in this manner.

The third mobility seldom led to the superintendency and was the one most likely to be held by women. This path began at the level of assistant elementary principal and moved to the elementary principalship. This path only ends in a superintendency in elementary districts, and then almost always it is a male who becomes the elementary superintendent.

These three paths are mobility patterns for both men and women, but for women the paths usually end at supervisory positions or elementary principalships. Unfortunately, these three routes in administration put very few women on the fast track. All are primarily dead-end positions on the hierarchy that don't lead to the powerful line positions of secondary school principal, assistant

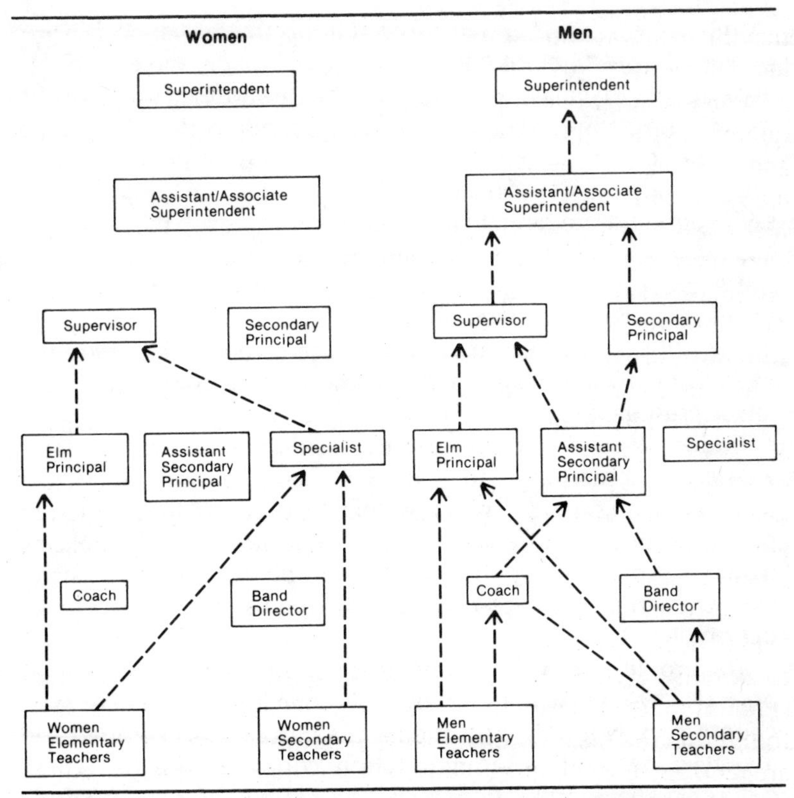

Figure 2.1 Typical Career Paths of Women and Men in Administration

and associate superintendent, and superintendent. Supervisory positions and the elementary principalship are not the positions in which mobile men are found, neither are they positions most women can use to reach the superintendency. Only in the case of the superintendency are the paths of men and women similar (Stockard, 1984).

Why these differences? There are three major views on women's lack of achievement of formal positions. The first two—that women lack aspiration or that sex discrimination in the form of a myriad of barriers keep women out—will be discussed in the next chapter. A third perspective is that women are not victims but rather have control of their lives and see their worlds in a larger perspective—one that allows room for achievement and affiliation. For many women, the superintendency is not a job that has appeal. It has power and prestige but it lacks, for these women, the day-to-day experiences that make work enjoyable. One woman said that she would "no sooner like to be a superintendent than I would a garbage collector. Both are jobs that seem undesirable to me." Interestingly, studies of male superintendents often quote them as saying, upon retirement, that the most enjoyable job they held was an elementary school principalship. And yet, they didn't remain in these jobs, preferring the lure of power and prestige to day-to-day satisfaction. For many women, perhaps, the glories of the top are not worth the sacrifices and they choose career paths where the quality of work life makes up for the lower salary, lower power, and lower prestige.

I add this caveat because we don't know all the reasons that women's career paths are the way they are. We know that discrimination exists and we know that the organizational structure precludes people in certain positions—positions usually held by women—from moving up. However, we do not fully understand why women themselves choose these paths when given other options.

The profile of the woman administrator presented in this chapter portrays a woman who differs by more than her sex from her male counterpart. Not only does she have a different background and life-style, her path in administration contrasts with his. These differences have implications for what we know about the "typical" administrator, as the typical male is most unlike the typical female.

REFERENCES

Barnett, R. C., & Baruch, G. K. (1979). *Multiple roles and well being: A study of mothers of preschool age children* (Working Paper No. 3). Wellesley, MA: Wellesley College Center for Research on Women.

Baron, E. B. (1976). The status of women senior high school principals in the United States. *Dissertation Abstracts International, 37*, 4259A. (University Microfilms No. 77-681)

Bell, A. P., & Weinberg, M. S. (1978). *Homosexualities: A study of diversity among men and women*. New York: Simon & Schuster.

Biklen, S. K. (1985, April). *Can elementary school teaching be a career? A search for*

new ways of understanding women's work. Paper presented at the annual meeting of the American Educational Research Association, Chicago.
Birmelin, B. T. (1984). *The superintendent*. New York: Schocken.
Bledstein, B. J. (1976). *The culture of professionalism*. New York: Norton.
Blumberg, A., & Greenfield, W. (1980). *The effective principal*. Boston: Allyn & Bacon.
Bock, D. J. (1976). Women in instructional middle management in California community colleges: A study of mobility. *Dissertation Abstracts International, 37*, 5624A.
Briner, C., & Iannaccone, L. (1966). Selected social power relationships in education. *Educational Administration Quarterly, 2*(3), 190-203.
Brooks, B.J.R. (1976). A profile of black females in selected administrative positions in the public school systems of Florida. *Dissertation Abstracts International, 36*, 6585A. (University Microfilms No. 76-9353)
Burton, J.M.H. (1976). An exploratory study of racially different female administrators in selected colleges and universities. *Dissertation Abstracts International, 37*, 825A. (University Microfilms No. 76-19, 094)
Carlson, R. O. (1972). *School superintendents: Careers and performance*. Columbus, OH: Merrill.
Carlson, R. O., & Schmuck, P. A. (1981). The sex dimension of careers in educational management: Overview and synthesis. In P. A. Schmuck, W. W. Charters, Jr., & R. O. Carlson (Eds.), *Educational policy and management: Sex differentials (pp. 117-130). New York: Academic Press.*
Crosby, J. W. (1973). An exploratory study of women superintendents. *Dissertation Abstracts International, 34*, 3742A. (University Microfilms No 73-31, 074)
Cuban, L. (1976). *Urban school chiefs under fire*. Chicago: University of Chicago Press.
Davis, M. C. (1978). Women administrators in southwestern institutions of higher education. *Dissertation Abstracts International, 39*, 1945A-1946A. (University Microfilms No. 7819168)
Donovan, F. R. (1974). *The schoolma'am* (2nd ed.). New York: Arno (Original work published 1938).
Doughty, R. (1980). The black female administrator: Woman in a double bind. In S. K. Biklen & M. B. Brannigan (Eds.), *Women in educational leadership* (pp. 165-174). Lexington MA: D. C. Heath.
Douglas, P. D. (1977). An analysis of demographic characteristics and career patterns of women administrators in higher education. *Dissertation Abstracts International, 37*, 653A. (University Microfilms No. 77-16, 705)
Drust, B. (1977). Factors related to the employment of women as junior high school and high school principals, assistant superintendents and superintendents in California public schools. *Dissertation Abstracts International, 37*, 5479A. (University Microfilms No. 77-4825)
Educational Research Service. (1981). *Survey: Attitudes toward women as school district administrators*. Arlington, VA: American Association of School Administrators.
Fansher, R. R. (1978). Job satisfaction and dissatisfaction of female public secondary school principals in the United States. *Dissertation Abstracts International, 39*, 7260A. (University Microfilms No. 7807880)

Gaertner, K. N. (1981). Administrative careers in public school organizations. In P. A. Schmuck, W. W. Charters, Jr., & R. O. Carlson (Eds.), *Educational policy and management: Sex differentials* (pp. 199-217). New York: Academic Press.
Giggleman, L.J.C. (1978). A comparison of the personality characteristics of women administrators and women teachers in selected community colleges. *Dissertation Abstracts International, 39,* 3397A. (University Microfilms No. 7824137)
Goerss, K.V.W. (1975). A study of personality factors of selected women administrators in higher education. *Dissertation Abstracts International, 36,* 1942a. (University Microfilms No. 75-22, 500)
Greenfield, W., & Beam, A. (1980). Power and opportunity in the principalship: The case of two women leaders in education. In S. K. Biklen, & M. B. Brannigan (Eds.), *Women and educational leadership* (pp. 47-62). Lexington, MA: D. C. Heath.
Gross, N., & Trask, A. E. (1964). *Men and women as elementary school principals* (Final Report No. 2). Cambridge, MA: Harvard University, Graduate School of Education.
Gross, N., & Trask, A. E. (1976). *The sex factor and the management of schools.* New York: John Wiley.
Hankin, C. G. (1978). The female elementary school principal. *Dissertation Abstracts International, 39,* 49A. (University Microfilms No. 7810883)
Haven, E. W., Adkinson, P. D., & Bagley, M. (1980). *Women in educational administration: The principalship.* Annandale, VA: JWK International Corporation.
Lortie, D. C. (1975). *School-teacher.* Chicago: University of Chicago Press.
Lovelady-Dawson, F. (1980). Women and minorities in the principalship: Career opportunities and problems. *NASSP Bulletin, 64*(4), 18-28.
Marable, J. M. (1974). The role of women in public school administration as perceived by black women administrators in the field. *Dissertation Abstracts International, 36,* 73A. (University Microfilms No. 75-14,316)
Marshall, C. (1984). Men and women in educational administration programs. *Journal of the National Association for Women Deans, Administrators, and Counselors, 48*(1), 3-12.
Martin, K.J.L. (1976). Directors of continuing education for women: A study of the personnel and the position in general extension and continuing education. *Dissertation Abstracts International, 37,* 1935A. (University Microfilms No. 76-22, 204)
Martin, W. J., & Willower, D. J. (1981). The managerial behavior of high school principals. *Educational Administration Quarterly, 17*(1), 69-90.
McCamey, D. S. (1976). The status of black and white women in central administrative positions in Michigan public school. *Dissertation Abstracts International, 37,* 6189A. (University Microfilms No. 77-7987)
McCorkle, E. M. (1976). Top-level women administrators in higher education: A study of women presidents, chief academic officers, and academic deans in Federal regions I, VI, and X. *Dissertation Abstracts International, 36,* 7238A. (University Microfilms No. 76-9715)
Meskin, J. (1974). The performance of women school administrators—a review of the literature. *Administrator's Notebook, 23*(1), 1-4.
Meskin, J. (1978). Women as principals: Their performance as educational administrators. In D. A. Erickson & T. L. Reller (Eds.) *The Principal in Metropolitan Schools* (pp. 323-347). Berkeley, CA: McCutchan.

Miller, G. L. (1976). A study of selected social processes on women's career motivation related to the declining number of women in elementary school principalship. *Dissertation Abstracts International, 37,* 3315A-3316A. (University Microfilms No. 76-27, 336)

Natera, M. (1977). The employment of California women line administrators in K-12 districts in the years 1968, 1972, and 1976. *Dissertation Abstracts International, 38,* 11, 6448A.

National Association of Secondary School Principals (1972). *Job descriptions for principals and assistant principals.* Resten, VA: Author.

Nieboer, N. S. (1975). The administrative woman in higher education. *Dissertation Abstracts International, 36,* 2550A-2551A. (University Microfilms No. 75-25, 971)

Ortiz, F. I. (1982). *Career patterns in education: Women, men and minorities in public school administration.* New York: Praeger.

Ortiz, F. I., & Venegas, Y. (1978). Chicana [female] school administrators. *Emergent Leadership, 2*(2), 55-60.

Paddock, S. (1978). Women's careers in administration. *Dissertation Abstracts International, 38,* 5843A. (University Microfilms No. 7802552)

Paddock, S. C. (1980). Women principals: The rule or the exception? *NASSP Bulletin, 64*(4), 1-4.

Paddock, S. C. (1981). Male and female career paths in school administration. In P. A. Schmuck, W. W. Charters, Jr., & R. O. Carlson (Eds.), *Educational policy and management: Sex differentials* (pp. 187-198). New York: Academic Press.

Patten, F. G. (1954). *Good morning, Miss Dove.* New York: Dodd, Mead.

Pharis, W. L., & Zachariya, S. B. (1979). *The elementary school principal in 1978: A research study.* Washington, DC: National Association of Elementary School Principals.

Picker, A. M. (1980). Female educational administrators: Coping in a basically male environment. *Educational Horizons, 58*(3), 145-149.

Quinn, K. I. (1977). Self-perceptions of leadership behaviors and decision-making orientations of men and women elementary school principals in Chicago public schools. *Dissertation Abstracts International, 37,* 6199A-6200A. (University Microfilms No. 77-9151)

Rideout, A. H. (1974). The upward mobility of women in higher education: A profile of women home economics administrators. *Dissertation Abstracts International, 35,* 2604A-2605A. (University Microfilms No. 7425, 865)

Robinson, O. T. (1978). Contributions of black American academic women to American higher education. *Dissertation Abstracts Internationa1, 39,* 2094A. (University Microfilms No. 7816079)

Robinson, W. C. (1978). Secondary school women principals and assistant principals in Ohio: Characteristics and aspirations. *Dissertation Abstracts International, 39,* 1976A. (University Microfilms No. 77-8028)

Rosser, P. (1980, March). Women fight "Old Boys" for school administrator jobs. *Learning, 8* (7), 31-34.

Scriven, A. L. (1974). A study of women occupying administrative positions in the central office of large school districts. *Dissertation Abstracts International, 34,* 6920A-6921A. (University Microfilms No. 74-9762)

Smith, J. A. (1977). A study of women who are certified and employed as principals and assistant principals in Pennsylvania. *Dissertation Abstracts International, 37,* 7463A-7464A. (University Microfilms No. 77-13, 527)

Stockard, J. (1984). Career patterns of high-level women school administrators. *Journal of the National Association for Women Deans, Administrators, and Counselors, 48*(1), 36-44.

Taylor, A. A. (1977). The current status of black women in American higher education administration. *Dissertation Abstracts International, 38,* 1261A-1262A. (University Microfilms No. 77-17,844)

Tessler, S. E. (1976). Profiles of selected women college presidents reflecting the emerging role of women in higher education. *Dissertation Abstracts International, 37,* 840A. (University Microfilms No. 76-18, 927)

Thomas, E. J. (1976). Career patterns of black women administrators in historically Negro senior colleges and universities. *Dissertation Abstracts International, 36,* 3459A-3460A. (University Microfilms No. 76-27, 763)

Vance, C. L. (1978). Comparison of the career development of women executives in institutions of higher education with corporate women executives. *Dissertation Abstracts International, 38,* 717A. (University Microfilms No. 7812980)

Walsh, P. A. (1975). Career patterns of women administrators in higher education institutions in California. *Dissertation Abstracts International, 36,* 3323A-3324A. (University Microfilms No. 75-27, 004)

White, D. B. (1976). A descriptive study of the status of women administrators in Texas public schools, 1968-1973. *Dissertation Abstracts International 36,* 5735A. (University Microfilms No. 76-6064)

Williams, R. H., & Willower, D. J. (1983). The school administrator in fiction. *Educational Forum, 47,* 353-363.

Willower, D. J., & Fraser, H. W. (1980). School superintendents and their work. *Administrator's Notebook, 28*(5).

Wolcott, H. F. (1973). *The man in the principal's office.* New York: Holt, Rinehart & Winston.

Part II

Getting Women Into Administration

A synthesis of the research on the barriers to women in administration is the focus of the first chapter in this section. This literature has been analyzed using a number of synthesis techniques (taking a vote, meta-analysis, averaging statistics) and is used to support the argument that the major barrier to women has been a culture characterized by male dominance because all of the specific barriers identified can be traced back to a society that supports and enforces a male-dominant system.

Although educational writing is replete with suggestions for overcoming the barriers, only the strategies that have some form of documented success are presented in the second chapter of this section. Hopefully, these strategies can be used to break down the barriers.

Both chapters in this section depart from the literature on men in ways different from the research in Part I. Because, as a group, white men don't face barriers to jobs just because they are men and therefore don't have to negotiate such barriers, a literature on barriers and strategies for overcoming discrimination is nonexistent in the research on male administrators. This means that the world of male administrators and the world of female administrators are different, if solely because sex discrimination and barriers to administration occur only for women as a group. This is not to say that individual men are not thwarted in their climb up the administrative ladder. However, because they are not held back because of their sex, males experience a different reality than females. The female reality is explicated in Chapters 3 and 4.

· 3 ·

Barriers to Women's Advancement into School Administration

As historical record has shown, women have always been second choice in the selection of school leaders. The barriers today are not much different than the barriers that kept women from becoming high school principals in 1900 or superintendents in 1930. What is different is that in the past 15 years, a number of studies in the social sciences have been undertaken to articulate more clearly both what barriers exist and how salient each barrier is for preventing women from entering school administration. The studies have documented that patience—wild or otherwise—has not taken women very far.

ROOT CAUSES OF BARRIERS TO WOMEN IN ADMINISTRATION

The telling of the story of women in school administration doesn't explain why, in a larger sense, women have been consigned to teaching while men are clustered in administration. Thus in recent years, we have identified specific barriers but have not examined in much detail the roots of these blockages, although a handful of models have been suggested in an effort to begin to understand how these barriers originated. The lack of women in administration has been explained by researchers using the following models: the Woman's Place Model, which assumes women's nonparticipation in administrative careers as based solely on social norms; the Discrimination Model, which "draws on the assumption that institutional patterns are a result of the efforts of one group to exclude participation of another" (Estler, 1975, p. 369); and the Meritocracy Model, which assumes that the most competent people have been promoted and thus women are not competent. Estler (1975) provides evidence for support of both the Woman's Place and Discrimination Models but finds that the Meritocracy Model does not fit reality.

Adkison uses competing explanations to account for women's lack of success in entering administration, illustrating that "the same data can be explained equally well by different concepts" (1981, p. 330). Thus, she analyzes women's career barriers from sex-role stereotyping, sex-role socialization, career socialization, organizational characteristics, and devaluation of women perspectives.

An additional framework for examining barriers is to place them within the domains of internal and external barriers. Internal barriers are those that can be overcome by individual change whereas external barriers require social and institutional change.

Hansot and Tyack (1981) discuss three explanatory models from the literature and provide support for the two latter frameworks. The first focuses on the individual woman as possessing internal barriers that keep her from advancing; socialization and sex stereotyping are seen as the guiding forces behind all her behavior. This perspective originates from a psychological paradigm and, essentially, blames the victim for her lack of achievement in school leadership. Its remedy is for women to be resocialized so that they will fit into the male world.

The second approach describes an organizational structure that shapes the behavior of its members. "The chief source of male hegemony lies not in the psychological makeup of individuals . . . but in the structure and operation of organizations. Women behave in self-limiting ways not because they were socialized as females but because they are locked into low-power, low-visibility, dead-end jobs" (Hansot & Tyack, 1981, p. 7).

The third model discussed by Hansot and Tyack portrays a world that is male defined and male run. According to this explanation, it is male dominance that has led to conditions that keep women from advancing into positions of power and prestige.

It is this third model that provides the most satisfactory explanation of the limits imposed upon women in school administration. Not only are all other models subsumed under this male-dominance explanation, but the cause of all barriers to women in school administration that have been identified in the social science literature can be traced to male hegemony.

For instance, barriers labeled as internal can be seen as an outgrowth of a social context in which white males hold power and privilege over all other groups. An examination of some barriers commonly identified as internal will illustrate this point. The most prevalent explanation of women's lack of achievement, both in the research literature and the popular press, has centered on women's inadequacy. Guided by this ideology, if the woman changes herself she will no longer experience difficulties. This approach blames the victim for her lack of achievement, as the following vignette reported by Schmuck indicates:

> A female junior high school vice principal filed a grievance and questioned her district's hiring two white males as vice principals. At a school board hearing, she testified: "I have been told frequently and earnestly by several building principals that, 'I'd hire a woman if I could find one interested or qualified.' I am reminded of the Seattle School Board memo of 1948 which read, 'Will hire Negro if a competent Negro can be found.'" At the same meeting the only female high school vice principal, a woman who had served in that capacity for many years, also testified. Upon completion of her testimony, she was asked by a male board member if she had ever applied for a high school principalship. When she said that she had not, the board member replied, "Well, you certainly have not helped your cause." (1979, p. 24)

Continuing to blame the victim, the internal barriers most often listed as contributing to women's lack of achievement in administration under this model are low self-image, lack of confidence, and lack of motivation or aspiration.

Internal barriers as an explanation for women's perceived lack of achievement seem inadequate. Internal barriers are seldom more prevalent for women than for men, and when they are it is not the woman's psyche that is at fault and thus needs changing but rather the social structure of society that is the root cause of inequities.

Internal barriers are merely camouflage for deeper, societal roadblocks to women's advancement. By accepting as fact that inequities toward women occur because of some lack of ability or action by women, we are not forced to look elsewhere for explanations, neither are we pushed to question the concepts and frameworks that conclude that the victim is at fault. Questioning these concepts and definitions helps to point out alternative ways of seeing women's condition—ways that find reasons other than the woman herself as the cause.

For instance, Schmuck (1976) among many others lists lack of confidence and low self-image as internal barriers reported by women that prevent them from considering school administration. Many women, her data assert, either do not see themselves as school administrators or lack confidence to pursue such an end. Although it is true that women have been shown to have lower self-confidence than do men in public sphere activities, studies of self-confidence often are confined to just that—public sphere activities. We have not studied self-confidence through the eyes of women but rather have forced women to be measured by male-defined standards of self-confidence. Thus it is not clear whether women have less self-confidence or if they only have less self-confidence in areas in which they are traditionally thought not to excell. It might be argued that any human will have lower self-confidence in areas where he or she is not experienced than would an individual who has experience. Low self-confidence might be viewed, then, as a product of a system that keeps women separated from experiences that would help build confidence in the public sphere.

Looking at self-confidence from this perspective, we see that women have self-confidence in areas in which they have experience (private sphere functions), whereas men have self-confidence in areas in which they have been allowed to participate (public sphere functions). The problem with labeling women as low in self-confidence is that it doesn't go far enough and define in which sphere this insecurity lies—once that is done, the problem can be redefined as lack of experience in public sphere activities rather than lack of self-confidence.

Andrews points out how self-esteem and self-confidence differ for men and women. For males, self-esteem and self-confidence go hand in hand. For women, high self-esteem is not consistently positively related to confidence in performing tasks. "Self-confidence is a narrower construct than self-esteem, focusing on performance expectancies and self-evaluation of abilities and completed performance" (Andrews, 1984, p. 3). Low self-confidence can affect aspiration level. A person with low self-confidence is much less likely to attempt an action than a person with high self-confidence: "If a person believes than he or she is capable of performing competently, such confidence may well contribute to a positive performance" (1984, p. 2). Self-confidence affects the way women are perceived as well as the ways they perceive themselves. Not suprisingly, Andrews found that a woman's self-confidence "has a substantial impact on an individual's chances of being perceived as a group's emergent leader" (1984, p. 9).

A number of researchers have tried to understand why women, more than men, lack self-confidence, and how self-esteem and self-confidence are nurtured. The salience of experience and positive reinforcement in nontraditional activities and its relationship to self-confidence and self-image is dramatically illustrated by Dweck et al.'s 1978 study of elementary school children. Dweck and her colleagues found that the types of feedback girls receive from teachers refers almost exclusively to intellectual inadequacies whereas the teacher feedback given to boys criticizes the nonintellectual aspects of their work. They further found that when boys were treated like girls (i.e. evaluated negatively on their intellectual abilities as opposed to their nonintellectual ones), they were more likely to believe that they did, indeed, lack ability. The authors concluded that "the pattern of evaluative feedback given to boys and girls in the classroom can result directly in girls' greater tendency to view failure feedback as indicative of their level of ability" (Dweck, 1978, p. 274).

Thus, what has often been seen as a personal failing of women—lack of self-confidence—might be more accurately seen as a consequence of a sex-structured society that generates a belief in females that they lack ability—a belief reinforced by an organizational system that prevents women from developing confidence in public sphere activities through both lack of opportunity and lack of positive feedback. This, then, is an external, not an internal, barrier to women and one that flourishes in and can be traced to a male-dominated society.

A number of studies (Dias, 1975; Goerss, 1975; Gross & Trask, 1964, 1976; Hilton, 1977; Huserik, 1975; Landon, 1975; Miller, 1976; Perrin, 1975; Sample, 1977; Whitten, 1975; P. J. Williams, 1977) suggest that women's lack of success in obtaining administrative positions is due to lowered aspirations or lack of motivation on the part of women. Although it is true that women have traditionally applied less often than men for administrative positions and that women, more often than men, need to be encouraged to enter administration, there is little evidence that the reasons for this can be found in lower aspiration and motivation. Further, most of the studies on women analyzed the career patterns of white women only. Studies comparing white and black women find most black women with higher levels of aspiration, although upper-middle-class black women are similar to white women (Reynolds & Elliott, 1980).

For all women, there are many ways to understand what has been called aspiration. Two contrasting positions will be discussed, both of which challenge the ways in which aspiration is categorized for women. The first posits that women aspire but that the traditional definition of aspiration fails to fit female experience and thus if measured by this definition it appears that women don't aspire. The second position argues that women aspire but organizational and societal barriers prevent women from acknowledging or acting upon, either overtly or covertly, their aspirations and thus it appears that women lack aspiration.

Like self-confidence, aspiration and motivation have only been defined using a male lens and male experience. Aspiration has been defined as moving up the hierarchy. For instance, in a study of aspiration, Reynolds and Elliott use an operational definition of aspiration that conforms to traditional male descriptions: "We defined most of the independent variables for this study in terms of dichotomous categories . . . for career aspiration level, aspiring for a principalship or higher and not aspiring for a principalship or higher" (1980, p. 7). Having career aspiration, then, means wanting to become a principal, not wishing to remain a teacher. These definitions leave out much of female experience and thus may not be accurate for describing women's participation in the work force. These definitions are also public sphere definitions and, like conceptualizations of self-confidence, they suffer by examining women's lives only within a public sphere defined by male experience.

Thus a way to understand women's perceived failure to aspire to "higher" levels of school service is to rethink the achievement norm inherent in this belief. The bureaucratization that took place early in the century was related to the premise that the business model was the right model. This kind of thinking led school boards to invite men into school administration, men who did not necessarily have educational backgrounds. There was a belief (one still subscribed to today) that management was management and there wasn't much difference between a factory and a school. Thus many men had little or no educational interest or knowledge. It might be that this lack of educational underpinning of the managers forced them to take care of the technical or clerical aspects of administration rather than the instructional and educational ones, thus molding administration into a managerial, rather than an educational or instructional enterprise. Whatever the reasons, a number of studies support the notion that the motivation for entering teaching differs for men and women: Most women enter teaching to teach but most men enter teaching to administer.

A study by Gross and Trask (1964, 1976) of principals nationwide reported that 65% of female principals and only 27% of males had decided upon teaching as a career as early as their senior year in high school. Further, 85% of the women responded that teaching was their first choice of occupations; only 46% of the male principals indicated that education was their primary interest. Typical of women administrators is the following quote from a study by Payne and Jackson (1978, p. 7):

> I never expected to be in the field of administration and that's natural for most everybody. I had a very humble beginning in administration. I happened to have wanted to be just a teacher.

Thus these women teachers are aspiring and achieving that for which they are aiming. A remark by a woman principal as quoted by Carlson and Schmuck would reinforce this notion. She said, "Success is not measured in moving from job to job in a vertical continuum . . . it is measured by the quality of any job held" (1981, pp. 122-123).

That women see teaching and administration as distinct and very different careers is reaffirmed by the work of Baughman (1977) who found that women perceived many administrative positions as entailing too much paperwork and not enough educational content and, therefore, these jobs were not of interest to them. These same women do not value administration and the role of administrators, neither do they desire a position that separates them from students. To translate this into lack of motivation or aspiration is to misunderstand or ignore the reasons women chose to enter teaching in the first place.

Reynolds and Elliott's work (1980) in many ways confirms that women want to achieve but that their definitions of achievement may differ from those commonly used to measure women's and men's career patterns. In their study of educators, Reynolds and Elliott found that women had higher achievement orientations than did men. Interestingly, and importantly, in measuring achievement, they chose measures and ways of thinking that took into account female experience. "Operationally, we defined achievement orientation as the z score on the subjects' descriptions of themselves on the ACL Achievement sub-scale ('self-achievement scores') adjusted through covariance for the z score on the subjects' descriptions of themselves on the ACL Nurturance sub-scale ('self-nurturance scores')" (Reynolds & Elliot, 1980, p. 9). In this study, then, women, more than men, had high achievement needs.

This expanded view of achievement was suggested by Oliver (1974) who described women's career aspirations as a combination of achievement-orientation and affiliation needs. Looking at women from their experiences and value perspective resulted in a clearer understanding of women's achievement.

Reynolds and Elliott explained women's high need for achievement but lack of interest in the principalship as low career aspiration. An equally logical explanation, and one that corresponds to women's reasons for entering teaching, is that women aspire to and wish to achieve in the career they chose for themselves years earlier—teaching. Thus not wanting to be a principal means just that, rather than serving as an indication of low aspiration.

Nevertheless, status has been defined by males and is organized hierarchically so that language mirrors a value system that describes administration as more important than teaching. Women who decide to teach, rather than administer, are judged from this framework.

> "Stepping *down*," "going *back* to the classroom," and "*just* teaching" are phrases which convey messages of lower value. Tucked away in the minds of those who use them is also a suspicion that those who choose this direction of change are forced to do so because of some inadequacy, because administration is higher than teaching, because we all strive to go up and, when up, to stay there. Faculty are accorded less pay, less prestige, less recognition, and less power. Who, after all, would voluntarily opt for that? (Mickey, 1984, p. 5)

Even if one accepts the male definition of aspiration, low aspiration may not be what is being measured. Three possible alternative explanations are that what is really being measured is a reality response, that it is a measurement error (respondents do not tell the truth), or that it is really a measure of low opportunity rather than low aspiration.

For instance, lack of aspiration or motivation in women may actually be an accurate reflection of reality in light of home and family responsibilities and job opportunities. If this is the case, it is not internal barriers that keep women from aspiring but rather the reality of a world that expects that if a woman works outside the home she will continue to do the major portion of work inside the home as well. The difficulties of juggling the full share of family responsibility with administrative tasks may just not seem worth it to many women. Although more women than men believe that women can do both successfully, in a study conducted by Fisher (1978) of 359 Michigan teachers, only 34% of the women teachers agreed that for women a successful marriage and a successful job as a school administrator are compatible. This means that 66% of the women teachers didn't believe that the two full-time jobs could be successfully carried out at the same time by a woman. For males to be fathers, husbands, and school administrators entails not two careers, but one. For most men, family responsibility is work responsibility—bring home the paycheck. For most women, work responsibilities are added to home tasks. Not wanting to take on two jobs says nothing about aspiration level but rather reflects an accurate assessment of the number of hours in the day and the very real limits of the human body.

A companion explanation for the seeming lack of aspiration of women in education is that they don't verbalize these desires for fear of reprisals. Ortiz found that women teachers who expressed interest in administration before receiving tenure often had difficulty getting tenure. One woman's story is illustrative:

> When I first started teaching, I knew I wanted to be an administrator. Like a fool, I told everyone how anxious I was for tenure so I could apply for an administrative position. During my third year at the school, the principal called me in. He said, "I know you'd be happier in a different working situation than teaching, so I'd like to tell you that you are not expected to get tenure this spring." (1982, p. 58)

Another woman, an associate superintendent, experienced the same problem early in her career:

> I realized that I had to leave the school district. I had told many persons I wanted to be a principal. The principal told me, "You can't fulfill your teaching obligations if you're preoccupied with becoming an administrator. I am therefore recommending that you not get tenure. It would be best for you, however, to resign and get another job somewhere else." I resigned, moved to another school district and believe me I just concentrated on getting tenure. No one ever suspected I wanted to be an administrator. (Ortiz, 1982, pp. 58-59)

Thus acknowledging aspiration may be a very dangerous thing for women and might be a reason some women prefer not to identify administrative goals publicly.

An alternate way to view women's achievement motivation in educational careers lies in the organizational structure framework. Rosabeth Moss Kanter, in *Men and Women of the Corporation* (1977), first presented the thesis that it was neither gender nor an individual's personal characteristics but organizational structure that limits the opportunities of women and minorities. In her five-year study of the Industrial Supply Corporation (Indsco), a pseudonym for a conglomorate that is one of the world's largest producers of industrial goods, Kanter examined how "opportunity, power, and relative numbers . . . have the potential to explain a large number of discrete individual responses to organizations" (1977, p. 246).

Kanter points out that "opportunity structures shape behavior in such a way that they confirm their own prophecies" (1977, p. 158). Thus people who have very little opportunity to move up the hierarchy (women teachers) disengage in the form of depressed aspirations. Those people who are highly mobile within the hierarchy (men teachers), however, "tend to develop attitudes and values that impel them further along the track: work commitment, high aspirations, and upward orientations" (Kanter, 1977, p. 158). Thus women's so-called lack of aspiration in administration might more accurately be seen as an expected response to lack of opportunity and be more fully explained by a framework that holds organizational structure as paramount in preventing women from moving into school administration.

Work by Donelson and Gullahorn (1977), Barnett and Baruch (1979), and Jovick (1981) support the argument that people who have a chance at being hired in administrative positions are more likely to aspire to those positions. Tibbetts (1979) also found that lack of job availability depressed aspirations; similarly, a black woman administrator in a study by Payne and Jackson (1978, p. 10) described her lack of desire for the superintendency as an outgrowth of lack of opportunity for black women administrators:

> This is the time of the Black male in my area and maybe this is true across the country. Where people have an opportunity to choose a principal or superintendent, they will almost invariably ask for a Black male. In that regard, I feel that women are at a very definite disadvantage. As Black people, we have got to find a way to accommodate Black women also.

Further evidence is supplied by Coffin and Ekstrom (1979) who found that lowered aspiration was really a response to lack of opportunity. Thus Kanter's assertion that "things may become evaluated as less desirable as they become less likely" (1977, p. 140) is crucial to understanding women's aspiration levels.

What has been called women's lack of aspiration may really be a very logical and effective mental health remedy. To desire something she believes she can never have may lead to bitterness and unhappiness. A more effective coping strategy—one more likely to ensure sanity—is to not want what is out of one's reach. For some women it may be better to say, "I don't want to be a school superintendent," than to long for a job that her experience and the experience of other women educators tell her she is unlikely to be given.

Kanter's thesis is further strengthened by recent studies documenting that once organizational or societal barriers are removed, women begin applying for positions in school administration. Edson (1981) determined that as positions opened up, as women were encouraged to apply, and as they saw other women achieving, women in her study began to aspire to administrative jobs. Picker also documented that aspiration has not only increased as women begin to believe that they have a chance in administration but that women are beginning to record higher aspiration levels than men. The results of her study showed that "female administrators, in contrast to the men who participated in the study, generally aspired beyond the position of principal as their ultimate career goal . . . when compared with their male counterparts, women showed greater desire to advance more than one step up the organizational ladder" (1980, p. 147).

Thus it would seem that women do not possess mystical internal barriers that keep them from becoming school administrators. Rather it is a combination of seeing administration as a different career than teaching, and of acknowledging the impact of structural and social forces which allow us to understand that so-called "internal barriers" do not explain women's heavy representation in teaching and not administration.

However, these forces don't present the whole picture. Whereas Kanter's work on the structural determinants of opportunity and power is most useful for explaining behavior in an organization, it does not address the cause of the initial inequity. Although many of the behaviors attributed to females—behaviors often cited as evidence for not promoting women into school administration—are shown to be behaviors exhibited not by females, per se, but by those who are low in organizational opportunity, power, and proportions, we are still left wondering why women, and not men, ended up in those low-power, low-opportunity positions in the first place.

The appropriateness of Kanter's model for schools, then, might be twofold: first, to help us understand why teachers of both genders might disengage from teaching, and second, to help us understand the behaviors of women and minorities once they achieve token positions in school administration. Kanter's work may be more helpful for understanding how people behave as workers in schools than for explaining barriers to women's advancement into school administration, as she doesn't address the reasons why such a gender-segregated structure exists to begin with. Despite more women than men in teaching, we are left wondering why, if gender is not the overriding explanation of a profession structured according to sex, are men managers and women teachers? How is it that women, more than men, are in positions low in power and opportunity? Why is it that teaching is a high opportunity profession for a man but not for a woman? Kanter's research has great utility for understanding the behavior of women administrators but is less useful for explaining how we got into this predicament in the first place.

Having found the first two frameworks inadequate for explaining why women remain in teaching and men become administrators, we turn to an explanation that describes society as male dominated. Explanations for this are ripe in the anthropological, psychological, sociological, biological, and political literature and a number of theories have been offered to understand a world in which men in most cultures occupy the positions that command the most prestige (see for example, Chodorow, 1978; Dinnerstein, 1976; Firestone, 1970; Greenberg, 1978; Morgan, 1972; Sherfey, 1966; Stockard & Johnson, 1979).

Whether resulting from biological or societal forces, these patterns of dominance have been consistently documented. Margaret Mead noted:

> Three primitive societies have grouped their social attitudes towards temperament about the very obvious facts of sex difference. . . . Our own society makes great use of this plot. It assigns different roles to the two sexes, surrounds them from birth with an expectation of different behaviour, plays out the whole drama of courtship, marriage, and parenthood in terms of types of behaviour believed to be innate and therefore appropriate for one sex or for the other. (1935, pp. viii-ix)

This sex division occurs in all societies and results in a sex-based division of labor. Although the specific tasks may differ by gender from society to society, two things do not change: Men and women divide the labor on the basis of sex and male tasks are more valued than female ones.

> In all societies the activities and positions that are considered to be the most important, that are accorded the highest prestige in that society, tend to be defined as especially (if not exclusively) appropriate for men. Moreover, in all societies positions of highest authority . . . tend to be the special province of men. (Stockard & Johnson, 1981, p. 236)

And to make matters worse, this highly valued world is not friendly to women. Jessie Bernard writes:

> Among human beings, though, there is clear evidence that although individual men may love individual women with great depth and devotion, the male world as a whole does not. (1981, p. 11)

Not suprisingly, male dominance explains much of the source of inequality in education, deeply imbedded as it is in both social institutions and individuals. Greenberg (1978) characterized the reality of school life in America as constructed by male dominance.

> After extensive searches and researches into the nature of school personnel practices, curricula policies, textbook and material content, and teacher-pupil interaction, the accumulated evidence suggests that educational practices support the social ideology with depressing obedience. Surprisingly, the social ideology the schools support is not democracy but patriarchy. Our schools . . . teach notions of a *priori* determined sex roles (one sub-, the other superordinate), of gross gender differences, and of differential libidinal drive; they support these notions with enthusiasm generally reserved for far worthier causes, coupled with a vigorous determination to remain unconscious of their harm. (1978, p. 44)

This ideology of patriarchy is also called androcentrism, meaning male centered. Androcentrism is the practice of viewing the world and shaping reality from a male perspective. It is the elevation of the masculine to the level of the universal and the ideal and the honoring of men and the male principle above women and the female. This perception creates a belief in male superiority and a masculine value system in which female values, experiences, and behaviors are viewed as inferior.

In an androcentric world, a hierarchy of status exists. Men and women must do different things; women and what women do are less valued than are men and what men do. Otherwise, gender as an ordering principle with someone above and someone below would not be possible. Thus in an androcentric world, there is a woman's place and that place is less valued, less honored, and less reinforced than man's place. If having a woman's place is not only acceptable but desirable, as it is in an androcentric world, then having two sets of rules, one for women and one for men, is also acceptable and desirable. Hence, discrimination on the basis of sex is necessary for the existence of an androcentric (male-defined) world to exist. The barriers that will be discussed throughout the rest of the chapter can only exist in a world that divides people into categories based on sex; thus these barriers need to be seen not as women's fault, not as a result of organizational structure, but as the outcome of a sexual hierarchy in which males are at the top and females are at the bottom. Thus it is this ideology of patriarchy resulting in an androcentric society that explains why men, and not women, occupy the formal leadership positions in school and society. The remainder of this chapter documents the ways that androcentrism is manifested in an effort to keep men dominant and in charge of schooling.

The literature on barriers differs dramatically for males and females—there is no literature on the barriers to white males in administration. Further, there is little literature for men on ways to advance. The strategies that women assume men have used to move into administration—mentors, networks, and so on—have seldom been articulated or universally used. Work by Edson (1981) indicates that the majority of men in her study had no mentor and interacted in no networks. Thus many men achieve without consciously using so-called advancement strategies simply because they are men. Only in an androcentric world can a man have a better chance than a woman of succeeding because of his sex. Carlson points out that for a male educator, perseverance helps in achieving the superintendency.

> Because men are very much in the minority in public schools, because their ranks are rapidly depleted by those dropping out of the

> occupation, and because they are advanced to administrative posts far more frequently than women, the men who simply persist in the occupation have a high probability of moving up the ladder. (1972, p. 9)

Sex discrimination is the name for business as usual in an androcentric world. This discrimination may be overt or covert; it may take the form of refusing to hire a woman because of her sex or it may be rationalized in a more indirect way. For instance, a school board might say that the reason no women were hired is because no woman applied or that women don't possess administrative credentials. What is missing in this rationalization is the acknowledgment that if these two conditions are true, it is because historically women were not encouraged or allowed to enter graduate programs in administration and were not encouraged to apply for administrative positions. The long and winding road of excuses always ends up at sex discrimination. A number of studies (Andrews, 1984; Baughman, 1977; Bonuso & Shakeshaft, 1983; Bunyi & Andrews, 1985; Capps, 1977; Drust, 1977; Fleming, 1974; Forsyth & Forsyth, 1984; Fox, 1975; Gardner, 1977; Gasser, 1975; Goldsmith, 1976; Holland, 1973; Hurlbut, 1978; LaBarthe, 1973; Mickey, 1984; Miller, 1976; Moore, 1977; Noll, 1973; Owens, 1975; Perrin, 1975; Poll, 1978; Porter, Geis, & Jennings, 1983; Powers, 1975; Pruitt, 1976; Quell & Pfeiffer, 1982; Rabenau, 1978; Ralston, 1975; O.T. Robinson, 1978; Schmuck, 1976; Stevenson, 1974; Tjosvold, 1975; Wain, 1976; Wood, 1975) document the existence of overt sex discrimination by school boards, boards of trustees, departments of educational administration and educational administrators. Other studies illustrate covert forms of discrimination that have prevented women from becoming school administrators. In the following section, both overt and covert discrimination will be discussed by focusing upon the barriers that arise from each in the context of the androcentric world that discriminates on the basis of sex.

THE BARRIERS OF OVERT SEX DISCRIMINATION

In many studies, the reasons given for not hiring or promoting women have only to do with the fact that they were female. Whether it is attitudes that were negative or practices that negated women, these studies document direct discrimination against women. A comment from an aspiring school administrator reflects the sexism that controls the staffing of schools:

> Silly as it seems, the fact that I was a woman seemed to be the biggest obstacle. My training is as good as many men. My track record in school positions is good. I was told by a university advisor not to get my administrative credentials if I wished to remain in this community. (Coffin & Ekstrom, 1979, p. 57)

The above quote came from a survey undertaken by Coffin and Ekstrom (1979); they reported that women had been given the following reasons for not being hired for positions for which they believed themselves qualified: Women were not hired because of custom; men do not want to take directions from a woman; the community was not ready for a woman administrator. These reasons have nothing to do with ability or competence; they all use as their reason the woman's sex.

Interestingly, competency is an adjective used to describe acceptable women and minority candidates but never white male aspirants. Only the Marines are looking for a few good men; school district personnel are notorious for looking for white men, competent women, and competent minority applicants. One black woman relates a typical experience:

> A few years ago in this district they were also saying that no qualified blacks were applying, and I was living right here and applying every year. Maybe school boards and principals would like to think of me as invisible, but I'm not. I want them to accept the fact that I am very visible. (Edson, 1981, p. 179)

In fact, competent women may be at more of a disadvantage than women of lesser ability when seeking a position. A study by Hagen and Kahn found that men discriminate more against competent women than against those who aren't:

> Men only like a competent woman from a distance; when men and women have to work together or against one another, they prefer an incompetent woman as much as a competent one. . . . when given a choice of who not to have around, for both sexes a competent

> woman is more likely to be excluded than a competent man. (1975, p. 371)

They conclude, "the implications of these findings for a competent woman are not pleasant. They suggest that a competent woman . . . will be more likely than an equally performing man to lose her job" (p. 372).

These findings may also help to explain why, when a woman or minority person is hired, it is often noted that the less competent woman or minority applicant is chosen, an action that may make white males feel more comfortable while at the same time providing evidence that women and minorities can't cut it.

Studies tell us that people tend to hire those like themselves. Thus white males hire white males. This is made easier in light of recent work that documents the lack of uniformity in administrative selection procedures nationwide. Baltzell and Dentler report that specific selection criteria for the hiring of administrators are seldom articulated.

> This lack of criterial specificity opens the way for widespread reliance on localistic notions of "fit" or "image," which emerged as centrally important. . . . Every district had a deeply held image of a "good" principal or a "top" candidate or "just what we're looking for." However, time and time again, this "fit" seemed to rest on interpersonal perceptions of a candidate's physical presence, projection of a certain self-confidence and assertiveness, and embodiment of community values and methods of operation. (1983, p. 7)

Because of lack of particular criteria, it becomes easy for a hiring committee to choose a white male without ever questioning on what basis this choice was made. Timpano and Knight (1976) documented specific behaviors in New York that discriminated against women in the hiring process. They called these filters and broke them into the five categories presented in Table 3.1

These practices that keep women out of administration have changed little in ten years. Studies of the very same school districts in New York (Shapiro, 1983) indicated that the discriminatory actions identified by Timpano and Knight continued despite laws that prohibit many of them. Female candidates for administrative jobs still report, as late as 1987, that they are asked questions about

TABLE 3.1
Sex Discrimination in Hiring

Recruiting Filters:
- Word of mouth recruiting through the old boy network
- Limiting eligibility to within the district when it is known that few women there are certified as administrators
- Notifying women's organizations of only certain openings, such as director of home economics
- Advertising in journals known to have primarily male audiences

Application Filters:
- Including questions on applications about children, ages of children, and marital status
- Questions about "lowest salary acceptable" which can lead to unequal pay for men and women
- Separating applications received by sex

Selection Criteria Filters:
- Using criteria with unproven validity as predictors of success, such as requiring a specific length of experience in a specific position
- Not allowing applicants to substitute comparable or superior alternative experience for specified requirements
- Permitting men to skip steps on the career ladder but expecting women to complete each one
- Requiring only women candidates to hold state certification

Interview Filters:
- Having only men as interviewers
- Asking women irrelevant questions about child care, how male subordinates might react to them
- Questioning applicants about personal matters that are excluded from application forms by law and rejecting candidates who remind the interviewer of this
- Focusing upon the applicant as a woman, rather than as a qualified professional as in, "Why would such a bright and attractive woman ever want to be a superintendent?"

Selection Decision Filters:
- Regarding an aggressive manner in men as desirable but regarding women who display such traits as unfit
- Establishing special sets of job titles for women at salary levels lower than those established for men.

SOURCE: Timpano & Knight (1976).

parental status and how it will affect their job performance. These very same school districts inquire into marital status for women on application forms and treat women as less serious candidates than men. For instance, one candidate for an elementary principalship on Long Island, New York, in 1983 reported that a male member of the selection committee kissed her when she attempted to shake his hand at the end of the interview. She didn't get the job.

In addition to these filters, the selection process, because it does not concentrate on specific behaviors, allows hiring committees to formulate criteria based on something as nebulous as fit. Fit can be as seemingly inconsequential to performance as appearance or body build. Recent work, which indicated that height and weight made a great deal of difference in the selection decisions of superintendents for secondary school principals (Bonuso, 1981), also documented that males and females were not evaluated differently (Bonuso & Shakeshaft, 1983). In this study, 472 school superintendents in New York State rated a resume of an applicant for the position of high school principal. Each superintendent received a packet that contained a direction page, a job description for a senior high principalship, a hypothetical resume of an applicant for this position including questionnaire items, and a photograph of the applicant in question. The direction page consisted of specific and detailed instructions for completing the survey. Superintendents were reminded to rate the listed credentials without regard to resume construction or format. The job description was a brief one-page listing of the major functions and responsibilities for the hypothetical position of senior high school principal, and the resume was one page in length with credentials listed under the headings of: (1) Education, (2) Experience, (3) Professional Memberships, Honors and Awards, and (4) Community Involvement. A five-point rating scale was included with reference to the above-mentioned job description. Superintendents could rate the candidates' credentials, in each of the areas, from excellent to unsatisfactory.

In an effort to analyze the effects of candidates' height and weight, in addition to their gender, on their appropriateness for the administrative position, a group photograph of males or a group photograph of females in six height-weight categories was included. In this manner, the gender of the hypothetical applicant was not only varied but the stature or body build as well. The six males or females pictured in the photograph were either Type I—tall and of "ideal" weight; Type II—tall and "overweight"; Type III—average height and of "ideal" weight; Type IV—average height and "overweight"; Type V—short and of "ideal" weight; and Type VI—short and "overweight."

The superintendents were randomly assigned to one of twelve groups, with each superintendent receiving the hypothetical resume for a male or female applicant. The appropriate group photograph was enclosed and indication was given as to which of the persons pictured (stature type) was the applicant in question. The resume remained identical except for changes in name and height and weight information. Additionally, a control resume was sent to another group of superintendents that included no height or weight information and no group photograph.

Validation of the resume and photograph had determined that, with the exception of height and weight, the people pictured were relatively alike in terms of dress, facial expression, attractiveness, and age.

Not surprisingly, the resumes of those candidates who were tall and of "ideal" weight—whether male or female—were rated significantly higher than were the resumes of any other stature type. The lowest ratings were received by the short "overweight" candidates.

These findings have implications for women and for members of minority groups, both of whom may not fit the white male stature type. If tall implies leadership, white males will more likely be seen as leaders.

In addition to stature as a determining factor, this study provided evidence that contradicted a number of earlier studies in which male resumes were rated more highly than female resumes. In this study, within height and weight groupings, males and females were not rated significantly differently. This prompted a new set of questions. Was sex discrimination at an end? Or did this study reflect a growing experiment awareness on equity issues by superintendents? Were they giving lip service to equity, but not hiring women? We decided to do a follow-up investigation to determine what was really going on.

The target population for this follow-up were 59 superintendents from the original study who had actually hired a secondary school principal in the year in which they responded to our first inquiry. These superintendents indicated that they and boards of education had made the final decision in the hirings and that, of the new principals hired, 92.3% were male and 7.7% were female. A look at second-level evidence, those who made it to the final interview stage, found 95.5% male candidates and 4.5% female candidates. Although a majority of superintendents claimed the the reason few females were hired was because there were "few, if any, qualified female applicants," work by Shapiro (1983), which documents a large pool of women administrative candidates in New York, would discredit that explanation. Thus we found that although superintendents in New York state were indicating no preference for one gender over another for the hypothetical job of secondary school principal, at the same time these same superintendents were filling 92.3% of their real openings for secondary school principals with men. Women were neither receiving the jobs nor participating in final-level interviews—this in a state in which more that 50% of all students in administrative certificate programs are women. In addition to giving us information about the ways discrimination takes form, this study also reminded us, as researchers, that what someone says they do and what they actually do may be very different things indeed.

So, despite changes in the law and the social context that might indicate that sex descrimination no longer exists, its presence is still being documented. There has been some work to demonstrate that laws passed to prevent sex discrimination are actually used to promote it. A number of researchers (e.g., Marshall & Grey, 1982) have pointed out that affirmative action policies are often misused—either through hiring a less qualified woman or minority applicant where a more qualified applicant exists or by failing to take into account a woman's personal career orientation or interests and, thus, misplacing her in the organization. Men's views on affirmative action reflect these distortions. A man interviewed by Oller said that "he was told he would not be considered for a position in his district, 'not that I'm not qualified, but my sex and skin color are not right'" (1979, p. 7). Another white male reported that he believed affirmative action would hurt him saying, "the idea has merit, but my attitude is negative" (p. 7).

The quote from another interviewee came closer to the truth when he said, "my experience has been that districts aren't all that anxious to hire women" (p. 7). However, lack of interest in the goals of affirmative action hasn't discouraged representatives of some school districts from quoting it chapter and verse. The use of affirmative action as a reason for not hiring one white male while hiring another white male was documented in 1978-1979 at Texas A & M University by David Gardner and me. A number of white male candidates returned from administrative interviews in anger because they had been told that although they were outstanding candidates, the district could not hire them because affirmative action regulations forced that district to hire a woman or minority. These were candidates for jobs in a variety of districts throughout the state of Texas. Understandably, these men were angry; they felt unfairly treated because, based only on their sex and race, they were being told they couldn't be seriously considered for a position. In response, they expressed negative views toward affirmative action, women, and minority people. What they didn't know and what was determined in a follow-up was that in *every* case, regardless of what the candidate had been told, a white male was actually hired. Not a single woman or minority person filled any of these positions!

This incident illustrates how affirmative action requirements have been used by cowardly administrators to let white male candidates down easily or, from a more sinister view, to sabotage the opportunities of women and minority people by making white male candidates feel directly threatened by affirmative action. As one woman noted: "The good old boy system of hiring and promoting employees has adapted itself to survive within the confines of affirmative action" (Oller, 1979, p. 8).

Ruth Benedict once observed that no person "ever looks at the world with pristine eyes." She or he "sees it edited by a definite set of customs and institutions and ways of thinking" (1934, p. 2). Nowhere is this more true than in looking at attitudes toward women in administration. Many, many studies have been done that purport to examine attitudes; very few of these can be called attitude measures in the strictest sense—most merely ask the respondents what they think about a particular issue. Thus in talking about attitudes, we're talking about a mix of attitude, opinion, and belief studies.

As is illustrated from the Bonuso and Shakeshaft work (1983), a belief given in a survey form doesn't always result in a similar action. However, three studies (Beck, 1978; Makulski, 1976; Ralston, 1975) draw a link between beliefs and attitudes and the ways in which the superintendents surveyed treated women. Makulski concludes that superintendents' attitudes are shaped by the experiences they have with women and that these attitudes have an effect on the promotion possibilities of women.

A synthesis of a number of attitudinal studies on women administrators (Shakeshaft, 1979, 1985) concludes that, when compared, the following groups have more favorable attitudes toward female administrators:

- females (teachers, administrators, school board members) versus males (teachers, administrators, school board members)
- older male administrators versus younger male administrators
- educators from medium to large districts versus educators from small districts
- those who have taught elementary and secondary education versus those who have not taught at those levels
- married administrators versus unmarried administrators
- non-southerners versus southerners

Although the link between attitudes and behavior is murky, studies of attitudes of superintendents and school board members have consistently shown that these two groups hold unfavorable attitudes toward women in administration. An AASA survey of superintendents and school board presidents finds attitudes toward women in administration to be slightly more favorable than earlier studies, but still reports a number of negative beliefs (Educational Research Service, 1981). Importantly, is the reaffirmation in this study of an occurrence documented in all attitudinal studies—women in any category are more favorable to women in school administration than are men. This finding gains significance in light of a commonly held belief that "women are their own worst enemy." Attitudinal, opinion, and behavioral studies do not bear this out.

In the AASA study, for instance, 94% of the male superintendents, 98% of the female superintendents, 90% of the male board presidents, and 100% of the female board presidents strongly agree that men and women should be given equal opportunity to participate in management training programs. On the other hand, 22% of the male school board presidents and 15% of the male superintendents still believe that it is not acceptable for women to assume leadership roles. A substantial proportion of these two groups of men also believe that to be a successful administrator means that women must lose their femininity (35% and 39%, respectively) and that pregnancy and administration don't mix (56% and 59%). Of male school board presidents, 53% believe that women would allow their emotions to rule a situation and 35% of them believe that menstruation negatively affects women's administrative behavior.

Another position held by male superintendents and school board presidents as reported in the AASA study, which reflects discriminatory attitudes, is the belief that some jobs should remain men's jobs whereas others should remain women's. At the same time that these men affirmed that a person of either sex could fill their own jobs well, they also believed that in their own districts promotional opportunities were greater for men. Further, 6.5% of the superintendents and 8.6% of the school board presidents resented women's attempts to change this imbalance in their districts. The studies provide evidence that attitudes of important gatekeepers in schools are still not altogether positive to women.

Minority women suffer doubly from these attitudes. For them discrimination occurs on two fronts: race and sex. Whereas Paddock's 1978 national survey found that minority women suffered more on account of sex than race, Doughty's (1980) research finds both statuses hinder minority women. Pitting race against sex as an explanatory variable often obscures the reality that despite myths to the contrary, minority women are still at the bottom of the career ladder in schools (Crain, 1985). A black woman respondent in Coffin and Ekstrom's study articulated the discrimination black women face:

> I am a black female and I feel that the factors that have contributed to my unsuccessful efforts to secure promotion and upgrading of salary have been sex and race discrimination. Most of the top administration jobs in this system are filled by white males. (1979, p. 57)

Clement (1980. p. 131) writes that the few women who hold "prestigious, visible superintendencies" are mostly black women, but they are "in positions of such overwhelming difficulty as to make success highly unlikely." Women of any race seldom get good administrative jobs: "Not for women are the so-called lighthouse districts, plausible suburban communities, or stable urban areas" (1980, p. 131). Or, as one black woman phrased it, "Blacks don't get jobs until whites have messed up the system totally and the courts or expediency requires change" (Coffin & Ekstrom, 1979, p. 57).

The studies thus far mentioned focus on the entry process where discrimination has most often been studied and documented—far more often than in the promotional or job performance arena. However, research by the Navy Personnel Research and Development Center (Sadler, 1984) may have currency in school administration. This study found that the evaluation reports of males and females differed greatly in the language used to describe the two groups. Women consistently tended to have aspects of their job that were considered less important to advancement highlighted, whereas men's reports directly discussed their leadership ability. Men were more likely to be described as competent and knowledgeable and as being leaders. Table 3.2 illustrates the differences in words used to describe males and females—words that had an adverse impact on women's promotions.

THE BARRIERS OF COVERT SEX DISCRIMINATION

Sex discrimination is also played out in a number of more subtle ways—ways that limit women's mobility and advancement but aren't directly traceable to sex discrimination. Most school people do not consciously discriminate, however, "the evidence suggests that sexual discrimination operates largely outside of conscious awareness" (Porter et al., 1983, p. 1036). A study of graduate students in my classes in an administrative training program found that to the person, they denied believing there were differences between males and females. And yet, when asked, "If you woke up tomorrow and discovered you were a member of the opposite sex, how would your life be different?," all of the students responded in sex-stereotypic ways. Men wrote that they would have to quit work and raise children and women reported that they could apply for positions in school administration.

Women often experience, but deny, sex discrimination. Erickson found that the denial of discrimination is a survival mechanism. If she acknowledges it, the woman might have to confront it directly, which might be deadly to her career. So she "ignores bias, heightens her social sensitiveness, and moves forward" (1984, p.

TABLE 3.2
Words and Phrases Used in Evaluations
of Male and Female Employees

Word/Phrases Used About Men	*Words/Phrases Used About Women*
Carries out duties effectively	Gets job done in timely manner
Handles job with skill and technical know-how	Instrumental in aiding division efforts
Directs subordinates	Has positive impact on unit
Provides information on EO	Supports EO
A true leader	Good manager/administrator
Displays common sense	Displays concern
Physically fit	Well groomed
Dynamic	Receptive
Forceful	Bright
Assertive	Valuable asset
Aggressive	Personable
Mature	Outgoing
Reliable	Sociable
Logical	Tactful
Motivated	Impeccable appearance
Perceptive	Articulate manner
Self-starter	

101). A number of studies document barriers to women that at first don't seem to indicate sex discrimination; however, a second look leads us to prior practices or conditions that hurt only women and not men. For instance, a number of researchers (Baughman, 1977; Drust, 1977; Gasser, 1975; Schmuck, 1976; Stevenson, 1974) have pointed out that women have traditionally had little support, encouragement, or counseling from family, peers, superordinates, or representatives of educational institutions to pursue careers in administration. A 1978 study by Fisher found that 40% of the men but only 17% of the women were encouraged by an administrator to apply for an administrative position. More often, these women have been given negative cues by family and work groups concerning such an endeavor. The importance of encouragement and support can be seen in light of studies (Shakeshaft, 1979) that indicate that of the women who have decided to pursue administrative careers, *most* have done so because some significant other (mother, lover, husband, father, principal, college professor) encouraged them.

In nine studies that explored the most important influences on women administrators' careers (Anderson, 1978; Drust, 1977; Hankin, 1978; Marable, 1975; McCamey, 1977; McCorkle, 1976; Paddock, 1978; Rideout, 1974; Walsh, 1975), the person most often credited with supporting the woman administrator was her mother. Others were teachers, central office personnel, current supervisors, other school administrators, and family members (including husbands). The research on the support of husbands is mixed. In three studies (Coffin & Ekstrom, 1979; Doughty, 1980; Payne & Jackson, 1978), *all* respondents underscored the importance of husbands, partners, and other family members in allowing them to continue to succeed, even in the face of other barriers. Many of these women attested to the importance of a husband's support but indicated they did not have the benefit of such support. On the other hand, many women felt their husband's encouragement completely. Responses that indicate the degree to which these women credit husbands with their success are reflected in the following quote by a woman administrator, "I don't know how I would have made it without my husband. He has always been supportive of everything I've become involved in. He's just a wonderful person."

The unanimity of the voices of married women who are administrators, concerning supportive husbands, is somewhat puzzling in light of the research that indicates that in dual-career families, women take on a *larger* share of the work in the home than they do in relationships where only the husband works outside the home. Perhaps the husbands of women in school administration are particularly unlike men in the rest of the world. Or, more likely, what women call support from husbands may be a lack of resistance to their aspirations. In these relationships, as long as the status quo is not upset, the husbands do encourage their wives. For instance:

> I am very fortunate, in that I'm married to a man who is secure and not threatened by me. It's really very soothing. On the other hand, he's very traditional. Although we are very supportive of each other, when I go home I am a wife. I can kid myself into thinking I'm in charge, but that just wouldn't work. (Payne & Jackson, 1978, p. 11)

Or, from another black woman administrator discussing the price she pays for "support" from her husband:

> I would think that this is a problem for all women. Perhaps I think that

> this is a very special problem for Black women because the problem of the Black male has been overly dramatized to the point that any Black man who is married to a woman in a leadership position has a tendency to be extra sensitive. In order to compensate for it on a very personal level, I bend over backwards to sort of feed my husband's ego. (Payne & Jackson, 1978, p. 12)

Clement et al. (1977) believe that women need more support than men because of the social context in which women exist; unfortunately, they tend to receive less (Gross & Trask, 1964, 1976). However difficult family conditions may be, once outside family circles, support appears even harder to obtain.

Women have been socialized not to pursue education. As a result fewer females than males have participated in certification, doctoral, or internship programs in administration in the past. Several researchers (Barry, 1975; Capps, 1977; Edson, 1981; Perrin, 1975; Sample, 1977; Schmuck, 1976; Tjosvold, 1975) have cited both lack of formal preparation as well as few administrative learning experiences while still a teacher vis-a-vis committees, unions, coaching, discipline duty, or extracurricular responsibilities, as areas that render women less experienced or less prepared for administration than men. Recent work (Edson, 1981; Picker, 1980) indicates that this barrier is being overcome as more women participate in internships, receive administrative certification, and earn doctoral degrees.

When women go to college to acquire these administrative degrees, they are less likely than males to find a supportive atmosphere. The majority of professors of educational administration are white males (Campbell & Newell, 1973; Schmuck, 1977). Contradicting a number of studies, Oller found that women in educational administration were encouraged by university professors in equal amounts but that this encouragement was more important to women than to men, perhaps because of lack of support in school districts and at home. When women professors were available, they provided the most support to both female and male students. One woman stated:

> Isn't it interesting that the encouragement for my present activity in the program came from women, most of whom were relative strangers, rather than from the men who worked alongside of me and indirectly identified me as competent? (Oller, 1979, p. 2)

Campbell and Newell reported in 1973 that professors of educational administration as compared to university professors generally are "a little older, prefer more frequently a Protestant faith, are more likely to be married, and have more children" (1973, p. 25). They go on to write, "there appears to be an alarming homogeneity within the professorship. The number of mavericks, those who are distinguished by great independence of thought and action, seems to be very small" (p. 137). Although there is some indication that the makeup of the professorate is changing, it is still largely a group of traditional white men. Silver points to a possible conflict between the women who come to graduate school in educational administration and who are "unusual people, having sought professional advancement despite all the odds" and the male professors who are "much more traditional, middle-class and conservative in orientation" (1976, p. 12).

Silver also discusses women's further isolation in graduate school as they can't identify with the male students either:

> The male students have typically been more conforming, more compatible with the existing power structure, more able to visualize themselves as part of the administration group. Thus, there are likely to be personality clashes between men and women in the graduate school situation: the women tend to be older, in many cases having raised families during the intervening years; they also tend to be more experienced and more socially deviant than the men. (1976, p. 12).

This interaction supports the notion by Adkison (1981, p. 323) that "men choose to sponsor women who conform to their stereotypes." University professors often don't find women who are acceptable as protegees and when they do, they may have chosen women who are the least likely to be competent and successful, women who "are passive and nonthreatening, or at least capable of appearing so" (1981, p. 323).

Besides lack of support by male faculty and male students, women experience a number of other conditions that combine to discourage graduate school participation and success. J. M. Williams (n.d.) found that subtle discrimination adversely affected women's success in college attainment, with the highest level of discrimination experienced by women in graduate school. Institutional barriers that were found to hamper achievement for women included lack of child care, poor medical services for female-related conditions, informal networks consisting of male students and male faculty, inadequate number of female role models, college courses and activities listed "for men only," and the lack of focus on women as students.

A not-so-subtle barrier for women graduate students in educational administration is the instructional material they must read. A number of researchers have commented upon the relationship between sexist curriculum materials and the dampened career goals of women. Several studies (Nagle, Gardner, Levine, & Wolf, 1982; Schmuck, Butman, & Person, 1982; Shakeshaft & Hanson, 1982; Shakeshaft & Hanson, 1986; Tietze, Shakeshaft, & Davis, 1981) have critiqued the textbooks and journals in the field for gender bias and have found a shocking proportion of sexist content in the research and writing of the field. Thus an additional barrier for women in administration is the lack of appropriate and positive curricular materials for them to read. Marshall concludes that graduate programs in educational administration develop and support "students in ways that do not promote equal opportunity" (1984, p. 10), a finding supported by S. W. Williams (1982), who concluded from his study of 119 programs in educational administration that most departments do little to serve their women and minority students.

Women, more than men, cite lack of finances as a reason for being unable to continue administrative training (American Association of University Women, 1985). Women in the general labor force earn 59 cents for every dollar earned by a man; women in public school teaching and administration also earn less than their male colleagues (Databank, 1982). Women have tended to sacrifice financially for their families, thus cutting short educational opportunities. Women are more likely than men to be financially disadvantaged and are more likely expected, and to expect, to sacrifice their education or needs so that the resources may be used for family purposes.

Although women receive less support from friends, family, and university professors, they appear to receive counseling more often than do men, according to a 1979 study by Oller; 50% of the women but only 25% of the men in her study sought formal counseling on career issues. Unfortunately for the women, their experiences were not always positive. Many described their sessions as "rotten" or "unsatisfactory." One noted that, "the counselor told me to drop out of educational administration and was unreceptive to what I wanted" (1979, p. 4).

Related to the issue of support for women are expectations of traditional roles for women. Not surprisingly, family and home responsibilities, including the major responsibility for child and home care, were listed as barriers to women's achievement in administration in a number of studies (Barry, 1975; Davis, 1978; Edson, 1981; Gasser, 1975; McCorkel, 1976; Schmuck, 1976; Stevenson, 1974). As a result, many women in administration have either never been married or are divorced or widowed. Whereas some of these women are undoubtedly in committed lesbian relationships, many are heterosexual women who find the demands of marriage and work incompatible. Illustrative is the explanation of one woman of her single state:

> I never married, and the more deeply committed I became in this one growing institution the less time I had for social activities. Men would generally take the position that I was too intellectual. So, most of my association was limited to professional kinds of activities. (Payne & Jackson, 1978, p. 11)

For those who had children—married or unmarried—the lack of reliable child care and limited pregnancy benefits were listed as obstacles to taking on additional administrative responsibilities. As a result, the profile of the "typical" woman administrator is of a woman who either (a) does not have children; (b) whose children are grown; or (c) who has private child care in the form of a full-time housekeeper or, more often, her own mother.

Although research does not support the notion that women's work suffers from these added responsibilities, it is believed by men in positions of power that family responsibilities adversely affect job performance. For instance, an AASA (Educational Research Service, 1981) survey of superintendents and school board presidents reports that 78% of male school board presidents and superintendents believe that women, more than men, put family ahead of jobs. Women were believed by 45% of the superintendents and 48% of the school board presidents to take more time off for personal reasons than did men. A majority of male superintendents and school board presidents (56% and 59%) stated that pregnancy and an administrative career don't mix, and 36% of male superintendents and 47% of male school board members supported the notion that "a woman who stays at home all the time with her children is a better mother than a woman who works outside the home at least half time" (1981, p. 12).

Thus home and family responsibilities provide obstacles for women in administration in two ways: The woman not only must effectively juggle all of her tasks, she must also contend with the bulk of male school board presidents and superintendents who erroneously believe that not only is she unable to manage the balancing act but that it is inappropriate for her to even attempt it.

Socialization and sex-role stereotyping have been cited by several researchers (Davis, 1978; Poll, 1978; Schmuck, 1976; Tjosvold, 1975) as explanations of why the women themselves, as well as others within society, do not immediately connect women with administration. Antonucci (1980) writes that teaching has been presented as a career compatible with traditional female sex-roles and thus becoming a teacher, for a woman, does not challenge her femininity. Administration, on the other hand, does put the role of female and the role of worker at odds. Women, themselves, identify sex-role stereotyping and socialization as problematic. Oller (1979, p. 7) reports that one woman said, "My internalization of what women can do and are *supposed* to do is my biggest barrier. I learned very early that 'good girls' take a back seat. Socialization haunts me to this day!" Not only have women been socialized in ways that have not made them administratively inclined, those who hire have been socialized to believe that those qualities frequently associated with females are antithetical to those qualities needed to manage and, conversely, that qualities needed to manage are ones not possessed by women.

Because of an androcentric worldview, traditional female qualities are not highly valued. By dividing the world into two kinds of behavior—those who are male and those who are female—and labeling behaviors of competence as male, women must choose between being called competent or being identified as female. Biklen (1980) points out the difficulties of women attempting to succeed in traditionally male fields: Either they are judged competent and unfeminine or incompetent and feminine, a choice that puts two strong and interconnected identities in conflict. Ortiz (1980, p. 7) offers examples of how competence in women is described negatively: "I don't want to ever be an administrator. When I look at Dr. Denton and when I hear about her coldness and how bright she is, I know I'd never be happy being like that. She's not feminine at all."

The socialization process of women results not only in role conflict for women but in behaviors that are traditionally feminine and that are not considered (but that in fact are) the behaviors of good administrators. For instance, assertiveness is a skill that women, by and large, have not been socialized to call their own. Relatedly, women's contributions are often ignored and women have reported feeling invisible in policymaking groups. Socialization is also partly responsible for the resentment, from both males and females, that women aspirants sometimes find directed at them.

Attitudinal studies indicate that males in all positions have less positive attitudes than do females toward women in school administration; many of these attitudes were based upon sex-stereotypic ideas—ideas that limit opportunities for women. For instance, Neidig (1973) found that male school board members believe that women cannot cope with the emotional and physical stress found in school administration. Male superintendents in this same study agree that due to a greater number of female teachers, it is important to have more male administrators in the schools. Rabenau (1978) found that superintendents expected women, more than men, to have interpersonal skills and to experience success in personal relationships.

Reflective of basic stereotypic views of women were the beliefs of male superintendents and school board presidents who described women as more likely than men to enjoy doing routine tasks, not to set long-range goals or work toward them; to want less responsibility; to be home rather than job oriented; to be more sensitive to criticism; to be less aggressive than males; to be less likely to stand up under fire; to be less independent and self-sufficient; to cry more easily; to be good at detail work; to be unable to understand financial matters; and to be unable to negotiate contracts (Educational Research Service, 1981). These attitudes, based on limiting and sexist views of women, if reflected in practice, would indicate that male superintendents and school board presidents are quite likely to discriminate against women solely because of their sex because they believe that women do things in a different, and *less effective*, way than men. As we will see in Chapter 5, it is not viewing women as different from men that harms women, but rather identifying women and women's styles of leadership as inferior to men and men's styles of leadership. Whether individual or organizational, socialization and sex-role stereotyping have been potent obstacles to increasing women's participation in the management of schools.

The lack of opportunity to see other women in a variety of administrative positions, to hear how these women describe their lives, and to compare themselves with women just one step farther up the hierarchy have been cited as reasons women have not moved into administrative positions in larger numbers (Davis, 1978; Gasser, 1975; Schmuck, 1976). The importance of role models in helping both the women themselves and others within the system to view women administrators as a normal occurrence, rather than an exceptional one, cannot be overstated. One woman articulates this: "I had earned my administrator's credential when I went back to school. But I never thought about becoming an administrator. Administrators are all men" (Schmuck, 1979, p. 25).

Oller in a study of male and female aspirants in educational administration notes that as they grew up, the men in her study had a wider range of role models than did the women. "While women looked to their families, friends and teachers close by, men saw beyond this inner circle to athletes, professionals, former presidents, religious leaders, and military superiors for models" (1979, p. 4).

Research has found same-sex role models to be crucial for women but not for men. Women often cannot envision patterning themselves after men, either because they identify men's behavior as "male" and therefore incongruent with their "female" self-images, or because male behavior seems inappropriate for them. Edson reported that women saw men as negative role models, as related by the women aspirants in her description of male principals. One said, "When I decided to go for this job, I looked around at the kind of principals there were. I thought Lord, I can do it at least as well as they're doing! If they can, *I* can" (1981, p. 184).

Unlike role models, which generally must be of the same sex and race in order for women to identify with the model, sponsors or mentors may be either male or female. A sponsor or a mentor is much more important to the individual woman than is a role model because it is the sponsor who advises the woman, supports her for jobs, and promotes and helps her. Sponsors and mentors, who have traditionally been white males, have tended to promote other white males. Minority women often suffer doubly in the area of sponsorship—first because they are female and second because of their minority status (Lovelady-Dawson, 1980). Although most women have not had either sponsors or mentors, most who have been successful in acquiring administrative titles have sponsors or mentors. Thus sponsorship or mentoring appears to be an important process in a woman's administrative career (Covel, 1978; Poll, 1978; Stevenson, 1974).

Related to sponsorship is the need to have access to a network that provides one with information on job openings and administrative strategies as well as visibility and a support group. Women have traditionally been excluded from these networks and thus have not heard about administrative positions, have not been known by others, and have had few people to approach for counsel (Davis, 1978; Gasser, 1975; Schmuck, 1976; Stevenson, 1974).

Whereas all the barriers identified do not affect all women, neither are they equally prohibitive at all career levels. Lack of sponsorship may be less of a problem at the department chair level than at the superintendency. Conversely, socialization and sex-role stereotyping may hinder a women who has not taken the first step toward becoming an administrator more than it hinders a woman who has served as an administrator. Relatedly, racial and ethnic minority women find that the barriers are compounded by their racial and ethnic identifications.

In this chapter, I have demonstrated how, in an androcentric society, an array of discriminatory practices converge to keep women from becoming school administrators. Strategies for demolishing these barriers are discussed in Chapter 4.

REFERENCES

Adkison, J. A. (1981). Women in school administration: A review of the research. *Review of Educational Research 51*(3), 311-343.

American Association of University Women. (1985). *Women and student financial aid*. Washington, DC: Author.

Anderson, E. B. (1978). The life-history correlates, work-related motivational characteristics, and role-identification factors of on-site women administrators in Hawaiian public schools. *Dissertation Abstracts International, 38,* 5809A.

Andrews, P. H. (1984). Performance—self-esteem and perceptions of leadership emergence: A comparative study of men and women. *Western Journal of Speech Communication, 48*(1), 1-13.

Antonucci, T. (1980). The need for female role models in education. In S. K. Biklen & M. B. Brannigan (Eds.), *Women and educational leadership* (pp. 185-195). Lexington, MA: D. C. Heath.

Baltzell, D. C., & Dentler, R. A. (1983). *Selecting American school principals: A sourcebook for educators*. Cambridge, MA: ABT Associates.

Barnett, R. C., & Baruch, G. K. (1979). *Multiple roles and well being: A study of mothers of preschool age children* (Working Paper No. 3). Wellesley, MA: Wellesley College Center for Research on Women.

Barry, C. S. (1975). The role of women in higher education administration in New York state in the 1980's. *Dissertation Abstracts International, 36*, 4886A. (University Microfilms No. 76-4173)

Baughman, M. K. (1977). Attitudes and perceptions of a selected sample of women senior high teachers toward becoming school administrators in Detroit public schools. *Dissertation Abstracts International, 38*, 6420A. (University Microfilms No. 7804644)

Beck, H. N. (1978). Attitudes toward women held by California school district board members, superintendents, and school personnel directors including a review of the historical, psychological and sociological foundations. *Dissertation Abstracts International, 38*, 3246A-3247A. (University Microfilms No. 7819511)

Benedict, R. (1934). *Patterns of culture*. Boston: Houghton Mifflin.

Bernard, J. (1981). *The female world*. New York: Free Press.

Biklen, S. K. (1980). Barriers to equity—women, educational leadership, and social change. In S. K. Biklen & M. B. Brannigan (Eds.), *Women and educational leadership* (pp. 1-23). Lexington MA: D. C. Heath

Bonuso, C. A. (1981). An examination of the influence of the physical characteristics of height and weight in the selection of secondary principals in public schools of New York state. *Dissertation Abstracts International, 42*, 1864A.

Bonuso, C. A., & Shakeshaft, C. (1983). The gender of secondary school principals. *Integrateducation, 21*(1-6), 143-146.

Bunyi, J. M., & Andrews, P. H. (1985). Gender and leadership emergence: An experimental study. *Southern Speech Communication Journal, 50*(3), 246-260.

Busch, J. W. (1983, November). *Mentoring in graduate schools of education: Does it happen?* Paper presented at the annual meeting of the American Educational Research Association Special Interest Group: Research on Women and Education, Tempe, AZ.

Campbell, R. F., & Newell, L. J. (1973). *A study of professors of educational administration*. Columbus, OH: University Council for Educational Administration.

Capps, J. A. (1977). The roles of assistant superintendents and supervisors in North Carolina relative to sex differences. *Dissertation Abstracts International, 38*, 1140A. (University Microfilms No. 77-18, 765)

Carlson, R. O. (1972). *School superintendents: Careers and performances*. Columbus, OH: Merrill.

Carlson, R. O., & Schmuck, P. A. (1981). The sex dimension of careers in educational management: Overview and synthesis. In P. A. Schmuck, W. W. Charters, Jr., & R. O. Carlson (Eds.), *Educational policy and management: Sex differentials* (pp. 117-130). New York: Academic Press.

Chodorow, N. (1978). *The reproduction of mothering.* Berkeley: University of California Press.

Clement, J. (1980), Sex bias in school administration. In S. K. Biklen & M. B. Brannigan (Eds.), *Women and educational leadership* (pp. 131-137). Lexington, MA: D. C. Heath.

Clement, J. P., Di Bella, C. M., Eckstrom, R. B., Tobias, S. T., Bartol, K., & Alban, M. (1977). No room at the top? *American Education, 13*(5), 20-23.

Coffin, G. C., & Eckstrom, R. B. (1979). Roadblocks to women's careers in educational administration. In M. C. Berry (Ed.), *Women in educational administration* (pp. 53-63). Washington, DC: National Association for Women Deans, Administrators, and Counselors.

Covel, J.I.M. (1978). Analysis of school administrators' careers in Riverside County from 1870-71-1974-75: A study of factors which affect career patterns for men and women in school organizations. *Dissertation Abstracts International, 38,* 7044A-7045A. (University Microfilms No. 7808275)

Crain, R. L. (1985). *Employer reactions to hypothetical candidates: The role of race and high school quality.* Paper presented at the annual meeting of the Eastern Sociological Association, Philadelphia.

Databank. (1982, March 10). *Education Week,* pp. 12-13.

Davis, M. C. (1978). Women administrators in Southeastern institutions of higher education. *Dissertation Abstracts International, 39,* 1945A-1946A. (University Microfilms No. 7819168)

Dias, S. L. (1975). A study of personal, perceptual, and motivational factors influential in predicting the aspiration level of women and men toward the administrative roles in education. *Dissertation Abstracts International, 36,* 1202A. (University Microfilms No. 75-20, 946)

Dinnerstein, D. (1976). *The mermaid and the minotaur: Sexual arrangements and human malaise.* New York: Harper & Row.

Donelson, E., & Gullahorn, J. E., (1977). *Women: A psychological perspective.* New York: John Wiley.

Doughty, R. (1980). The black female administrator: Woman in a double bind. In S. K. Biklen & M. B. Brannigan (Eds.), *Women and educational leadership* (pp. 165-174). Lexington, MA: D. C. Heath.

Drust, B. (1977). Factors related to the employment of women as junior high school and high school principals, assistant superintendents and superintendents in California public schools. *Dissertation Abstracts International, 37,* 5479A. (University Microfilms No. 77-4825)

Dweck, C., Davidson, W., Nelson, S., & Enna, B. (1978). Sex differences in learned helplessness: II. The contingencies of evaluative feedback in the classroom and III. An experimental analysis. *Developmental Psychology, 14*(3), 268-276.

Edson, S. K. (1980). Female aspirants in public school administration: Why do they continue to aspire to principalships? *Dissertation Abstracts International, 41,* 7-8, 3345A.

Edson, S. K. (1981). "If they can, I can": Women aspirants to administrative positions in public schools. In P. A. Schmuck, W. W. Charters, Jr., & R. O. Carlson (Eds.), *Educational policy and management: Sex differentials* (pp. 169-185). New York: Academic Press.

Educational Research Service. (1981). *Survey: Attitudes toward women as school district administrators.* Arlington, VA: American Association of School Administrators.

Erickson, H. L. (1984). Female public school administrators and conflict management. *Dissertation Abstracts International, 45* (5), 1251-A.

Estler, S. (1975). Women as leaders in public education. *Signs: Journal of Women in Culture and Society, 1*(3), 363-386.

Firestone, S. (1970). *The dialectic of sex*. New York: William Morrow.

Fisher, F. P. (1978). A study of the relationship between the scarcity of women in educational administrative positions and the multiple factors which influence the career aspirations of women teachers. *Dissertation Abstracts International, 40,* 574A.

Fleming, J. T. (1974). Assessment of employment practices towards women administrators in institutions of higher education. *Dissertation Abstracts International, 35,* 4184A. (University Microfilms No. 75-488)

Forsyth, D. R., & Forsyth, N. M. (1984, April). *Subordinates reactions to female leaders*. Paper presented at the annual meeting of the Eastern Psychological Association, Baltimore, MD.

Fox, F. J. (1975). Black women administrators in the Denver public schools. *Dissertation Abstracts International, 36,* 7089A. (University Microfilms No. 76-11, 574)

Gardner, L. C. (1977). Employment status of female administrators and attitudes toward employment of female administrators in the community college system of North Carolina. *Dissertation Abstracts International, 38,* 3833A-3834A. (University Microfilms No. 77-27, 984)

Gasser, M. H. (1975). Career patterns of women administrators in higher education: Barriers and constraints. *Dissertation Abstracts International, 36,* 7893A-7894A. (University Microfilms No. 76-13, 240)

Goerss, K.V.W. (1975). A study of personality factors of selected women administrators in higher education. *Dissertation Abstracts International, 36,* 1942A. (University Microfilms No. 77-16, 424)

Goldsmith, H. B. (1976). The categorical dominance of sex, race and national origin in the preferences of white, black, hispanic male and female New York City elementary school teachers for white, black, hispanic male, female elementary school principal candidates by means of a simulation activity. *Dissertation Abstracts International, 38,* 1148A-1149A. (University Microfilms No. 77 32864)

Greenberg, S. (1978). Preschool and the politics of sexism. In B. Sprung (Ed.), *Perspectives in non-sexist early childhood education* (pp. 40-56). New York: Teachers College Press, Teachers College, Columbia University.

Gross, N., & Trask, A.E. (1964). *Men and women as elementary school principals* (Final Report No. 2). Cambridge, MA: Harvard University, Graduate School of Education.

Gross, N., & Trask, A. E. (1976). *The sex factor and the management of schools*. New York: John Wiley.

Hagen, R. L., & Kahn, A. (1975). Discrimination against competent women. *Journal of Applied Social Psychology, 5*(4), 362-376.

Hankin, C. G. (1978). The female elementary school principal (Volumes I-VI). *Dissertation Abstracts International, 39,* 49-A. (University Microfilms No. 78 10883)

Hansot, E., & Tyack, D. (1981). *The dream deferred: A golden age for women school administrators* (Policy Paper No. 81-C2). Stanford, CA: Stanford University School of Education, Institute for Research on Educational Finance and Governance.

Hilton, J. M. (1977). The relationship between sex-role stereotypes and career aspirations of elementary and secondary women teachers. *Dissertation Abstracts International, 38,* 3843A-3844A. (University Microfilms No. 77-28,041)

Holland, J. L. (1973). Relationships between the chief school administrator's selection of principal candidates and the candidates' qualifications, attitudes on educational issues and sex. *Dissertation Abstracts International, 34,* 2213A-2214A. (University Microfilms No. 73-26, 720)

Hurlbut, J.A.A. (1978). Attitudes and other concerns related to women being employed as public school administrators in Texas. *Dissertation Abstracts International, 39,* 3951A. (University Microfilms No. 7824648)

Huserik, M. C. (1975). Career aspirations and promotional opportunity for women administrators in California school districts. *Dissertation Abstracts International, 36,* 3290A. (University Microfilms No. 75-28, 633)

Jovick, T. D. (1981). Ambitions and the opportunity for professionals in the elementary school. In P. A. Schmuck, W. W. Charters, Jr., & R. O. Carlson (Eds.), *Educational policy and management: Sex differentials* (pp. 153-168). New York: Academic Press.

Kanter, R. M. (1977). *Men and women of the corporation.* New York: Basic Books.

LaBarthe, E. R. (1973). A study of the motivation of women in administrative and supervisory positions in selected unified districts in Southern California. *Dissertation Abstracts International, 34,* 3695A-3696A.

Landon, G. L. (1975). Perceptions of sex role stereotyping and women teachers' administrative career aspirations. *Dissertation Abstracts International, 36,* 1214A. (University Microfilms No. 75-16, 317)

Lovelady-Dawson, F. (1980, July). *Women and minorities in the principalship: Career opportunities and problems.* Paper presented at the American Association of School Administrators Third Annual Summer Instructional Leadership Conference, Chicago.

Makulski, M.J.D. (1976). Case studies of the attitudes of superintendents and school board members of selected school districts in the State of Michigan toward the employment of women as school administrators. *Dissertation Abstracts International, 37,* 6186A. (University Microfilms No. 77-7979)

Marable, J. M. (1975). The role of women in public school administration as perceived by black women administrators in the field. *Dissertation Abstracts International, 36,* 73A. (University Microfilms No. 75-14, 316)

Marshall, C. (1984). Men and women in educational administration programs. *Journal of the National Association for Women Deans, Administrators, and Counselors, 48*(1), 3-12.

Marshall, C., & Grey, R. (1982). Legal rights of women seeking administrative positions in local school districts. *Journal of Educational Equity and Leadership, 2*(4), 253-259.

McCamey, D. S. (1977). The status of black and white women in central administrative positions in Michigan public schools. *Dissertation Abstracts International, 37,* 6189A. (University Microfilms No. 77-7987)

McCorkle, E. M. (1976). Top level women administrators in higher education: A study of women presidents, chief academic officers, and academic deans in Federal regions I, VI, and X. *Dissertation Abstracts International, 36,* 7238A. (University Microfilms No. 76-9715)

Mead, M. (1935). *Sex and temperament in three primitive societies.* New York: William Morrow.

Mickey, B. H. (1984). You can go home again, but it's not easy. *Journal of the National Association for Women Deans, Administrators, and Counselors, 47*(3), 3-7.

Miller, G. L. (1976). A study of selected social processes on women's career motivation related to the declining number of women in the elementary school principalship. *Dissertation Abstracts International, 37,* 3315A-3316A. (University Microfilms No. 76-27, 336)

Moore, S. E. (1977). Opportunities for women in the field of public school administration in the New Jersey counties of Cumberland, Hunterdon, and Passaic. *Dissertation Abstracts International, 37,* 7451A-7452A. (University Microfilms No. 77-13 , 468)

Morgan, E. (1972). *The descent of woman.* New York: Stein and Day.

Nagle, L., Gardner, D. W., Levine, M., & Wolf, S. (1982, March). *Sexist bias in instructional supervision textbooks.* Paper presented at the annual meeting of the American Educational Research Association, New York.

Neidig, M. B. (1973). Women applicants for administrative positions: Attitudes held by administrators and school boards. *Dissertation Abstracts International, 34,* 2982A. (University Microfilms No. 73-30, 959)

Noll, N. L. (1973). Opinions of policy-making officials in two-year public educational institutions toward the employment of women administrators. *Dissertation Abstracts International, 34,* 1100A-1101A. (University Microfilms No. 73-20, 447)

Oliver, L. W. (1974). Achievement and affiliation motivation in career-oriented and home-making-oriented college women. *Journal of Vocational Behavior, 4*(3), 275-281.

Oller, C. S. (1979, April). *Differential experiences of male and female aspirants in public school administration: A closer look at perceptions within the field.* Paper presented at the annual meeting of the American Educational Research Association, San Francisco.

Ortiz, F. I. (1980, April). Career change and mobility for minorities and women in school administration. Paper presented at the annual meeting of the American Educational Research Association. Boston.

Ortiz, F. I. (1982). *Career patterns in education: Women, men and minorities in public school administration.* New York: Praeger.

Owens, E. T. (1975). Perceived barriers to employment for women as educational administrators in South Carolina public schools. *Dissertation Abstracts International, 36,* 7107A-7108A. (University Microfilms No. 76-10, 478)

Paddock, S. (1978). Women's careers in administration. *Dissertation Abstracts International, 38,* 5834A. (University Microfilms No. 7802552)

Payne, N. J., & Jackson, B. L. (1978). Status of black women in educational administration. *Emergent Leadership: Focus on Minorities and Women in Educational Administration, 2*(3), 1-15.

Perrin, E. H. (1975). Perceptions of women college faculty members toward careers in academic administration. *Dissertation Abstracts International, 35,* 7574A-7575A. (University Microfilms No. 7816079)

Picker, A. M. (1980). Female educational administators: Coping in a basically male environment. *Educational Horizons, 58*(3), 145-149.

Poll, C. (1978). No room at the top: A study of the social processes that contribute to the under-representation of women on the administrative levels of the New York City school system. *Dissertation Abstracts International, 39,* 3165A. (University Microfilms No. 7821905)

Porter, N., Geis, F. L., & Jennings, J. (1983). Are women invisible as leaders? *Sex Roles,* 9(10), 1035-1049.

Powers, B. F. (1975). Perceptions of the gender of leadership behaviors of effective high school principals. *Dissertations Abstracts International, 35,* 7575A-7576A. (University Microfilms No. 75-8637)

Pruitt, G. S. (1976). Women in leadership of alternatives schools. *Dissertation Abstracts International, 37,* 80A. (University Microfilms No. 76-14, 655)

Quell, M., & Pfeiffer, I. L. (1982). Instances of sex bias rated by women administrators. *Journal of Educational Equity and Leadership,* 2(4), 268-273.

Rabenau, M. L. (1978). The perceptions of superintendents of the importance of selected variables used to evaluate male and female applicants for the positions of public school administration. *Dissertation Abstracts International, 39,* 1242A. (University Microfilms No. 7814624)

Ralston, Y. L. (1975). An analysis of attitudes as barriers to the selection of women as college presidents in Florida. *Dissertation Abstracts International, 35,* 6992A. (University Microfilms No. 75-10,687)

Reynolds, B., & Elliott, B. (1980). *Differences between men and women in their aspirations for careers in educational administration.* Unpublished manuscript.

Rideout, A. H. (1974). The upward mobility of women in higher education: A profile of women home economics administrators. *Dissertation Abstracts International, 35,* 2604A-2605A. (University Microfilms No. 74-25, 865)

Robinson, O. T. (1978). Contributions of black American academic women to American higher education. *Dissertation Abstracts International, 39,* 2094A. (University Microfilms 7816079)

Sadler, G. C. (1984). Two languages in FitReps: Male and . . . *Proceedings (110/12/982),* 137-139.

Sample, D. E. (1977). Some factors affecting the flow of women administrators in public school education. *Dissertation Abstracts International, 37,* 6201A. (University Microfilms No. 77-8208)

Schmuck, P. A. (1976). Sex differentiation in public school administration. *Dissertation Abstracts International, 36,* 5791A. (University Microfilms No. 76-5204)

Schmuck, P. A. (1977, August). *Sex differentiation in educational administration in the United States: A political and educational appraisal.* Paper presented at the National Conference of the Australian Council for Educational Administration. Brisbane, Qld, Australia.

Schmuck, P. A. (1979). *Sex equity in educational leadership: The Oregon story.* Eugene: University of Oregon, Center for Educational Policy and Management.

Schmuck, P. A., Butman, L., & Person, L. R. (1982, March). *Analyzing sex bias in Planning and Changing.* Paper presented at the annual meeting of the American Educational Research Association, New York.

Shakeshaft, C. (1979). Dissertation research on women in educational administration: A synthesis of findings and paradigm for future research. *Dissertation Abstracts International, 40,* 6455A.

Shakeshaft, C. (1985). Strategies for overcoming the barriers to women in educational administration. In S. Klein (Ed.), *Handbook for achieving sex equity through education* (pp. 124-144). Baltimore: Johns Hopkins University Press.

Shakeshaft, C., & Hanson, M. (1982, March). *Androcentric bias in the Educational Administration Quarterly.* Paper presented at the annual meeting of the American Educational Research Association, New York.

Shakeshaft, C. & Hanson, M. (1986). Androcentric bias in the *Educational Administration Quarterly. Educational Administration Quarterly, XXII*(1), 68-92.

Shapiro, C. (1983). *Employment applications survey for discriminatory questions. Long Island school districts.* Port Washington, NY: Women on the Job.

Sherfey, M. (1966). *The nature and evolution of female sexuality.* New York: Random House.

Silver, P. F. (1976). *Women in educational leadership: A trend discussion.* Columbus, OH: University Council for Educational Administration.

Stevenson, F. B. (1974). Women administrators in big ten universities. *Dissertation Abstracts International, 34,* 5553A-5554A. (University Microfilms No. 74-6141)

Stockard, J., & Johnson, M. M. (1979). The social origin of male dominance. *Sex Roles, 5*(2), 199-218.

Stockard, J., & Johnson, M. M. (1981). The sources and dynamics of sexual inequality in the profession of education. In P. A. Schmuck, W. W. Charters, Jr., & R. O. Carlson (Eds.), *Educational policy and management: Sex differentials* (pp. 235-254). New York: Academic Press.

Tibbetts, S. L. (1979). Why don't women aspire to leadership positions in education? In M. C. Berry (Ed.), *Women in educational administration: A book of readings* (pp. 1-11). Washington, DC: National Association for Women Deans, Administrators, and Counselors.

Tietze, I. N., Shakeshaft, C., & Davis, B. N. (1981, April). *Sexism in texts in educational administration.* Paper presented at the annual meeting of the American Educational Research Association, Los Angeles.

Timpano, D. M., & Knight, L. W. (1976). *Sex discrimination—the selection of school district administrators: What can be done?* (NIE Papers—Education and Work: Number Three). Washington, DC: Department of Health, Education and Welfare. (ERIC Document Reproduction Service No. Ed 133917)

Tjosvold, M. M. (1975). An analysis of selected factors in personnel management decisions which superintendents perceive as affecting the employment and promotion of women in public school administration in Minnesota. *Dissertation Abstracts International, 37,* 89A. (University Microfilms No. 76-14, 972)

Wain, J. A. (1976). Attitudes of teachers toward women school administrators and the aspirations of teachers for administrative positions in the state of Minnesota. *Dissertation Abstracts International, 36,* 4951A. (University Microfilms No. 76-4082)

Walsh, P. A. (1975). Career patterns of women administrators in higher education institutions in California. *Dissertation Abstracts International, 36,* 3323A-3324A. (University Microfilms No. 75-27, 004)

Whitten, J. E. (1975). Women teachers' perceptions concerning career aspirations of the elementary school principalship in selected schools in Texas. *Dissertation Abstracts International, 36,* 2566A-2567A. (University Microfilms No. 75-23, 952)

Williams, J. M. (n.d.). *The impact of subtle discrimination on a group of college women.* Unpublished manuscript.

Williams, P. J. (1977). Career aspirations of selected women teachers as related to their perceptions of the chances of success in becoming a school administrator. *Dissertation Abstracts International, 38,* 4507A. (University Microfilms No. 77-30880)

Williams, S. W. (1982). *A study of selected programs in educational administration in the United States and Canada.* (ERIC Document Reproduction Service No. ED 217 525)

Wood, J. L. (1975). An historical and contemporary chronicle of women faculty and/or administrators at Miami University. *Dissertation Abstracts International, 36,* 2069A. (University Microfilms No. 75-21, 690)

. 4 .

Demolishing the Barriers

Change strategies, whether implemented or imagined, vary depending upon which conceptual lens is used to view the barriers. If one believes in internal barriers, an approach that tries to change the woman is required. For instance, therapy might be suggested for the woman as a way to learn to cope with a hostile world, and assertiveness training courses prescribed to learn how to work in a male environment. Both strategies are based on the same belief—that the woman needs to change to adapt. On the other hand, if one believes that the barriers are primarily the result of the devaluation of women, the strategy for increasing women in educational administration will take a more global perspective than if one is working from the premise that it's a woman's problem. All of society, not just individual women, must be altered.

Change strategies are formulated based both on the barriers that are believed to exist and on the causes of these barriers. For instance, if a person believes that women's own efforts are the cause of barriers and also believes that lack of networks is a barrier, she or he would tell the woman to build a network. On the other hand, if lack of networks is believed to be a barrier but the cause of this barrier is believed to be male hegemony, then strategies for building those networks would be quite different and more wide ranging than merely telling the woman to find a few colleagues with whom to work. To devise solutions and assess their possibility of success, one must not only know the particular barrier but must also be clear about what is the root of that barrier.

In Chapter 3, I have argued that all barriers to women in administration are a result—either directly or indirectly—of an androcentric society. To eliminate the barriers, one must change the androcentric nature of the culture in which they flourish. To do this, behavioral changes in men and women, structural and legal changes in school and society, and attitudinal changes in everyone must be achieved. No one strategy will accomplish this revolution; many approaches must be used.

It is not surprising, then, that change strategies that have been used to increase the number of women in school administration are not mutually exclusive and that their combined effects have caused change. There have been a number of federally funded projects as well as individual and organizational efforts to increase the representation of women in administration. Although the research on the effectiveness of these strategies is limited and although not all effective strategies will be discussed, the remainder of this chapter is devoted to describing a variety of tactics that have been documented for combating the barriers to women in administration.

Descriptions of the specific projects that have evaluative data can be found in the Appendix. Although these projects are the basis of the recommendations for effective strategies to use to demolish barriers to women in school administration, a caution on their effectiveness is in order. The suggestion that the effectiveness of the programs can be measured warrants some discussion of the difficulties of such a task. At this point, there is certainly more evidence to document the barriers than there is to evaluate the solutions. There are several reasons why this is the case. It is too soon, in many instances, for the evidence to be in; there is a necessary and expected time lag between receipt of administrative certification or training and offer of an administrative job. Additionally, the general decline in enrollment, cutbacks in school budgets and federal financing of education, and the reluctance of many to retire from teaching and administration has made it even more difficult to measure the effects of the programs. Even if this were not the case, methodological weaknesses in the evaluations render assessments difficult: Control groups are seldom used; participants are not randomly selected; and existing instruments and measures are inadequate to uncover subtleties in attitudes, beliefs, self-concept, and confidence. Concomitantly, more support (funding, institutional, peer) has been provided for documentation of the issues than for developing and testing change strategies. Finally, it is nearly impossible to separate the programs from the larger context in which social change issues, particularly those concerning sex equity, are debated. Compartmentalizing the effects of larger social movements is not only impossible but probably not desirable. It is too soon to determine if there has been long-term individual, organizational, and social change that shapes a world in which women as well as men play substantive roles in all facets of schooling.

Most of the strategies that have been tested are formulated from an individual perspective or from an organizational approach. Very few have tried to change the larger societal context, neither have most acknowledged this as problematic. For instance, a number of courses and workshops have been offered to give the individual woman skills to survive in a sexist world. It is the woman who is targeted and taught assertiveness training, taught strategies to balance home and office, networking, catching of a sponsor, interviewing techniques that negotiate sexist and racist questions, and presentation of self.

Organizational changes include the recruitment of women into university administrative training programs (but not changing those programs in any way to meet the needs of women), the institution of internships that allow women experience and visibility in a number of organization positions, and the creation of jobs in schools for women.

Efforts at changing the system, although less widespread than individual or organizational approaches, have been attempted. These include providing women with financial assistance so that they can attend graduate school, increasing the number of women professors in educational administration, providing support systems and networks for women, organizing consciousness-raising sessions for women, working through the political process to change the power structure of organizations, and changing laws so that they include women.

Very little has been done to change the nature and behavior of male school board members and administrators. Nor has there been any uniformly organized effort to change the experiences of male and female children so that future generations are guided by their own expectations, rather than society's. To make changes in curriculum and teaching means first changing the ways teachers and administrators are trained. As Sadker and Sadker (1982), among others, have noted, schools of education have been among the most resistant to women's studies, gender issues, and gender equity concerns, although schools of education tend to have the highest percentage of women students.

Given the enormity of the task, it is little wonder that the strategies used have been modest in nature. They have had achievable goals. These "winnable" battles are the ones that have been undertaken. The Appendix provides a list of specific programs that have been successful and that have used a combination of strategies to achieve equity for women. Unfortunately, most of these programs are no longer in existence. When federal funds were depleted, many of these efforts ceased. Some left training and curricular materials, many of which are inaccessible. Further, there are few forums in which to use such materials. Thus, most of these programs stand as models of change to be copied rather than as examples of ongoing change strategies. The following describes each of the pieces that needs to be in place if gender is to become irrelevant in the selection of school administrators.

GETTING WOMEN TRAINED AND CERTIFIED IN ADMINISTRATION

One argument traditionally used against hiring women is that there are no qualified female candidates. Although this has never been true in school administration (there have always been qualified and capable women teachers), it is true that women were once less likely than men to have administrative training or certification. Thus a major strategy for increasing the number of women administators was to increase the number of women with administrative training. This took two major initiatives: convincing women to enter administrative programs and providing the training itself.

Recruitment of Women into Preparation Programs

For many of the reasons discussed in Chapter 3, women have traditionally not been found in administrative training programs.

Therefore, recruitment into these programs is one strategy necessary to increase the number of women in administration. In an effort to overcome the initial resistance of women to the nontraditional career of school administrator, a number of methods have been used to reach women teachers and students and provide them with information that might encourage their entrance into school administration. For instance, Women in School Administration (WISA), A Project of Internships, Certification Equity—Leadership, and Support (ICES), and Sex Equity in Education Leadership (SEEL) personnel all gave talks to education groups composed mainly of women teachers in an effort to reach prospective women administrators. Additionally, WISA provided field-based courses in an attempt to recruit women in rural areas and to provide a statewide recruitment and selection pool. In St. Paul, a recruitment program within the school district identified women for a special administrative training program. The strategies used in all of these programs have ranged from large-scale awareness programs to asking administrators to nominate individual women for training programs, but all have the goal of finding and encouraging women to have the paper credentials to become administrators.

Financial Aid for Women in Preparation Programs

Once recruited for school administration or made aware of training options, women often confront the problem of lack of financial support to fund training programs. Thus one approach to helping women become school administrators is the provision of scholarships and stipends to women pursuing careers in educational administration. FLAME (Female Leaders for Administration and Management in Education) interns, for example, were paid a monthly stipend while taking leaves of absence to pursue full-time graduate work; ICES awarded scholarships to women to attend university summer sessions and ICES workshops.

Traditional Administrative Training for Women

So that women could gain knowledge about administrative skills and/or acquire certification credentials, programs provided administrative knowledge either via formal university educational administration courses or in the form of skill workshops. FLAME interns, for instance, enrolled in full-time doctoral administration programs whereas ICES interns took administration courses during the summer. WISA (Women in School Administration) offered workshops on conflict management, the study of power and leadership, time management, and grant writing, along with other topics. ICES workshops concentrated on conflict management, business management, and the politics of education. Higher Education Resource Service (HERS), through their The Next Move program, provided a leadership and management clinic for women in higher education. These general courses, available to both males and females, are essential for women entering school administration. In some states, they are required for administrative certification whereas in others they are recommended. Whatever the case, skill courses in administration are invaluable for the woman administrator.

Providing Internships Experiences for Women

Once women began receiving training or decided to become administrators, it became clear that most lacked actual experience in administrative situations. Thus many programs implemented internship experiences for the women involved. FLAME provided participants with a variety of internship experiences both in and out of education; ICES interns spent 10 months in a school district experience; WISA interns trained in rural and small urban settings.

Recruitment, financial aid, training and internships have been successful in increasing the number of women trained to be administrators. However, these strategies weren't the only reasons that university educational administration programs opened their doors to women. Less noble, but equally important to the increase of women students, has been the need for departments of administration to stay in business. As enrollments have declined in recent years, schools of education turned to other "markets," and departments of administration were no exception. Thus women were seen as a way to keep the student body robust.

Others have pointed out that women have moved into administration training programs and public school administration in general at a time when the field is suffering a particular beating—declining enrollments, competition by private schools, decreased public support, and decreased federal government support. This analysis explains women's participation as a function of the undesirability of education as a career. In other words, only when the future of a profession seems hopeless are women allowed to enter. Whatever the reasons, the increase in women in administrative training programs has been dramatic. So much so that it can no longer be said that women aren't prepared for jobs in administration.

CHANGING THE TRAINING PROGRAMS TO ADAPT TO THE NEEDS OF WOMEN STUDENTS

Whereas women need much of the same training as men, many need additional or substitute information in order to be successful administrators. Relatedly, the entrance of women into administration also means that men need to understand the implications of gender for effective management. Programs designed by men for men are not suitable for women for a number of reasons: Their sexist content makes the environment uninviting for women; the knowledge base taught presents much information that only works for men or for women who can pass as men; all male faculties aren't aware of the issues that women need to discuss, neither can they serve as role models or confidants for female concerns.

Schmuck reports an incident that happened with the SEEL program in Oregon, which illustrates the sexism in universities:

> An administrator in an Oregon school district called the SEEL Project director. He was angry that SEEL would be investigating school district hiring practices without addressing the sexist nature of preparatory programs. His advice was, "Clean up your own shop before you address school district problems." Of course, he was correct. Preparation programs for administrators serve as an important barrier to equal employment or affirmative employment practices. Personnel, resources, and student concerns perpetuate sex stereotyping and do little to make programs attractive to women. (1979, p. 33)

Because of these factors, it was acknowledged by many who designed change strategies that it wasn't enough just to get women into traditional programs—these programs needed to be changed to reflect the backgrounds and experiences of the women students. The change strategies most often used were to increase the number of women professors, add courses especially for women, and change already existing courses to include women's experiences.

Increase the Number of Women Professors of Administration

As women began to take courses in educational administration, they were confronted by the lack of female role models and advisors in the professorship; this was compounded by the misogynous attitudes of some male professors. Thus one strategy that has been used to provide aspiring women administrators with role models and sponsors at the university is that of increasing the number of women professors. Three federally funded projects made this a specific strategy of their efforts. In addition, universities have begun to hire women for faculty positions in educational administration. Unfortunately, these gains are small; the percentage of women professors in educational administration went from 2% in 1975 to 8% in 1983 (Marshall, 1984). Most of these women are in junior, untenured positions and their futures are uncertain. However, in universities where there are women professors, women students tend to believe that their needs are either being met or have a good likelihood of being satisfied.

Addition of Courses Specifically for Women

In addition to the lack of female professors to serve as role models in formal university programs, women also encountered the absence of courses to meet their particular needs as women entering a male-dominated field. Using the model of "remediation," which has prompted many administration departments to add courses in human interaction to provide male students with skills most were not socialized to have, courses specifically for women were offered within training programs, supported by universities or federal funding. With few exceptions, most of these courses are not regular departmental offerings in universities but rather are "special" courses or programs.

SEEL offered yearly conferences and workshops for women whereas ICES provided workshops on educational equity issues.

WISA's activities included sessions on assertiveness training, sex-role stereotyping, socialization, and balancing one's life. Assisting Women to Advance through Resources and Encouragement (AWARE) provided a number of workshops through their six project sites as well as through separate conferences and sessions at annual AASA meetings on such topics as networking, self-concept, resume writing, how to enlist sponsors, discovering job potential, interviewing techniques, and employment negotiation.

The Florida State University offered a program in goal setting, self-knowledge, and awareness of career opportunities to women in an effort to encourage participation in nontraditional fields. AASA provided career training to 75 upper-level administrative women in an attempt to help them develop positive self-concept, become professionally visible, enlist influential sponsors, discover potential jobs, analyze jobs to determine their professional desirability, write letters of application, prepare resumes, prepare for interviews, and discuss conditions of employment.

Hofstra University offers a course to women annually as part of the certification program in educational administration in an effort to confront barriers to women through the teaching of skills related to job searches, assertiveness, networking, resume preparation, interviewing, recognizing sex discrimination, presentation of self, sponsorship, and importance of self-confidence. Brayfield developed a workshop in social literacy training to overcome internal factors that inhibit the pursuit of administrative careers by women, and The Next Move included sessions addressing barriers to women. Women in Leadership Learning (WILL) and the St. Paul school district both provided similar training to women so that they might learn strategies for confronting obstacles to school administration.

Each of these workshops or courses provides job-seeking and job-getting information tailored specifically to women's particular situations. Very few confront the issues that women face once hired as administrators. These "second-level" courses have yet to be developed. Sadly, too, most of the workshops were given for a short period of time; of those introduced into university curriculums, very few have gained permanent acceptance in the curriculum and most lasted only as long as a particular crusader was on site to give the course. The option of being able to take a course that addresses the specific needs of women in administration is therefore not available to the overwhelming majority of women students.

Change the Curriculum of Traditional Courses to Include Women's Experiences

Neither have traditional courses seen a change to include the experiences of women, although this has been a strategy attempted in several federal projects and by women professors. Supervision courses still continue to ignore gender in supervision issues, for instance. Theory courses continue to center on theories that tell us only about male administrators and most courses use instructional materials—books, case studies, films—that are offensively sexist.

To counter these offenses, many federal projects had as their goal the development of curriculum materials. Within both general administrative courses and workshops, and those directed specifically at women, a lack of appropriate materials on women's issues, sex-role stereotyping, socialization, and barriers and strategies for women in administration is evident. Thus one approach to the larger problem of women's absence in the administration of educational institutions is the development of awareness and training materials for use in classrooms or at conferences with both women and men.

DICEL, for instance, produced four training modules for women on androgyny, assertion, power, and leadership, as well as a videotape on women in administration. ICES developed a 30-minute videotape of five women administrators discussing their careers, a role-playing videotape, and two videotapes describing their project. SEEL staff published a textbook, *Sex Equity in Education* (Stockard, Schmuck, Kempner, Williams, Edson, & Smith, 1980), prepared a slide show on the issues surrounding women in administration, and provided a quarterly newsletter to inform people of the issues as well as to raise awareness. The University Council of Educational Administration (UCEA) in conjunction with teams at six universities developed six multimedia instructional modules for women preparing for educational administration, for professors of educational administration, for policy and decision makers in K-12 systems, for other educators, for male and female trainees, and for policy and decision makers in postsecondary systems in an effort to alter conditions for girls and women in educational institutions. WILL developed modules for training in balancing personal/professional life, conflict resolution, competition, cooperation, developing strategies and diagnosing organizations, team building, developing support networks, and understanding maintenance systems. WISA published a hiring procedures manual for school trustees.

Although the content of these materials has been judged favorably, the actual impact is unknown. Few professors admit to using any of these materials in administrative training programs, and most, if adopted at all, are available in special programs or courses for women (Williams, 1982).

CHANGING THE ORGANIZATIONAL CONTEXT IN WHICH WOMEN WORK

Training women isn't enough. Even well-trained, well-prepared women aren't hired for administrative positions, as was documented in Chapter 3. Therefore, the organizational context in which women work and in which hiring occurs must be changed. Ways of changing this hiring context that have proven successful have included providing support systems and networks for women, offering consciousness-raising groups that allow women to analyze the culture in which they work, teaching women the male world, altering the structure of traditional professional education organizations while developing ones specifically to meet the needs of women, and, finally, creating jobs for women that change the balance and nature of the internal administrative context.

Support Systems

Women traditionally have not had the support and encouragement needed to attempt a career, let alone a career that has been identified as belonging to men. Consequently, an early strategy was to build systems that could help women sustain the often disillusioning and difficult process of finding an administrative job and keeping it. Once trained, these women still find a need for a support system that reinforces their aspirations and provides a mechanism for ventilation, generating strategies, and professional companionship. In an effort to deal with the frequent problem of lack of family support, FLAME instituted a program that reached out to families of interns so that they could understand what the women in the program were trying to achieve as well as to be able to anticipate and confront many of the problems this might bring to the family. Additionally, family counseling was made available.

In an effort to deal with the lack of sponsors and mentors for women, many projects set up formal sponsorship arrangements in which influential educators would take aspiring women administrators "under their wings" and help them in the job search. These formal relationships were developed to provide women with the kinds of official support and sponsorship that men are often said to have but that have seldom been available to women. For instance, FLAME created an advisory group composed of powerful educators to act as sponsors for their interns. The ICES interns identified support teams in their districts with which they could meet regularly, and SEEL formed support groups for women in educational administration in Oregon.

Networks

Family and work support, although crucial, need to be supplemented with a large system of contacts so that women can both learn about job availability and about how other women handle similar administrative situations. There needs to be a system that can compete with the Old Boys' Club. A common vehicle for providing women with both contacts and information is a network. Both SEEL and UCEA offer directories of women in educational administration. AWARE, FLAME, and Hofstra University have all instituted formal networking systems. Additionally, SEEL linked women administrators in Oregon through the Oregon Women in Educational Administration group and then linked this group with existing state and national organizations to expand the network. NECEL/CCEL provide these services in New England. Related to networking is the method of providing a formal and institutionalized vehicle for bringing job information to women's attention as well as bringing women to the attention of employers. SEEL published *A Directory of Administrators,* which included both men and women, in an effort to highlight women candidates. Another approach to visibility was used by both WISA and FLAME whose interns were sent to districts and other states so that they might be both seen and heard.

Crucial to networking for women have been a variety of administrative organizations for women and, to a lesser extent, those for all educators. These groups, such as local branches of the National Council for Administrative Women in Education and

NECEL, have provided women with both support and a network, developing job sharing newsletters as well as systems for finding out about districts in which there are job openings. The Women's Caucus of the American Association of School Administrators has been equally effective in promoting its members and in demystifying the selection process for school administration, as has the National Coalition of Women School Executives and the National Association of Women Deans, Administrators, and Counselors.

Whereas it is important to have men in the networks and to have men as sponsors (because there aren't enough women in key positions to help everyone), traditional administrative groups that have had large male memberships have been unreliable for helping women. Although they might help an individual woman here or there (and almost all women who have advanced have credited some help from a man), there has not been any systematic support for equity from these groups. As Schmuck points out:

> Different administrator associations have leadership with varying levels of awareness about equity issues and different attitudes toward women's role as educational leaders. Whether or not the leadership of the group is "sensitive" or "aware," the fact is that equity issues will probably never become a major objective of such groups. . . . Administrator associations are primarily composed of men and will not adopt equity issues as a major goal. Perhaps it is because their members fear female competition. Perhaps it is because other educational concerns are pressing. Or perhaps it is because members hold traditional views about "women's place." Certainly in Oregon it was concluded that the association would not be the legacy for change. (1979, pp. 37-38)

The strategies, then, in dealing with these groups have been to try to put pressure on them to act, usually through women's caucuses or committees, as has been done in AASA, or to attempt to gain some sort of organizational power through increased female membership or influence. The latter tactic has yet to be successful.

Consciousness-Raising and Technical Assistance to Organizations and People Who Affect Hiring Policies and Practices

Giving women support and networks might help them brave a hostile world, but the hostile world has to be confronted at some point. Therefore, a next step was to try and change the attitudes of the members of that world. Consequently, one strategy has been to make organizations and others who hire aware of the bias against women as well as providing these groups and individuals with technical assistance and materials to help them evaluate and change their own policies and practices. This has been done using a number of approaches. UCEA and WISA developed materials, including a WISA handbook for hiring procedures for school boards. Other strategies include workshops for policymakers at local, regional, and national meetings. The effectiveness of this strategy has not been determined. Although evaluations of the materials and workshop presentations rate them as high quality endeavors, participation at workshops by the targeted audiences has been low and actual use of the materials by these same audiences is undetermined. In other words, changing attitudes is a difficult task, made even more difficult if those whose attitudes need changing aren't at all interested in the transformation. By and large, the folks who came to the sessions or read these materials were converts already. Because participation was voluntary, those who really needed to hear the message never replied to the invitation.

Learning Male Rules

A major preoccupation of organized programs for women has been to teach them the male rules of the game. From books such as *Games Mother Never Taught Me* (Harragan, 1977) to teaching how to dress for success, these strategies have urged women to be more like men. Some of these approaches have provided women with useful information whereas others have not worked. All rest on the assumption that the male way is the best way—or at least the only way to enter the male system. The inadvisabilty of this notion will be discussed more fully in Chapters 6 and 7.

Create Jobs

Despite these efforts and in large part because of the effects of declining enrollments in schools, many qualified women are unable to obtain administrative positions. A strategy that FLAME pioneered was teaching interns to create their own jobs by writing and getting funding for new programs in school districts, which they can then administer. Creating new jobs within an organization has its limits and, as many have found, once the federal funding stops, so does the district support. Therefore, it should be seen as a short-term chance to gain administrative experience, not a long-term career option.

Alter the Structure of the Organization

As Kanter (1977) has pointed out, unless the hierarchical structure of the organization is flattened, opportunity and power for women and minorities will be limited. Jovick (1981) studied schools in which women teachers had extensive decision-making freedom versus those that were more authoritarian and in which the women teachers had very little power. Organizations that allowed decisional flexibility for the teachers were also the ones in which the teachers had more interest in administration and in taking control. Thus changes in the structure of teaching may well lead to changes in the number of women in administration. This approach has not been utilized specifically to achieve a gender equitable workplace but has been used for pedagogical reasons, resulting inadvertantly in a more welcoming workplace for women educators.

CHANGING THE STRUCTURE OF SOCIETY

For long-term change, the stucture of American society must be changed. Educational, political, and legal methods have all been attempted with some success.

Changes in K-12 Education

If the attitudes toward women are to change substantially, people need to change. Many believe that the best place to begin to change beliefs about women is in the school. To do this, change must be directed at two groups of people: First, teachers and administrators must be made aware of sexist attitudes, teaching materials, and teaching strategies that limit female students; next, students must be allowed to learn and grow in an educational environment that is nonsexist. In the *Handbook for Achieving Sex Equity Through Education* (Klein, 1985), a number of researchers have examined the sexist nature of schooling and have written about tested and effective strategies for changing schools so that they will become non-sexist environments. This is the most comprehensive compilation of proven approaches to changing the school and it documents that a non-sexist education is good for both males and females.

Political Clout

Moving from the women themselves to the larger world, many strategists believe that before women will be hired in greater numbers, the issue of the underemployment of women administrators must be taken seriously and that political pressure must be put on school boards. Many point out that no matter how qualified women are, if political conditions aren't supportive for their selection, they won't become school administrators. The history of women in school administration in the first part of this century illustrates this point dramatically (Gribskov, 1980). At that time, women had begun attending universities in large numbers and had attained the backgrounds to become school administrators. Yet, it was the organized political efforts of women teachers and women's organizations that provided the pressure that forced school boards to hire women. When this overt political and feminist pressure disappeared so, too, did women in administration.

A political approach demands that insiders work with outsiders to make changes in the structure of the work force. It has been noted that women inside school systems can often do much more than they do to make a difference in the hiring practices of the district. Tenure, often supported for the purposes of academic freedom and job security, often seems to be forgotten when teachers grumble about sexist practices. In schools where women teachers have formed caucuses and action groups to get more women into administration, the result has been that women have been hired. Further, serving as a spokesperson for such groups has given those women the visibility that they need to be recognized by male administrators as leaders. It is safe to say that in few districts have women organized and used the clout they have as teachers to help to change the system. This is the first kind of political action that needs to be taken if a district is to be divested of the male hierarchy.

Nevertheless, there is only so much that insiders can do (and very few have done it) and, therefore, for major transformations to take place, insiders need to work with outsiders to pressure school boards and superintendents to hire women. A number of outside groups have been very effective in some communities in helping women to become school administrators. SEEL, for instance, has been effective in providing a strong voice that keeps the issue of underrepresentation of women in administration in the public's eye in Oregon. The National Organization of Women, the Women's Political Caucus, and the American Association of University Women have provided the pressure in many communities to force school boards to consider women candidates. On Long Island, New York, Women on the Job, a not-for-profit organization that promotes equity in women's employment, has served as a watchdog on school district hiring practices. Women on the Job has conducted studies of local districts that have documented illegal practices, written articles for newspapers and journals on these activities, and organized lawsuits where discrimination has occurred. Working with such an organization helps to force school district change from the outside, while at the same time keeping women's job prospects on the inside safe.

Burt (1975) points out that of all national, state, and local efforts to increase equal opportunity, local school boards and parent/student pressure groups are the most effective in placing minorities. Thus using the political process to elect activist school board members as well as using existing structures, such as parent groups, is an important and effective way to help women into administration.

Legal Remedies and Affirmative Action Programs

The use of the legal system ranges from indirect action such as teaching the intricacies of antidiscrimination laws to women, administrators, and school boards, to writing and passing legislation that prescribes equity, to the more direct approach of forcing districts to comply with those laws.

A number of the special workshop courses for women have presented discussions of women's legal rights as well as exercises that help women recognize sex discrimination. Nevertheless, for a variety of reasons, most women do not choose litigation when confronted by sex discrimination. Many believe that if they sue, they will ruin any chance of an administrative position. A case on Long Island would challenge that notion and support the belief that women can probably do more than they think they can before causing damage to themselves. A math chairperson sued her district for sex discrimination. A few years after filing suit and only a few months after having the suit settled in her favor, she was promoted from math chairperson to acting superintendent while a search was being conducted for a superintendent. After the new superintendent was appointed, she became the assistant superintendent for business.

The laws that are available to pursue justice vary. Comprehensive employment practice laws have been passed in nearly all 50 states. Many of these are modeled on federal laws, thus an examination of federal legislation that has been passed to help end sex discrimination is useful for understanding the kinds of protection women have. The major federal legislation to help end sex discrimination is listed in Table 4.1

Both Title VII and Title IX have been used to challenge sexist practices in school districts. The results have been mixed. Shapiro (1984) reports that of three complaints under Title IX, only one actually resulted in any change—and that was minor. Nevertheless, some women have achieved equity using Title IX and other laws. In Los Angeles, a suit under Title VII produced a federal court agreement that insured goals for administrative hiring and promotion of women into administration and that will substantially increase management opportunity for women ("Los Angeles Agrees," 1981).

The impact of legal strategies is largely unknown; no studies are available that chart the relationship between such strategies and increased employment for women in administrative positions. Marshall and Grey (1982) point out that sex equity in schools is complicated by ambiguity of job entry requirements, professional norms of loyalty, lack of political support for enforcement, and insufficient resources and expertise for enforcement. They conclude that "laws like EPA and Title VII have not been useful to

TABLE 4.1
Federal Legislation to End Sex Discrimination

Title VII of The Civil Rights Act of 1964 (42 U.S.C. 2000e, et seq.) prohibits discrimination on the basis of sex, race, color, religion, or national origin and applies to all aspects of employment. Title VII prohibits the classification of a job as male or female, disallows separate seniority or career progression lines based on sex, prohibits sexual harrassment and allocation of fringe benefits based on sex. Title VII established the Equal Employment Opportunity Commission (EEOC), which provided a framework for bringing individual and class actions in federal court.

Executive Order No. 11375 (1967) which amended executive order No. 11246 (1965) and prohibits discrimination on basis of sex, race, color, religion, or national origin by institutions (or parts thereof) with federal contracts (or grants) of $10,000 or more and requires contractors to take affirmative action to ensure nondiscriminatory employment practices.

Revised Order No. 4, revising Executive Order No. 11375 (1967), requires written affirmative action plans submitted by institutions (or parts thereof) receiving federal contracts (or grants) of $50,000 or more and having 50 or more employees.

Education Amendments (Higher Education Act 1972), prohibits sex discrimination in salaries and most fringe benefits of educational institutions. Title IX of this act prohibits sex discrimination against students and employees in educational programs and activities, but was not enforced until guidelines were published.

Women's Education Equity Act (1974), establishes a Council on Women's Educational Programs in the Department of Education to do a range of research, development, dissemination and training activities to eliminate sex bias in education.

Guidelines for Title IX (1975) published, which allowed enforcement of Title IX.

individuals excluded through subtle discriminatory practices, and that Title IX implementation requires continuing efforts at persuasion and offers little immediate relief for women" (1982, p. 257).

A further strategy within the legal realm involves a change of teacher education competencies to include knowledge of antidiscrimination laws and mandates. This was done in Oregon so that now all aspiring teachers must learn about sex discrimination and judicial recourse.

THE FUTURE FOR WOMEN IN ADMINISTRATION

The political climate of the mid-1980s is not encouraging for those who hope that the gender structure of school employment will change. Activist work seems to have quieted and gains once made are in danger. Because federal funding has been cut for projects like those used to target the barriers and because no other system has emerged to carry on these goals of sex equity, it may be that we will see the same kind decline that occurred in the 1930s. Gribskov (1980) has demonstrated that feminist, activist energy is necessary for moving women into educational administration. As women teachers, administrators, and community members have become tired of the struggle—believing it either impossible or finished—the schools may remain in the hands of male administrators.

Despite the lack of large-scale change, several approaches to increasing women in school administration have been formalized and have proven, in varying degrees, to be successful antidotes. How successful each program or stategy has been is still to be determined. The real measure of success will be seen both in an increase in the number of women in administration and in allowing those women to function as females, not as imitation men. This change, if it occurs, will take time. The essential concept to internalize when examining the strategies used to counter barriers to women in administration is that no one strategy will solve the problem. Unless an approach that links equipping women with needed skills and mind-sets to changing the structure in which they work is used, it is unlikely that overall, large-scale change will occur. No matter how qualified, how competent, or how psychologically and emotionally ready women are to assume administrative positions in schools, they are still living and working within a society and school organization that is both sexist and racist. If we are to make any lasting change, we must confront a system that is white male centered and white male dominated and change that system. Molding ourselves to be imitation men or becoming successful while the doors are closed to other women will do nothing to restructure society so that the barriers will cease to exist.

REFERENCES

Burt, W. L. (1975). The impact of the 1964 Civil Rights Act—Title VI and Title VII—on employment of black administrators in Michigan school districts from 1964-74. *Dissertation Abstracts International, 36*(10), 6386A.

Gribskov, M. (1980). Feminism and the woman school administrator. In S. K. Biklen & M. B. Brannigan (Eds.), *Women and educational leadership* (pp. 77-91). Lexington, MA: D. C. Heath.

Harragan, B. L. (1977). *Games mother never taught you.* New York: Warner.

Jovick, T. D. (1981). Ambitions and the opportunity for professionals in the elementary school. In P. A. Schmuck, W. W. Charters, Jr., & R. O. Carlson (Eds.), *Educational policy and management: Sex differentials* (pp. 153-168). New York: Academic Press.

Kanter, R. (1977). *Men and women of the corporation.* New York: Basic Books.

Klein, S. S. (1985). *Handbook for achieving sex equity through education.* Baltimore: Johns Hopkins.

Los Angeles agrees to increase numbers of women in administrative posts. (1981, May). Phi Delta Kappan, *62*, 683.

Marshall, C. (1984). Men and women in educational administration programs. *Journal of the National Association for Women Deans, Administrators, and Counselors, 48*(1), 3-12.

Marshall, C., & Grey, R. (1982). Legal rights of women seeking administrative positions in local school districts. *Journal of Educational Equity and Leadership, 2*(4), 253-259.

Sadker, M. P., & Sadker, D. M. (1982). *Sex equity handbook for schools.* New York: Longman.

Schmuck, P. A. (1979). *Sex equity in educational leadership: The Oregon story.* Eugene: University of Oregon, Center for Educational Policy and Management.

Shapiro, C. (1984). We'll sue your school board to win equity for women administrators. *American School Board Journal, 171*, 43-37.

Stockard, J., Schmuck, P. A., Kempner, K., Williams, P., Edson, S. K., & Smith, M. A. (1980). *Sex equity in education.* New York: Academic Press.

Williams, S. W. (1982). *A study of selected programs in educational administration in the United States and Canada.* (ERIC Document Reproduction Service No. ED 217 525)

Part III

Female Culture and Educational Administration

This section begins with an analysis of organizational theory and research illustrating how women have been left out of the picture. Next, the differences between the female and male worlds of school administration are documented. Research tells us that women not only experience the day-to-day world of the school differently than do men, but—perhaps because of these different experiences—approach administrative tasks from a female worldview.

Beyond discussing some of the differences that women bring to the administration of schools, this section uses what we know about women in administration to challenge some of the theories and beliefs currently touted by organizational theorists. Part III challenges the research community to rethink how we have come to know what we know about school administration; it urges the researcher to ask, "Does this research or theory include or explain the experiences of women?" And if not, how might those experiences alter theory in educational administration?

. 5 .

Androcentric Bias in Educational Administration Theory and Research

When examining theory in educational adminstration, we must ask, "Does theory make any assumptions about male and female roles?" The answer supplied by the research is yes. The underlying assumption is that the experiences of males and females are the same, and thus research on males is appropriate for generalizing to female experience. In developing theories of administration, researchers didn't look at the context in general and, therefore, were unable to document how the world was different for women. When female experience was different, it was ignored or diminished. Jessie Bernard describes the construction of knowledge as the construction of the male world:

> Knowledge has been overwhelmingly male in subject matter, in assumptions, in methods, in interpretations; . . . a disproportionate share of human knowledge in all the disciplines has dealt with a world viewed through a male prism; . . . not only equity but also the human legacy calls for a correction of this situation in order that the lacunae be filled and distortions corrected. (1979, p. 268)

Theory in educational administration has undergone a number of methodological critiques. Central to these is the understanding that educational administration is a field of inquiry and, as such, employs a number of perspectives to interpret situations. Willower (1982, p. 5) summarized the role of theory for the administrator in this way:

> He or she needs an array of concepts and theories that portray human behavior in social, political, organizational, psychological and economic terms, and that have the potential both to enhance and help explain what the administrator sees.

Unfortunately, practitioners and scholars alike have complained that the organizational theory they have been taught rarely explains what happens in schools. A number of attempts have been made to discover why organizational theories and concepts are inadequate for school people. Researchers have pointed out that these theories are often based on research and conceptualizations centering on the corporate world and the military—environments that they believe differ from schools in important ways (e.g., see Seiber, 1975). Others have examined the research in the field in light of methodological weaknesses and found it lacking (Haller, 1979; Shakeshaft & Saffer, 1984). In neither of these approaches has the issue of gender been considered. Indeed, these critiques ignore an important quality of school environments—their character as predominantly female workplaces and the effects of such environments on the quality of theoretical arguments derived from male-based theories.

Unlike their educational counterparts, scholars in the disciplines informing the study of educational administration have been critical of male-based theory and research. At the very time when the field of educational administration has come to recognize its reliance upon this range of social science disciplines, researchers in these fields have begun to question the validity of the theoretical constructs that undergird their perspectives. Recently, researchers in the social sciences have uncovered theoretical foundations, conceptualizations, and methodological practices that have resulted in impoverished theories (Daniels, 1975; Eichler, 1980; Miller, 1976; Parker & Parker, 1979; Parlee, 1979; Sherif, 1979; Slocum, 1980; Smith, 1979; Smith-Rosenberg, 1983; Spender, 1981). These scholars have shown that theories and concepts emerging solely from a male consciousness may be irrelevant for the female experience and inadequate for explaining female behavior.

It is not new to say that women have been excluded from the production of knowledge; neither have they had a part in the construction of the ideological apparatus that selects, studies, and makes pronouncements upon key social questions, problems, and issues (Harway, 1978). Science and science-making tend to reinforce and perpetuate dominant social values and conceptions of reality. The funding of research, the objects of study, the use of research have to date been dominated by white males. Not unexpectedly, they have forged forms of thought within an all-male world and, perhaps without realizing it, have mistaken it for a universal reality. Those outcomes become the standards and norms by which all experience is measured and valued. Women are just one of many nondominant groups that have not been represented.

In an attempt to understand the dominance of the white male worldview in research and knowledge, scholars first needed a way of naming, and thus knowing, male-defined scholarship. Differing labels have been given to such work (some call it patriarchal, others sexist). The term used in this book to refer to the practice of viewing the world and shaping reality from a male lens is androcentrism. Viewing the world through this male lens has not only affected theories in the social sciences but has shaped reality in organizational behavior theories as well.

Existing paradigms, theoretical models, or concepts in organizational theory create imprecise, inaccurate, and imbalanced scholarship. Correcting weaknesses in this scholarship is a methodological issue of enormous importance as bias affects conceptual formulation as well as issues of reliability and validity.

It is important to understand that all research reflects particular worldviews. The harm comes not so much from the worldview but rather from a belief that it is the only lens through which to understand human behavior. Studying male behavior is not in and of itself at issue here. What is at issue is the practice of studying male behavior and then assuming that the results are appropriate for understanding all behavior. Of paramount importance is the ability to recognize bias and explain the methods and findings in ways that make it unmistakably clear to the consumer just what that bias is. The accumulated body of knowledge up to the present has not identified the bias of androcentrism and has thus distributed distorted ideas and ideological forms based on observations and assumptions drawn primarily by males from male experiences.

Dorothy E. Smith writes of this peculiar eclipsing of women from man's culture:

> Let us be clear that we are not talking about prejudice or sexism as a particular bias against women or as a negative stereotype of women. We are talking about the consequences of women's exclusion from a full share in the making of what becomes treated as *our* culture. We are talking about the consequences of a silence, an absence, a non-presence. What is there—spoken, sung, written, made emblematic in art—and treated as general, universal, unrelated to a particular position or a particular sex as its source and standpoint, is in fact partial, limited, located in a particular position and permeated by special interests and concerns. (1978, p. 283)

To label a piece of research or a theory, concept, or model "androcentric" is merely to identify the framework within which the thinking and work occurred. It is an attempt to establish for the consumer a set of parameters to be used in accepting, internalizing, and applying the results of such research as well as a way of addressing what is missing, what has been overlooked, what has not been stated. It heightens the awareness of both producer and consumer and reveals the limitations and restrictions of a one-sided system of knowledge. Its purpose is to assist in the re-envisioning of our world.

To begin the examination of the influence of gender on theory and research in educational administration, five theories/concepts that are cited most often in educational administration textbooks will be discussed, using the criteria in Table 5.1 as a framework for analysis. These theories/concepts are comprised of Jacob Getzels and Egon Guba's Social Systems Model, John Hemphill and Alvin Coon's Leader Behavior Description Questionnaire, Andrew Halpin's Organizational Climate Description Questionnaire, Fred Fiedler's Theory of Leadership Effectiveness, and Abraham Maslow's Theory of Human Motivation and Self-Actualization.

The theories provide illustrations of the ways that knowledge has been created, ways that exclude female experience and the female voice. All theories in educational administration suffer from this one-sided view of the world—the five chosen for examination are being used only to illustrate how theory is constructed in a way that leaves women out; many others could have been used, equally effectively, to illustrate the androcentric nature of theory and

TABLE 5.1
Framework Guiding the Examination of Selected Theories, Concepts, and Models of Organizational Theory for Androcentric Bias

Problem Selection and Conceptualization
1. Are the experiences, attitudes, values, and behaviors of females considered?
2. Is gender examined as a significant variable?
3. Are the effects of sex-role and sex-characteristic stereotyping examined?

Research Design
1. Are tests for sex differences or similarities included?
2. Are females included in the population and sample?
3. If excluded, is the exclusion of females explained?

Measurement
1. Are sex-neutral scales or measures used?
2. Have scales been validated on both sexes?
3. Is nonsexist language used?

Interpretation and Generalizability of Results
1. Are the results interpreted as pertaining primarily to the target population?
2. If not, are the limitations of the generalizability of the findings to both sexes discussed?

research. However, the particular theories analyzed are still seen, at least in textbooks and classrooms, as central to the field of educational administration; not surprisingly, they inform a great deal of our dissertation and field research. These theories were analyzed for androcentric bias using the categories displayed in Table 5.1.

The most significant conceptual weakness found in this array of theories, concepts, and models of organizational behavior is the researchers' narrowness of perspective. Females are viewed as "other" or rendered invisible in this male-defined perspective. Whether or not the process is intentional or subliminal, the end result is the same in the majority of the work examined: Women are not included.

Getzels and Guba's (1955) work on roles and role conflict deals with the occupational roles of men and the role conflicts they encounter on the job. Women are totally excluded from this problem formulation. They base their work on that of Talcott Parsons (1951), defining social behavior as organizational and occupational behavior, excluding the family altogether. Parsons simply could not conceptualize women as occupational actors but saw them as the keepers of a "private realm" instead. Getzels and Guba's conceptualization of the formal organization extends Parson's work and thus defines it exclusively as a male sphere populated by males and given over to male concerns.

The central constructs of role and role theory within the organization that they examined have naturally reflected the roles and role conflicts of males. Given Getzels and Guba's indebtedness to Parsons and the subsequent exclusion of females and the female experience from their conceptualization of social behavior, it is not surprising that they omitted gender and gender-related issues in their conceptualization of role mismatch. When they included females and studied role conflict of teachers, they saw no role conflict at all. Indeed, no attempt was made to illuminate or even to suppose that there might be a female counterpart to male-role definition.

> For women, teaching is a respected occupation often representing a top level vocational goal. They can be more tolerant of the inconsistencies in expectations since it is not likely they could do better professionally elsewhere, and in any case, many of the constraints represented by the expectations are already placed upon females *qua* females anyway. (Getzels & Guba, 1955, p. 39)

Getzels and Guba's exclusion of females and the female experience in their conceptualization of a model of social behavior renders it, at its best, as essentially imbalanced and incomplete. It lacks a feature—namely, gender of individual—intrinsic to the conduct of human interactions, especially in Western cultures. The Getzels-Guba model of social behavior presents only half a case.

Another example of male conceptualization can be found in the development of the Leader Behavior Description Questionnaire (LBDQ; Halpin & Winer, 1957)—an important research instrument for students of school leadership. The Ohio State Leadership Studies represented an ambitious and far-reaching undertaking arising from dissatisfaction with human trait theories of leadership. The new approach emphasized an examination and measurement of leader performance and behavior. The questions they sought to answer were:

> (1) *What* does an individual do while he operates as a leader?
> (2) *How* does he go about what he does? (1957, p. 6)

Although the questions of what leaders do and how they do it are central to a study of leadership behavior, a more elemental precursor to such an inquiry must be the question, what is leadership? The research team of the Ohio State Leadership Studies focused on a very narrow band of leadership given the numerous possible settings that might have been investigated. They chose to look at "head men" in mainstream formal organizations. Hemphill and Coons, forerunners in the development of the LBDQ, have written that "the study of leadership may be viewed as that of observing the behavior of individuals who have, by some specified criterion, been designated 'leaders'" (1957, p. 6).

These designated "leaders," judging by the team's research efforts, were those persons occupying positions of formal authority in corporate, academic, or military systems. The process of watching what "head men" do and characterizing that behavior as "leadership" is as much of a conceptual leap as determining that the personalities of "great men" constituted the traits leaders should possess. A strong argument can be made against the notion of leadership as being an action of formal managers in formal organizations. No distinction is made between leadership and mere management. Thus the LBDQ reflected a conception of leadership as that which men who are designated as leaders do. This tautological argument ignores, among other things, the actions of females and possible female conceptualizations of leadership behavior.

Fiedler (1967, p. 11) defines leadership as, "an interpersonal relation in which power and influence are unevenly distributed so that one person is able to direct and control the actions and behaviors of others to a greater extent than they direct and control his." Although this definition is not in and of itself sex specific (if one ignores the sexist pronoun), it is, nonetheless, an example of masculist reconstructed logic or reality reconstruction. Thus the term "leadership" is derived contextually and, in this instance, from the male-dominated corporate world of big business. Had Fiedler looked to another setting, his definition of leadership may have taken on a far different shape.

The major limitation of Fiedler's conception of leadership effectiveness inheres in its incapacity to reveal the salience of the gender of the leader in the group situation. This is not to say that Fiedler excluded women from his studies. On the contrary, there were female participants in his samples. A remarkable oversight, however, was his complete disregard of the importance of gender to his theory. Indeed, a 1961 study produced results showing that "sex differences seemed to have a consistent effect upon interpersonal perception" (Kohn & Fiedler, 1961, p. 162). "Females perceived significant persons in their environment in a less differentiated and in a more favorable manner than did males" (p. 162). Fiedler identified high-LPC leaders as being more concerned with people and as perceiving their coworkers in favorable, positive terms. Still, he chose not to view gender as a variable in his research.

In addition, this study revealed that older females and younger men and women shared more perceptions with one another than they did with their older male colleagues. Indeed, Fiedler came close to labeling women's responses as immature.

> Women, to a greater extent than men, may rely on stereotypy in forming impressions of people, and that they may, therefore, tend to categorize people rather quickly without fully evaluating their characteristics. If true, this formulation may help to explain why women are often said to have more "intuitive" reactions to others and why they supposedly find it difficult to offer logical reasons for their impressions. . . . It is possible that females, at least within the population here sampled, perceive significant persons in their environment more favorably than do males because they tend to be treated more kindly by the world, and because they are less exposed to disillusioning interpersonal experiences. Alternatively, females may report more favorable attitudes because our culture teaches them to mask genuine feelings . . . it should also be considered that these differences may reflect constitutional dissimilarities which cause women to be more conservative than men. (Kohn & Fiedler, 1961, pp. 162-163)

The androcentric explanation of this phenomenon is central to the issue of masculist conceptualization. In the foregoing statement, the comments on women's tendency to make quick judgments, their illogical reasoning, their insincerity, and their frailty illustrate a lack of knowledge or interest in female behavior. Moreover, only an uninformed interpretation of reality would view women as being treated kindly by the world and as being less exposed to disillusionment than men, given the centuries of oppression and female genocide that have occurred.

Fiedler noticed differences between males and females in his research but neglected to evaluate his own thinking on the dissimilarities between the sexes. He attests to discrepant behaviors between males and females, stating that females in general view others more favorably than males do; but he disregards this factor as it pertains to a key element in his research, namely, preference for coworker and its effect on women as leaders.

Fiedler's failure to perceive the sex of the leader as a moderating variable of leadership behavior, and his implicit assumption that women could not make differences that mattered, is compounded by his failure to recognize sex-role and sex-characteristic stereotyping as elements affecting situational favorableness. Because of this, female leaders in interacting, coacting, or counteracting groups, are likely to perform in situations in ways markedly different than are male leaders. Fiedler should have been attentive to any or all effects relative to gender of the leader and/or respondent as they may very well represent important contextual or situational variables.

Like the theories discussed previously, Abraham Maslow's theory of motivation and self-actualization is problematic for women. The effect of his conceptualization of the levels of needs that motivate people lead women to believe that their self-actualization is prescribed by sex-role fulfillment or sex-role denial; it leads men to devalue the experiences of hearth and home; and it denies both sexes participation in the full range of human expressions. Of particular note are the affiliation, self-esteem, and self-actualization needs of Maslow's hierarchy. Although Maslow states that the individual moves back and forth among these needs as they become more or less potent, he definitely implies a value scale to the differing needs—that is, the self-esteem need is on a higher plane than the affiliation need, and the self-actualizing need is on a still higher level than the self-esteem level. This prepotency configuration matches traditional male values. Whereas some females embrace this value system as well, one must question its applicability to the female experience. The female socialization process has placed tremendous emphasis on the love, affection, and belongingness needs. Although the attainment and satisfaction of these needs may be important to men, the maintenance of these needs is of critical importance to women. A woman's sense of self and fulfillment historically have been tied to her needs for affiliation and intimacy.

Contrast this with Maslow's (1970) description of the esteem needs:

> These are, first, the desire for strength, for achievement, for adequacy, for mastery and competence, for confidence in the face of the world, and for independence and freedom. Second, we have what we may call the desire for reputation or prestige, . . . status, fame and glory, dominance, recognition, attention, importance, dignity, or appreciation. (1970, p. 45)

The work of Ann Wilson Schaef (1981) and Carol Gilligan (1982) call into question these assumptions for women. Jean Baker Miller, too, would disagree:

> The parameters of the female's development are not the same as the male's and . . . the same terms do not apply. Women can be highly developed and still give great weight to affiliation. (1976, p. 86)

Such a perspective calls for a different theory of motivation, one that speaks to, listens to, and draws from women's need for affiliation and attachment.

Maslow's conceptualization of a self-actualized human also needs rethinking. The view of the fully self-actualized female in Maslow's conceptualization as one who makes it in a man's world is echoed in his comments on utopias:

> Now that females, at least in the advanced countries, have been emancipated and self-actualization is possible for them also, how will this change the relationship between the sexes? (Maslow, 1968, p. 149)

Here Maslow alludes to the fact that the opportunities for and avenues to self-actualization, which long had been a male privilege, were now available to women who wanted to achieve in the same ways. What Maslow totally disregards is that masculine means to and ends of self-actualization may not be the choices of females. A female utopia would not necessarily be based on "the masculine ethic." Maslow never explored the differences between the public world of men and the private world of women. The women he did study were women who succeeded in the public world. Self-actualization according to Maslow was possible for females if women: (a) opted to function in the male milieu and adopted male modes of behavior and values or (b) stayed within the boundaries of patriarchal convention and the code of feminine behavior. Maslow never realizes the contradictory stance of his standards of self-actualization for women. Here his message is: Act like a traditional female or act like a traditional male. Men, on the other hand, are not encouraged to act like traditional females to attain self-actualization.

These two positions of woman in woman's place and woman in man's world coalesce in Maslow's introduction to his opus *Motivation and Personality*:

> It is possible for a woman to have all the specifically female fulfillments (being loved, having the home, having the baby) and *then*, without giving up any of the satisfactions already achieved, go on beyond femaleness to the full humanness that she shares with males, for example, the full development of her intelligence, of any talents that she may have, and of her own particular idiosyncratic genius, of her own individual fulfillment. (1970, p. xvii)

Aside from the disturbing inference one draws from this statement that female work does not require intelligence, talent, or genius, Maslow, in effect, is devaluing the female experience. He espouses male superiority by encouraging females to reach further once the "feminine" fulfillments are complete. Meaningful self-actualization for men, however, cannot be accomplished through women's work. Maslow does not exhort males to go beyond their maleness to self-actualization because Maslow's implication is this: Excellence in humanity is, therefore, excellence in masculinity.

It is evident from Maslow's writing that he was perplexed about women's roles. He sends many conflicting messages. On the one hand, he puts forth the idea that women can reach self-actualization by performing motherly, domestic, service duties. Conversely, he contends that women can attain full humanness by appropriating male methods of self-actualization. A further confusion is his invitation to women to embrace both styles; to move from the female to the full humanness of the male. This mixture of incongruous elements in defining self-actualization for women reveals an imprecise and imbalanced conceptualization in Maslow's theory formulation, particularly in light of his belief that the only way for men to self-actualize is through public modes of achievement.

The examples discussed thus far provide instances of concepts that were formulated using a male lens but that have been subsequently applied to both males and females. When female behavior ran counter to the theory, it was the female rather than the theory who was found inadequate. Thus from a conceptual point of view, female behavior was ignored, not because females weren't studied but because their experience, by definition, had to parallel male behavior; if it didn't, the females were labeled deficient and the theory was left unchallenged. A similar result occurs even if the problem is formulated in a gender-inclusive manner but the methods used to test the questions emerge from an androcentric perspective.

Many theories upon which the field of educational administration relies heavily are based on all-male samples. For instance, Fiedler, in developing his Contingency Theory of Leadership, chose the business, military, and industrial spheres from which to draw his samples. Fiedler used men from B-29 bomber crews, army tank crews, antiaircraft artillery crews, infantry squads, open-hearth steel shops, sales display teams, service station managers, high school basketball teams, and ROTC units, among many others, to test his theory. Samples drawn were representative of their fields and thus the preponderance of the subjects were white males. Fiedler did not provide a rationale for restricting these samples to a single sex. Even as late as 1977, Fiedler and his associates were still conducting studies using all-male samples from the military. Although the majority of the studies used male participants only, a few included some women in the sample. As an interesting note, the one all-female sample in Fiedler's research required the participants to be hypnotized. The purpose of this study was to modify attitudes related to LPC scores through hypnotic suggestion.

Similarly, the research setting selected by Getzels and Guba for their first studies on role theory was reflective of their female-exclusive conceptualization. Their research was funded by the Air Force, and their opportunity sample consisted of military personnel at Air University, Maxwell Air Force Base. When Getzels and Guba's subsequent research finally did include women in the sample, no breakdown was given by sex. All we know is that the sample consisted of 344 elementary and secondary school teachers. Getzels and Guba chose an all-male research setting for their initial empirical studies and ignored gender as a variable even in subsequent research. Such a research design, which is exclusive of females and the effects of gender, is an outgrowth of a male-only conceptualization that presumes the universality of the male experience.

The samples chosen for the Ohio State Leadership Studies were drawn from the corporate and military worlds. These samples consisted of: Air Force bomber commanders and crew members, commissioned officers, noncommissioned personnel and civilian administators in the Department of Navy, foremen in a manufacturing plant, executives in regional cooperative associations, college administrators, school superintendents, and principals. Such samples were not surprising given the list of organizations that supported the research: the Air Force Personnel and Training Research Center, the Office of Naval Research, the Rockefeller Foundation, International Harvester, the Kellogg Foundation, the Ohio Farm Bureau Cooperative Wholesale, and several other farm cooperatives.

As has been previously mentioned, Maslow focused upon "Great Men." Although Maslow's initial conceptualization of his work was based on two persons, one female and one male, of the 46 cases, partial cases, and potential cases listed by Maslow as studied, 42 were male. This is not surprising in light of the way Maslow identified those people whose lives he examined. Maslow sought to examine the "growing tip," the fraction of 1% of the total population who were the self-actualizing type. Respect for privacy prevented him from disclosing the names of his contemporaries whom he considered to be self-actualizing, so Maslow looked to reknowned figures of the past and examined the letters, biographies, and documents by and about them. However, by defining self-actualization as a public sphere activity, his subsequent sample was bound to be predominantly male because historically females have been denied public sphere participation.

In addition to using predominantly male samples, researchers of organizational life have tended toward male-defined measures of the concept under question. For example, Getzels and Guba's study of role conflict in the teaching situation used an instrument that asked participants to make judgments regarding given school situations. Their responses served as indicators of role conflict. The following phrases were incorporated into the scenarios: Maintain a standard of living comparable to a minor executive or salesman, stop in a tavern for a drink, and support a family single-handedly. The mores of the 1950s cast such behaviors as masculine, and, although these items would be more sex-neutral today, such phrases as those listed above obviate women in the research issue. The role conflicts that women might have experienced were never explored.

Although originally formulated from work based upon a study of female juvenile delinquents (Jennings, 1950), the LBDQ was validated using predominantly white male samples. Further, the LBDQ uses male-exclusive language. Research has shown that the use of the masculine generic conjures up a male image (Schneider & Hacker, 1973) and that this can bias responses (Campbell, 1981). Therefore, LBDQ respondents asked to describe an actual or ideal leader would be more likely to envision a male rather than a female when reading the questionnaire that repeatedly used "he." This procedure reinforces the androcentric bias evident in problem formulation.

To judge the effectiveness of leadership, Fiedler used radar bomb scores, percentage of company net income over three years, stock controls, percentage of basketball games won, creativity ratings, and time to hit targets among many others. Fiedler saw effectiveness in terms of numbers, contests, ratings, counts, dollars, minutes, accuracy, and physical output. This emphasis on production and competition is reflective of the settings in which Fiedler chose to do his work. Some researchers have pointed out that the tasks used in Fiedler's studies were not sex-neutral; that is, due to prior experience and/or conditioning, males and females would not be able to identify with the task with equal ease. Hence, their performance on the task may be an artifact of the conditioning due to sex-role stereotyping (Schneier, 1978).

Leadership effectiveness has evolved from a consciousness that prizes the drive to compete, to win, to beat everyone else. An alternate perspective, however, might focus on the quality of the group interactions rather than the quantity of the outcomes. This was a conceptualization and a measure never entertained in Fiedler's work.

A common response to criticism of research in the field of educational administration is, "So what?" There is a belief that a majority of the theories, concepts, and models have been proven dysfunctional for the administrator already and that an additional critique is of no more than academic interest. I believe that the discussion of androcentric bias in organizational research serves a far more important purpose than as a critique of these particular theories, concepts, and models. They have been used only to illustrate some salient issues that need to be addressed in future research if we are to understand human behavior in organizations more clearly.

Even when subsequent research has tried to account for the effects of gender, the findings and interpretations were tainted by the androcentrism of the primary research. Women were measured against male standards and were presented with implications that might have been of more detriment than benefit to them. Not surprisingly, the androcentrism documented in these theories can be found in the research of the field in general. A study of ten years of research in the *Educational Administration Quarterly* identified androcentric conceptualizations and methods in a majority of the articles (Shakeshaft & Hanson, 1986). For instance, the literature upon which most authors based their work was never reviewed or discussed in light of gender issues. Thus many researchers based their investigations of both males and females on theory formulated only on males. Similarly, studies of aspiration, motivation, roles, and job experience failed to review literature on females, thus ensuring that these studies would continue to replicate androcentric conceptions.

Surveys and instruments used in the *EAQ* studies were often biased. This bias fell into four categories: maintenance of traditional roles, failure to measure aspects of a construct that might relate to women's concern's or perceptions, direct transfer of instruments from a predominantly male field to a predominantly female field, and exclusion of female experience from the study.

The studies themselves were similarly male identified. Of those in which the samples were described, 90% were all-male samples. Unfortunately, the results of these studies were generalized to both males and females without any discussion of the possible limitations of the research.

Not only does research exclude women from its traditional subject matter in educational administration, it does nothing to explain women's experiences outside the norms of male society. It is clear that the traditional theory and research in the field is inadequate for accounting for the phenomenon of discrimination and for the persistent fact that women's lives as school employees differ from men's. When the theories don't fit female experience, researchers admit puzzlement but they don't question the theory. Very much like George Bernard Shaw's Mr. Stead who, when confronted with a woman who did not fit his definition of womanliness, rejected the woman, not the theory. Shaw says of Mr. Stead's response to a woman utterly incompatible with the account of a woman's mind given to him by his ideal, "he was confronted with a dilemma that either Marie was not a woman or else his ideal did not correspond to nature. He actually accepted the former alternative" (1965, p. 224). Thus, we find that, like Mr. Stead, the majority of researchers continue to perpetuate, without question, research that does not help us understand the experiences of two-thirds of the players in school settings. Some leaders in the field have noted the peculiar configuration of the research and its inability to account for female experiences. In an article entitled "Intellectual Turmoil in Educational Administration," Daniel Griffiths suggested better definitions of environments surrounding organizations "in order to understand what is happening to women in organizations" (1979, p. 47). Unfortunately, most researchers in the field have not caught up with Griffiths.

If women and men were the same, if they behaved in similar ways, then leaving women out of the formulation of theory wouldn't be a problem. However, we have seen that the history of women and men in school administration differs, as do their career paths. Further, the profiles of women and men administrators vary in important ways. And, as we shall see in Chapter 6, the management styles of women and men in schools offer interesting contrast.

REFERENCES

Bernard, J. (1979). Afterword. In J. A. Sherman & E. T. Beck (Eds.), *The prism of sex* (pp. 267-275). Madison: University of Wisconsin Press.

Campbell, P. B. (1981). *The impact of societal biases on research methods* (Contract No. NIE P-79-0120). Washington, DC: National Institute of Education.

Daniels, A. K. (1975). Feminist perspectives in sociological research. In M. Millman & R. M. Kanter (Eds.), *Another voice* (pp. 340-380). New York: Anchor Press/Doubleday.

Eichler, M. (1980). *The double standard*. New York: St. Martin's.

Fiedler, F. E. (1967). *A theory of leadership effectiveness*. New York: McGraw-Hill.
Getzels, J., & Guba, E. (1954). Role, role conflict, and effectiveness: An empirical study. *American Sociological Review, 19*(2), 165-175.
Getzels, J., & Guba, E. (1955a). Role conflict and personality. *Journal of Personality, 24*(1), 74-85.
Getzels, J., & Guba, E. (1955b). The structure of roles and role conflict in the teaching situation. *The Journal of Educational Sociololgy, 29*(1), 30-40.
Gilligan, C. (1982). *In a different voice*. Cambridge, MA: Harvard University Press.
Griffiths, D. E. (1979). Intellectual turmoil in educational administration. *Educational Administration Quarterly 15*(3), 43-65.
Haller, E. J. (1979). Questionnaires and the dissertation in educational administration. *Educational Administration Quarterly, 15*(1), 47-66.
Halpin, A. W., & Winer, B. J. (1957). A factorial study of the leader behavior descriptions. In R. M. Stogdill, & A. E. Coons (Eds.), *Leader behavior: Its description and measurement* (pp. 39-51). Columbus: The Ohio State University, Bureau of Business Research.
Harway, D. (1978). The struggle for a feminist science. *Women: A Journal of Liberation, 6*(2), 20-26.
Hemphill, J. K., & Coons, A. E. (1957). Development of the leader behavior description questionnaire. In R. M. Stogdill, & A. E. Coons (Eds.), *Leader behavior: Its description and measurement* (pp. 6-38). Columbus: The Ohio State University, Bureau of Business Research.
Jennings, H. H. (1950). *Leadership and Isolation*. New York: Longmans, Green and Co.
Kohn, R. A. & Fiedler, F. E. (1961). Age and sex differences in the perceptions of persons. *Sociometry, 24*, 157-164.
Maslow, A. H. (1968). Some fundamental questions that face the normative social psychologist. *Journal of Humanistic Psychology, 8*(2), 143-153.
Maslow, A. H. (1970). *Motivation and personality*. New York: Harper & Row.
Miller, J. B. (1976). *Toward a new psychology of women*. Boston: Beacon.
Parker, S., & Parker, H. (1979). The myth of male superiority: Rise and demise. *American Anthropologist, 81*(2), 289-309.
Parlee, M. B. (1979). Psychology and women. *Signs, 5*(1), 121-133.
Parsons, T. (1951). *The social system*. New York: Free Press.
Schaef, A. W. (1981). *Women's reality: An emerging female system in the white male society*. Minneapolis: Winston Press.
Schneider, J. W., & Hacker, S. L. (1973). Sex role imagery and use of the generic "man" in introductory texts: A case in the sociology of sociology. *The American Sociologist, 8*(1), 12-18.
Schneier, C. E. (1978). The contingency model of leadership: An extension to emergent leadership and leader's sex. *Organizational Behavior and Human Performance, 21*(2), 220-239.
Seiber, S. D. (1975). Organizational influences on innovative roles. In J. V. Baldridge & T. E. Deal (Eds.), *Managing change in educational organizations* (pp. 75-97). Berkeley, CA: McCutchan.
Shakeshaft, C., & Hanson, M. (1986). Androcentric bias in the Educational Administration Quarterly. *Educational Administration Quarterly, XXII*(1), 68-92.

Shakeshaft, C., & Saffer, S. (1984, April). *Does dissertation research have anything to do with scholarship?* Paper presented at the annual meeting of the American Educational Research Association, New Orleans.

Shaw, G. B. (1965). The womanly woman. In D. H. Laurence (Ed.), *Selected non-dramatic writings of Bernard Shaw*, (pp. 224-230). Boston: Houghton Mifflin.

Sherif, C. W. (1979). Bias in psychology. In J. A. Sherman & E. T. Beck (Eds.), *The prism of sex* (pp. 93-133). Madison: University of Wisconsin Press.

Slocum, S. (1980). Woman the gatherer: Male bias in anthropology. In S. Ruth (Ed.), *Issues in feminism* (pp. 214-222). Boston: Houghton Mifflin.

Smith, D. E. (1978). A peculiar eclipsing: Women's exclusion from man's culture. *Women's Studies International Quarterly, 1*(4), 281-295.

Smith, D. E. (1979). A sociology for women. In J. A. Sherman, & E. T. Beck (Eds.), *The prism of sex* (pp. 135-187). Madison: University of Wisconsin Press.

Smith-Rosenberg, C. (1983). The feminist reconstruction of history. *Academe, 69*(5), 26-37.

Spender, D. (Ed.). (1981). *Men's studies modified: The impact of feminism on the academic disciplines*. Oxford, England: Pergamon Press.

Willower, D. J. (1982, May). *Some "yes, buts" and educational administration*. Paper presented at the University Council on Educational Administration Conference on Educational Leadership in honor of Jack Culbertson, Austin, Texas.

. 6 .

Differences Between the Ways Women and Men Manage Schools

If one looks at the literature on the experiences of men in administration versus the literature on the experiences of women in administration, one might easily conclude that the two work at different occupations in dissimilar settings. Not only are women's day-to-day interactions different from men's, women's styles of administration offer contrast—sometimes subtly, sometimes dramatically—to the ways men manage schools.

This chapter examines the literature on differences between the worlds men and women inhabit and the ways they administer. It demonstrates that theory and research that examine only male behavior will result in very different conclusions from research that includes women because women and men manage in markedly different ways.

Although there is a literature that documents "no differences" between men and women in the ways of management, I have not chosen to focus upon the "no differences" research for a variety of reasons but primarily because it doesn't extend itself beyond the world of white males. All of the "no-difference" literature looks at the ways men manage and then asks, "Do women do these things, too?" Not surprisingly, for the most part women do, indeed, do them. A justifiable conclusion of this research, then, would be that women do most of the same things that men do when they manage schools. Unfortunately, authors of this type of inquiry don't stop there but go on to conclude that there are no gender differences in school administration. What is not investigated in these studies, what isn't even conceptualized, are the activities that women undertake and their motivation for doing so that are in addition to and different from those that men perform. These studies have only viewed women within a male framework and from a theoretical background formulated on male behavior. It is no wonder, then, that few differences between male and female school administrator behavior are discovered in this literature.

Anne Wilson Schaef (1981) has written about the world of white males and the world of women. She points out that all people must know the world of white males because it is the dominant perspective in society. In addition to that world, women and minority people also live in worlds that exclude white men. They know and understand these worlds—worlds that white men seldom know exist. Thus for women to be able to negotiate the world of white males is to be expected. They wouldn't have been selected for school administration if they didn't comprehend and master that culture. In addition, however, they have knowledge of a female culture and socialization that they bring to the job. It is this world that researchers have failed to investigate when they have studied male and female differences, and their absence of knowledge on the female world has led them to assume that differences don't exist. It is also these worlds—the worlds of women and people of color—that must be examined if we are to really understand differences in the ways that those other than white males negotiate organizations.

There are a number of reasons why these perspectives have not been the lens through which women have been studied. However, it must be noted that it was politically desirable, some say necessary, for the research to report no differences between men and women. As those who didn't want women to become school administrators often based their biases upon the unproven argument that women weren't suited for the job, it was crucial for advocates of women in administration to be able to point to literature that refuted the notion that women were less effective than men. Thus at that time the best political strategy for helping to break down the barriers was to show that women were as competent as men in management positions. Unfortunately, the literature that measured effectiveness was often generalized to mean no difference in style, although all it really documented was that a female was rated in identified administrative competencies as high as, or higher than, a male. But describing male and female behavior as "equally effective" is saying something very different from "identical to."

Interestingly, even the literature that looked at male and female performance within the male sphere and found differences has an odd reporting history. When women surpassed men on the measures used, these differences were often not reported in the conclusions. For instance, a study by Hemphill, Griffiths, and Frederiksen (1962), which showed women performing better than men on a number of variables, ended with the conclusion that men should "probably" not be favored over women for positions in school administration.

> In considering the question, "Should men be appointed as elementary school principals in preference to women?" it would appear that the answer is *probably no.*
>
> This study does not present evidence that a woman principal should always be preferred over the man who may also be a candidate. It does indicate, however, that as a class men are not overwhelmingly superior to women as elementary school principals. The evidence appears to favor women if the job of the principal is conceived in a way that values working with teachers and outsiders; being concerned with objectives of teaching, pupil participation, and the evaluation of learning; having knowledge of teaching methods and techniques; and gaining positive reactions from teachers and superiors. (1962, p. 334)

An answer more consistent with the data provided by the researchers would be to the question, "Should women be appointed as elementary school principals in preference to men?" And that answer, based upon their findings, would be *probably yes.*

Frasher and Frasher (1979) and Fishel and Pottker (1977) have written that the bulk of the literature comparing males and females shows either no differences or differences favoring women. That this argument has not been more widely disseminated is curious from a political standpoint. It is as if women don't want to embarrass men in school administration, so instead of saying, "The research says we do your job better than you do," they merely say, "We do your job as competently as you."

The purpose of this chapter is not to make the case that women are better suited to school administration than are men. Methodologically, many of the studies that would support such a claim are weak. The foremost criticism of the studies that find women superior to men might be that in comparing males and females in school administration, researchers are not comparing similar groups. The few women who have made it into school administration have persevered in spite of the odds. Additionally, women teachers have tended to be brighter and more competent than men teachers if only because bright men had many career avenues to pursue whereas bright women had but a few (Adams, 1981). Thus the two populations may not be similar at all, with gender being the least important variable for accounting for differences.

If these "no difference" studies can't be used to prove the case for the superiority of women administrators, studies showing differences between the sexes—even within male models and conceptualizations—can be used to offer some evidence of the differing patterns between the two sexes, patterns that may bode well for school improvement. Few studies have been done that examine a solely female view of the school world; until this research is done, we have only findings reported within a male framework.

The purpose of the remainder of this chapter is to present the research which does find gender differences, in an effort to begin to document the existence of a female organizational culture. The existing literature on differences falls into the categories of work environment, leadership, communication, decision making, and conflict resolution, and some of it has been done on women in the corporate world. In the latter case, Benedetti (1975) cautions against assuming that the two groups are comparable because she found that women in the corporate world score higher on structure dimensions whereas women in educational administration score higher on consideration. Nevertheless, the differences are small and, in other areas, the two groups are similar. Therefore, this literature will be included.

WORK ENVIRONMENT

Although the activities that men and women undertake to fulfill their job responsibilities are primarily the same, there are some differences in the ways they spend their time, in their day-to-day interactions, in the priorities that guide their actions, in the perceptions of them by others, and in the satisfaction they derive from their work. These differences combine to create a work environment that is different for women than for men.

Only a few studies document what administrators actually do during the day. Cuban (1976, p. xii) pointed out that "while we know to the penny what salaries . . . administrators received, what degrees they earned, and where they were born, we know very little about what they, as executives, actually do each day." Perhaps as a consequence, a few studies have been undertaken since Cuban's observations that do give us a glimpse of the day-to-day activities of school administrators. Unfortunately, most of these studies examine only the behavior of males; very few include females in the sample.

These Mintzberg-type studies, which document the activities that fill up a school administrator's day, conclude that the structure of work for these people is made up of desk work (writing notes, completing reports, correspondence, and so forth), phone calls (internal via intercom and external), scheduled and unscheduled meetings, exchanges (brief verbal encounters with one other person lasting one minute or less), monitoring (watching a particular part of the building such as the cafeteria), tours (walks throughout the building with brief stops for a variety of reasons), trips to places outside of the school building, observations of teachers, personal business, announcing (introductions, intercom announcements), teaching, and support chores (clerical or janitorial tasks).

Although we still don't understand the substance of the tasks, studies on males and females find that women conduct more unscheduled meetings, monitor less, take fewer trips away from the building, and observe teachers more often. Comparing male and female principals, Berman reports that women secondary principals have

- a higher percentage of contacts initiated by others
- shorter desk work sessions during the school day and more time spent during after-school hours

- a higher percentage of total contacts with superiors
- longer average duration for scheduled meetings, phone calls, and unscheduled meetings
- cooperative planning more often taking place during scheduled meetings (1982, p. 2)

A study of elementary principals by Kmetz and Willower (1982) documents similar findings. The woman principal spent more time in unscheduled meetings, made fewer trips from the school building, and observed teachers considerably more often than male principals. Whereas both of these studies need to be replicated using larger samples, they provide support for the notion that the day-to-day activities of principals may differ depending on whether the principal is a male or a female.

Pitner, in a study of male and female superintendents, found that women "prepared their written correspondence and dictation in the evening at home" whereas men did theirs during school hours (1981, pp. 287-288). She also found that women superintendents toured their buildings more often, observing teachers and students.

> Female superintendents averaged seven tours per week, each lasting about 30 minutes; males averaged five tours per week, each lasting about 12 minutes each. More importantly, females used their time to visit classrooms and teachers, keeping abreast of the instructional program, while males used the time to walk the halls with the principals and the head custodians, requesting that they follow up on particular concerns.... Male superintendents did not visit classrooms during the observation phase of the study except in the case of teachers who had quasi-administrative assignments. (Pitner, 1981, p. 288)

Thus although men and women overall tend to do the same things in carrying out their work, they may put a different emphasis on the importance of the tasks. These differences in emphasis mean that whereas all the work gets done, some work gets more attention than other work depending upon the gender of the administrator.

Additionally, the time spent may be with different members of the work staff. As Berman points out, women are more likely to have more contact with superordinates. They are also more likely to interact with women than with men. However, women principals interact with male teachers much more than male principals interact with female teachers (Gilbertson, 1981). Pitner (1981) found that superintendents are more likely to interact with people—both within and without the school system—who are the same sex as they are. Thus women superintendents, more than men superintendents, interact with mothers, female teachers and administrators, members of parent-teachers' associations, and female community leaders. They are also more likely to eat with women or to lunch in restaurants with predominantly female clientele.

Female superintendents and principals interact more with teachers and students than men do. They spend more time in the classroom or with teachers in discussions about the academic content of the school than do males and they spend more time outside of school hours with teachers (Fauth, 1984; Gilbertson, 1981; Gross & Trask, 1964, 1976; Pitner, 1981). Additionally, studies have found that female principals are more likely to assist beginning teachers with instructional problems and direct their initial teaching experiences (Fishel & Pottker, 1977).

Pitner points out that women superintendents also spend more time than men with community members who are not parents and that they interact more frequently with their professional colleagues but, again, almost exclusively with female counterparts. Women superintendents in her study

> were formally involved in the training of administrators holding positions as adjunct professors in local universities and in sponsoring women teachers within the district for leadership positions within and outside of the school district. Women generally spent their unscheduled time handling curriculum and instruction matters, while men were involved with political activities—campaigning for a candidate for office in the state affiliate of AASA, eating lunch in local restaurants, maintaining liaisons with the state department of education, and trying to capture the state teacher-of-the-year award for the district. Women superintendents normally ate alone in their offices or at home rather than in restaurants in the community, while men used luncheon invitations for exposure, visibility, and to make connections. (Pitner, 1981, p. 289)

The other side of the coin for women superintendents and principals is a good deal of loneliness in the role (Williams & Willower, 1983). Women principals and superintendents, because they are tokens and because they are not included or do not choose to be included in all-male activities, often report less colleagueship with male administrators and a deep awareness of "loneliness at the top."

Not only do women administrators interact more frequently than men with teachers, parents, and women, they also exhibit a different style of interaction. Pitner (1981), for instance, found that women superintendents are more likely to use an informal style than are men. Subordinates more often address women by their first names. Women superintendents develop more flexible agendas for meetings and have more limited control over them than do male superintendents. Finally, women superintendents are more casual in their dress, more often refusing to adopt the corporate image of the female executive.

These differences in tasks and in day-to-day interactions reflect differences between men and women administrators in the priorities they carry to the job. A number of researchers (Fauth, 1984; Fishel & Pottker, 1977; Frasher & Frasher, 1979; Gross & Trask, 1964, 1976; Neuse, 1978) have described the different ways women and men conceptualize the purpose of their work. Women give more attention to the importance of individual differences among students, they're more concerned with delinquency-prone pupils, and they pay more attention to the social and emotional development of the child. In terms of teacher supervision and evaluation, women principals are more likely to emphasize teachers' technical skills and their responsibility to the total school (Gross & Trask, 1964, 1976). Fauth (1984, p. 67) reports that women "have been found to be more concerned than men about the academic achievement of students; to be more knowledgeable about curriculum; to value the productivity of their teachers; to demonstrate greater concern for individual differences, developmental problems, and social/emotional development of students." Women, then, have been found to view the job of principal or superintendent more as that of a master-teacher or educational leader whereas men more often view the job from a managerial-industrial perspective.

Neuse (1978), in a study of public service workers, found that females enter such work to be of service to people, to use professional skills for creative management, and to work with highly qualified and motivated people, whereas men choose such work to meet important people and to have high prestige in the public eye. His analysis sheds light on the motivation of women who move into public school administration—motivation that is informed by a service, as opposed to a status acquisition, perspective. A study by Williams and Willower reinforces these work philosophies. They found that women superintendents follow a "Log Cabin Ethos" or "The Students Come First" philosophy.

> The descriptor [the Log Cabin Ethos] was used to encompass virtues traditionally valued by our society; typical responses mentioned doing one's best, being honest, fair and open, and treating everyone equally. . . . The second largest category was "the students come first" given by 22 percent of the women. One respondent felt that making decisions on the basis of "what is best for the kids helps you keep your perspective." Another vowed, "I'll always be a student advocate." Some responses reflected the superintendents' views of administration. For instance, one said, "I really believe, as hokey as it sounds, that administration is a service. Its purpose is to assist people in providing the best education for the community". (Williams & Willower, 1983, p. 11)

Similarly, Palmer (1983) reports that women managers in his study favored more people-oriented projects than did the men. Bachtel and Molnar (1981) found that women community leaders were more often supportive of affirmative action for minority people and health and safety issues than men, issues on which they took a service perspective. A study of general male and female values reinforces these findings, reporting that women value the orientations of beauty, freedom, happiness, self-respect, independence, intellectualism, and loving more highly than do men (DeVito, Carlson, & Kraus, 1984). This approach to the job as a service to the community or to society results in an administrator who is different from a job holder who sees the job as an indicator of personal status or achievement or who views the school from a corporate perspective.

It is not only the woman administrator's perception of herself and her mission that makes her environment a different one from that of her male counterpart; the perceptions of others about who she is shape a different environment to live in for the female school administrator than for the male. Fishel and Pottker (1977) point out that studies have demonstrated that male teachers prefer to work with male administrators, whereas female teachers prefer to work with female administrators. Although it is true that males who have worked under a female administrator are more favorable toward females than are males who have not worked under a woman administrator, the preferences for males is male. Williams and Willower (1983, p. 19) report that "lack of confidence in women as organizational leaders may not dissipate once a woman has assumed the superintendency. More than one-third of the superintendents reported lack of acceptance by segments of the community, staff members 'unaccustomed to working for a woman,' or male colleagues." Kahn (1984) found that in female-led groups, more hostility is exhibited toward the female leader, specifically if she is a low-disclosing, high-task person. Alderton and Jurma (1980, p. 59) report similar patterns, documenting that both males and females disagreed "more with female leaders than with male leaders." Booth-Butterfield (1984) points out that female executives may not be listened to as closely as are their male colleagues, thus creating environments in which women must try harder to stay equal.

Kanter's research (1977) does much to explain how the environment for women administrators changes depending upon the number of males and females she works with directly. If she is the only female, or one of a few, a woman administrator assumes token status. Tokens get extra attention, are the subject of more gossip, stories, and rumors, and are always in the spotlight. This attention produces feelings of isolation and anxiety in the woman who is the token; it also may force these women to behave in ways that might not be good for them or the organization.

Because women are often marginal and unwanted, their worlds may reflect the minutiae of discrimination. Although by themselves these events are not worthy of fuss, together they combine to create a world that carries an undercurrent of stress and anxiety. A woman who quit administration articulates the effect of this world in the following passage:

> These are tiny, individually insignificant examples. But when they occur day after day, week after week, month in and month out, they constitute a dreadful drain on any woman administrator's morale, a kind of abrasion of the spirit for which there is no readily available remedy. My experiences were not unique. Any woman administrator . . . can cite dozens of similar examples. By and large they are not intended to be malicious or hurtful. Quite the contrary, in fact. I would characterize the attitude they exemplify as a kind of institutional paternalism. But it is a dreadful, smothering paternalism which confounds, confuses and further isolates the female administrator. . . . For example, central administration support and professional staff on our campus traditionally address college-level administrators as "Doctor" or "Mister." I was always "Lorayne". . . . In a budget

> meeting, after my detailed analysis of the cost of critically needed equipment for our theatres, I was asked, "Lorayne, honey, can't you find yourself a sugar daddy to buy all that stuff for you?" Other department heads could charge supplies purchased at the University Center to their departmental accounts. Clerks who waited on me invariably insisted on calling the departmental office so that my secretary could verify my identity. . . . Much more disheartening, however, was learning that my behavior was often construed as sexually motivated. When I protested that a mid-year raise for a female faculty member . . . was patently unfair to two male faculty members in my department who had identical rank, exactly the same low salary and exactly the same number of years of service as the woman had, I became one of those . . . types intent on keeping other women in their places so I could have all the likely young men to myself. My refusal to accede to a central administration request to enlist the faculty in the department to cover up the sexual indiscretions of a male faculty member unless that same courtesy were to be extended to an equally indiscrete female faculty member resulted in the conclusion that I was a "ball-busting female, probably a lesbian." (Lester, 1984, pp. 43-44)

A number of women have written that they have left administration because of the toll taken by these minor assaults. One woman shares some of her reasons for giving up on her administrative position when she says she left because of "the overexpenditure of personal capital in a tense world, attitudes toward women in administration and changes occurring in the expression of such attitudes" (Mickey, 1984, p. 4).

Williams and Willower discovered from their interviews of women superintendents that these women have similar experiences. However, their responses are constrained by their own recognition that the futures of other women often depend upon how well the superintendents perform, adding yet another layer of burden.

> Some female executives feel that they must face and survive a special trial in which they and their kind are at risk. As individuals, but more importantly, as women, they must succeed not just for themselves, but for the sake of their gender. (1983, p. 19)

Thus, for the woman administrator, the sex composition of the teaching force has implications for the environment in which she works and the job she does.

This sex composition often affects the level of satisfaction that women administrators feel from their jobs. Doughty (1980) suggests that this is even more of a problem for black women. She reports the experiences of the first black woman assistant principal in a large urban high school, whose responsibilities were staff and curriculum development:

> She found that the opposition to the programs were not due to their content, but to the inability of some teachers to have a black woman "telling them what to do". . . . These teachers, mostly male, did not take orders from their wives and additionally were unaccustomed to black leadership. (1980, p. 170)

Gross and Trask (1964, 1976) found that women derive more satisfaction from supervising instruction than do men, whereas men derive greater satisfaction from administrative tasks. Young (1984) also found that women superintendents receive greater satisfaction from supervising than do men superintendents. This preference for people tasks is supported by Williams and Willower, who found that "working with people was a favorite aspect of superintending" (1983, p. 9). In addition to interacting with faculty and students, women superintendents enjoy public and community relations. In contrast, these same women bemoaned the time spent on noninstructional matters:

> One woman complained, "I wanted to be involved in leadership toward educational excellence. Instead, I have tons of paperwork." The minutiae of superintending, like "handling band-aid crises" (also described as "putting out brush fires") and "deciding who makes the best garden tractor," were perceived by superintendents as inevitable and time-consuming. (Williams & Willower, 1983, p. 7)

These differences in working conditions, in administrative style, and motivation mean that for women the work environment is qualitatively different than it is for men. This "altered" environment combines with differences in leadership, communication, decision-making, and conflict resolution styles—all of which mold a feminine culture.

LEADERSHIP AND MANAGERIAL STYLE

A number of researchers have examined traditional leadership theories and looked for sex differences. Weaknesses in the conceptualization of these theories challenge their basic usefulness as was discussed in Chapter 5. Nevertheless, a discussion of some gender differences will be presented in an effort to demonstrate that on male-conceptualized definitions of leadership, men and women differ.

A meta-analysis of the results of 12 dissertations that examined sex differences on the Leadership Behavior Description Questionnaire—Form XII (LBDQ) found no differences between males and females (Shakeshaft, 1979, 1985). The LBDQ is composed of a series of 100 short, descriptive statements of leadership behavior. Those participating in the survey indicate the frequency with which the leader uses each form of behavior on a five-point scale: always, often, occasionally, seldom, or never. The LBDQ has divided leadership behavior into the following 12 dimensions: representation, demand reconciliation, tolerance of uncertainty, persuasiveness, initiation of structure, tolerance of freedom, role assumption, consideration, production emphasis, predictive accuracy, integration, and superior orientation. The meta-analysis indicated no differences between males and female on any of these dimensions.

Gross and Trask (1964, 1976), Leonard (1981), and Charters and Jovick (1981), using data collection instruments other than the LBDQ found differences in the leadership styles of males and females. Gross and Trask report higher task attention of female principals. For instance, they found that women exert more control of teacher's professional activities by requiring teachers to discuss classroom problems, by asking teachers to report all major conferences with parents, by requiring teachers to keep the principal informed about "problem" children, by closly directing the work of teachers experiencing difficulties, by requiring that teacher's classroom behaviors conform to the principal's standards, by checking to see that teachers had written lesson plans, by knowing what is taking place in the classrooms during the day, and by determining what the objectives of the guidance program should be in the school. Leonard (1981) found women to be high on both task and consideration dimensions, whereas Charters and Jovick concluded that women outranked men on the trust and consideration subscales of the Organizational Climate Description Questionnaire.

Behavioral studies—as opposed to perceptual ones—also find some differences in behavior, but few such studies have been done. Although Hemphill, Griffiths, and Frederiksen (1962) didn't use the LBDQ when they conducted a simulation study that has been used to discuss the "real" behavior of administrators as opposed to their perceived behavior, the results of their study might lead one to conclude that had the LBDQ been used, women might have scored higher on such LBDQ dimensions as persuasiveness, initiation of structure, tolerance of freedom, consideration, production emphasis, predictive accuracy, integration, and superior orientation, if the LBDQ had been normed on female as well as male samples. Thus behavioral studies, as opposed to perceptual studies, do indicate differences in the ways male and female principals might be described using traditional leadership categories.

COMMUNICATION STYLES

Communication is one of the major tasks of the administrator. As far back as Barnard (1938), verbal communication was documented as an important activity in the work of managers. Subsequent studies in the corporate and industrial worlds have shown that oral communication consumes over half of the manager's workday (Burns, 1954; Mintzberg, 1973; Stewart, 1976).

It has been found that the work behavior of school administrators is not unlike that in the corporate world. Kmetz and Willower (1982), Martin and Willower (1981), and Berman (1982) have all documented through Mintzberg-type studies that communication is the major activity engaged in by school administrators. Kmetz and Willower, for instance, found in a study of elementary school principals that an average of 18.6% of these principals' time was spent on desk work activity that "involved writing notes, completing reports, processing correspondence and similar chores" (1982, p. 7). Telephone calls consumed 8% of their time, with unscheduled meetings taking up another 8.4% of the week. Communication of an unscheduled nature required 32.5% of the principal's time and exchanges 6%. Thus more than 70% of an elementary principal's time in this study was involved in communication of one sort or another. Whereas the secondary principals spent differing amounts of time on communication tasks than did elementary principals (Berman, 1982; Martin & Willower, 1981), like them, the majority of the day was given over to communication.

The kinds of communication in which school administrators engage are both oral and written. However, oral communication is far and away the most prevalant. As Kmetz and Willower (1982, p. 17) note:

> The principals' worlds at work were basically verbal. They spent more than two-thirds of their time talking with people. They appeared to prefer the verbal medium, initiating more than 10 times as many verbal contacts as they did written ones. They also showed a preference for live action. Their face-to-face contacts exceeded the more formal telephone contacts by a ratio of nearly four to one.

Both oral and written communication, then, is essential to administration.

A number of researchers have documented differences between male and female language (Kramer, 1974a, 1974b; Lakoff, 1973; Thorne & Henley, 1975). Research on differences has explored both the perception of differences as well as the behavioral evidence of differences. In both cases, the written and spoken language of women and men has been described as being different. Perceptual studies indicate that both men and women attribute differences to written and spoken language, even if there are none. Observational studies support that in many cases, there are recognizable differences.

In verbal communication, women have been found to use correct speech forms more often than men. They are less comfortable with slang and more precise with standard grammatical usage. If the correctness of their language limits them, women show variety in other ways. For instance, they tend to exhibit a wide range of pitch, variations in loudness, and changes in the rate of speaking.

They also use different words than men. Women are more likely to use expressive language and intensifiers such as "so," "such," "adorable," and "lovely." Additionally, women are more likely than are men to use questions for a variety of purposes. For instance, women use questions to express opinions as in, "It's a lovely day, isn't it?" Women also use question intonations in answer statements; in this case, women would answer the question "When's the principal's meeting?" with a question, "It's Tuesday, isn't it?" or just "Tuesday?"

This tentativeness can be found in women's use of hedging constructions such as "apparently," "it would seem," "you could say." Women shy away from universal pronouncements that would indicate that there is only one way of seeing things or that the way they understand the world is the only way.

Women tend to use language that encourages community building and is more polite and cheerful than the language of men. A number of studies have documented that in verbal discourse, women are more likely than men to express courtesy, gratitude, respect, and appreciation. Women show respect for their audience through listening, echoing, summarizing, polite speech, and nonantagonistic responses.

Hyman (1980) reports that women use language that indicates more consideration and concern than the language of men. Baird and Bradley (1979), in a study of communication styles of men and women in a hospital, a clerical department of a large manufacturing firm, and a production line of a small manufacturing firm, found that female managers gave the workers with whom they spoke more information, encouraged effort more, and stressed interpersonal relations through communication more than did males. Interestingly, male subordinates' job satisfaction and morale were lower when they worked under male, rather than female, managers. The workers in this study rated women managers as better communicators than men managers.

Women's politeness is exhibited in their listening behavior. Women listen more than men; women remember more of what all participants in a conversation say. Men interrupt more often and are less able to recall what females say. Women look at a speaker when she or he is talking, whereas men don't. Women tend to hear the emotional and personal issues in a conversation, whereas men listen for "facts."

A further way that women build community through language is by the use of personal communication, using more affiliation words than men (Kahn, 1984). Women more often give testimony and speak about personal issues. They use more emotional language than do men, although they don't generalize from their personal experiences to others'.

Whereas men joke more often, when women joke they tend to make fun of themselves, to use their personal experiences as examples for humor. Men's humor tends to poke fun at others, to look outward, not inward. Kotthoff (1984) found that the jokes of women are less often laughed at than are the jokes of men. In other words, female humor is given less acceptance than is male humor.

Men more often use hostile verbs, interrupt in conversations with females, and talk more. Their language tends to be third person, rather than personal, and lacks emotional content. Men say, "I think," rather than,"I feel." A woman might end her argument with "I feel this is right," whereas a man would end his with "It's right." Men also more often talk about sporting, contesting, and combating—to be terse, to give evidence of fact rather than feeling, and to provide argumentative openings rather than narrative ones.

Scott (1979) has characterized the literature on male and female spoken language according to what research has documented as female and male styles. Table 6.1 presents these differences.

Differences in written language echo those in spoken discourse. Women tend to hedge and use expressions of uncertainty, use hypercorrect grammar, be less likely to use humorous examples, use words that express participation in a psychological state, and to give more justification for statements. Women use more verb than noun forms in descriptions (Warshay, 1972) and use modal auxiliaries (could, would, and might) more often than men (Key, 1975). Hiatt (1977), in an examination of women's and men's writing styles, concluded that women's style is more perceptive, moderate, consistent, and evenhanded than men's. Women nonfiction writers write shorter sentences than men, use parentheses more often, and repeat more. Hiatt also found that women draw fewer conclusions and give fewer illustrations. Goldman (1981) documented women's practice of using qualifiers to simple statements, using "may" or "could" in places where is or were would have been used by a man, justifying their arguments more often (using "because" or "since" more frequently in sentences), using parentheses, and a greater use of italics. Hughes (1981) documented the use of "I" and "we" and the reference to primary territory in the writing of girls in the United States (but not in England), whereas boys more often wrote in the third person and about secondary territory.

Not all communication is written or spoken. People communicate with expressions and bodily movement, and in this arena, as in

TABLE 6.1
Female and Male Spoken Language

Female Stereotypic Language Characteristics	*Male Stereotypic Language Characteristics*
Enunciate clearly	Demanding voice
High pitch	Deep voice
Use hands and face to express ideas	Boastful speech
Gossip	Quantifying modifiers
Concern for listener	Use swear words
Gentle speech	Dominating speech
Fast speech	Loud speech
Use of intensifiers	Show anger rather than concealing
Talk about trivial topics	Straight to the point
Wide range in rate and pitch	Militant speech
Friendly speech	Hostile verbs
Talk a lot	Use slang
Emotional speech	Authoritarian speech
Use many details	Forceful speech
Smooth speech	Lounge, lean back while talking
Open, self-revealing speech	Aggressive speech
Enthusiastic speech	Blunt speech
Smile a lot when talking	Interrupt women
Good grammar	Sense of humor in speech
Polite speech	Passive voice
Question intonation	Preference for impersonal or third person generalizations
Tag questions	Evidence of fact rather than feeling
Use of qualifiers	
Superlatives, diminutives	

SOURCE: Scott (1979).

written and spoken communication, men and women differ.

Studies have demonstrated that in American society, women and other lower-status people take up less space than men and high status people. Women usually take less space in a room, sitting with legs together and arms to the side, whereas men spread out, claiming more territory. Relatedly, men intrude upon women's space significantly more often than on other men's (Borisoff & Merrill, 1985).

Touch reflects the power relationship between two people. High power people touch those without power, whereas the reverse usually does not happen. For instance, Nancy Henley (1975) found that in work situations men touch women more than women touch men.

Dominant members smile less than nondominant members. Women smile more than do men both because they are taught to smile and because it continues to be expected of them. Submission is also enforced through eye contact. Henley (1977) points out that women look at others more but avert their eyes when looked at. These responses are representative of low-power positions.

Very little research has been undertaken to document differences in male and female school administrators' written and spoken communication. And nonverbal communication and gender has not been examined at all. Kmetz and Willower (1982) and Berman (1982) did find that women administrators spend more time communicating with others, more time in scheduled meetings, phone calls, and unscheduled meetings than male principals. Leonard (1981) documented more people orientation among women higher education administrators as well as the use of more personal adjectives in their speech. Examination of the precise words and expressions that women school administrators use has not been undertaken, but it is logical to assume that they are probably not much different from the other women professionals who have been studied and who have been shown to use language substantially different from men.

Overall, this literature says a lot about the differences between male and female speech. In particular, women talk more to subordinates than do men. In these conversations, women managers supply more information and are more receptive to subordinates' ideas.

The content of female speech is more likely to be centered on emotional and personal issues than on impersonal, factual subject matter. In conversation, women will be more polite, being less likely to interrupt or to use language that is aggressive or puts down others. They will also be more tentative in their assertations, usually not generalizing based on their own experience. Finally, women talk less and listen more than men.

What do these differences mean? When sex differences in communication were first reported, women's language patterns were presented as deficient. For instance, Lakoff (1975) concluded that female speech is inferior to male speech and that women should develop male language patterns in order to become more effective communicators. Books for women in management told them that they must communicate like men if they were to become successful. However, no one ever tested this assumption; neither did early writers question the belief that if it was male it must be right.

Scott, in an effort to see if women's speech was really ineffective, pinpointed 20 language and speech characteristics linked with typical female speakers and 16 typically linked with male speakers (see Table 6.1) and in two experiments attempted to determine the social desirability as well as the perceived competence of those using the language. What she found was that the majority of the participants in her study judged all 20 of the female stereotypic language characteristics and only 9 of the male characteristics as socially desirable. Next she examined the effectiveness of the speech and found that "stereotypic female characteristics rated more positively than stereotypic male characteristics for effective communication among competent adults" (Scott, 1980, p. 206) and that "the characteristics of effective females were more like those of effective adults than were those for effective males" (p. 206). Her studies refute the notion that male speech is superior and calls into question the advice urging women to talk more like men.

Rather than adopting male speech patterns, it may be that all managers—both male and female—could benefit from learning women's speech. Pearson (1981) has pointed out that management styles are focusing more upon the consensual and that managers will have to motivate workers rather than just direct them. Four areas in which it has been predicted that management style will need to change have relevance for women's speech. It has been recommended that managers engage in less autocratic downward communication and that they develop noncoercive motivational and persuasive skills, humanized feedback, and threat-reducing strategies. Women's styles respond to this need very nicely. As mentioned before, women use imperative statements less often than do men. Thus instead of saying, "Give me your report tomorrow," as some men do, a woman might say, "Please give me your report tomorrow," or "Won't you please give me your report tomorrow?," or "Let's talk about your report tomorrow." Less autocratic speech more often occurs when speakers use hedging construction, personal style, and stay away from generalizations.

Pearson notes that another trend in communication for effective managers in the 1980s will be "integrative decision-making and group problem-solving behaviors" (p. 64). She then points out that women's habit of admission "of limits on the speaker's knowledge recognition of the complexity of the problem, heavy qualification of assertions and muting of argumentative intent, and deliberative order" (p. 65) go a long way in accomplishing this integration.

Nondefensive communication techniques and conflict reduction skills are additional areas in which managers will need to be proficient. Women's provisional language, such as questions ("What if?"), qualifiers and hedging ("Possibly," "I would guess that"), avoidance of strong assertion, tentative tone, preference for personal rather than universal generalizations, and explicit references to areas of ignorance or uncertainty, helps to avoid conflict. Further female patterns such as the inclusive we, I-you statements, feedback, mutual question and answer exchanges, judgments couched in descriptive rather than evaluative terms, and signals of courtesy, respect, and support also help.

Finally, she writes that listening skills, receptivity to variant views, and audience analysis will all be necessary for good management. Women's listening skills are different than are men's and, specifically, offer women a better "read" of what the speaker is actually saying because they take into consideration both verbal and nonverbal clues, including factual and emotional information.

From this literature, it seems clear that women and men communicate in different ways. Further, it would seem that women's traditional and stereotypic styles of communication are more like those of a good manager than are men's stereotypic styles. Perhaps this is why many administrative training programs have courses on good communication and try to teach communication skills. If men have traditionally not had these skills, then it becomes necessary to include them as a regular part of the curriculum so that they can be learned. Rather than urging women to forgo female styles and emulate men, then, it seems that we should advise men to watch how women speak and listen and try to make those styles their own if they want to be effective school administrators.

DECISION-MAKING STYLES

Research contrasting differences between males and females in decision-making approaches indicate considerable difference in the way the sexes come to a decision. Most of the studies that examine this issue are either self-report studies or perceptual studies, asking subordinates how their principals or superintendents go about making decisions. Some studies, however, actually observed behavioral differences.

A number of researchers have found that women are perceived as being more democratic and participatory than are men. Hemphill, Griffiths, and Frederiksen found that women are preferred as decision makers because of the way they make decisions.

> The work of women principals was characterized to a greater degree than that of men by asking subordinates for information. Women tended to do more work on in-basket items, discussed problems more with superiors or outsiders, and used information found in the background materials somewhat more frequently than men. . . . In general, the difference between men and women in their performance on in-basket problems is that the women involved teachers, superiors, and outsiders in their work, while the men tended to make final decisions and take action without involving others. (1962, p. 333)

Similarly, Hines and Grobman (1956) found that self-reports of principals indicate that women principals are more democratic than are men principals. Berman (1982) in an observational study found that women use more cooperative planning strategies in meetings than do men. Fairholm and Fairholm (1984) note that the predominate power tactics among women principals are coalition building, cooptation, and personality. Women, much more than men, use coalitions to reach their desired goals.

Neuse (1978) documents that women are less committed to the formal hierarchy and are more willing to submerge displays of personal power in an effort to get others to participate in the decision-making process. This behavior is not unexpected. Studies of children's play have found that girls play more cooperatively to win, sharing the game. These cooperative skills seem to be carried into the decision-making process when girls grow into women and become administrators.

Pitner (1981) examined female superintendents' administrative styles and describes women who don't

> dominate the discussion [in a meeting] thus increasing the participation of subordinates. In addition, women seemed to use meetings with subordinates as a forum for considering possibilities. They used verbs like *think, guess,* and *wonder,* which require a specific response and imply uncertainty and hesitancy. (1981, p. 293)

The use of language to encourage participation was discussed previously in this chapter, but it is important to note that the language patterns of women do much to create a consensual and participative atmosphere for decision making.

Charters and Jovick (1981, p. 316) also documented women's collegial decision-making styles: "In large and small schools alike, more decisions than expected were of the collegial variety under female principals, while more decisions were made by the principal alone under male principals." They concluded that: "More participatory decision making appeared in female-managed schools" p. 322).

This participatory style appears to enhance rather than threaten the power base of female administrators. Charters and Jovick point out that the same women who are seen as collegial and participatory are also seen as the most powerful actors in their schools:

> Female principals were regarded as more influential with respect to the affairs of their school than male principals were, and they seemed more likely than males to be dominant in the school's internal power system. (1981, p. 322)

Thus it would appear that women decision makers are more inclusive than exclusive, using participatory management styles both to their advantage and to the advantage of the educational system.

In addition to more collegial approaches to making decisions, there is evidence that women think about and evaluate their decisions more often than do men (Hoyle, 1969; Morsink, 1970). Women are more likely to use strategies that include long-range planning and evaluative data in making decisions and thus have been rated as better planners.

CONFLICT RESOLUTION

Studies of women and men find that women approach the resolution or management of conflict somewhat differently than men. Although both males and females use a variety of conflict management styles, women are more likely to withdraw from conflict or use collaborative strategies, whereas males use authoritarian responses more often (Bendelow, 1983; Hughes & Robertson, 1980). Women have been evaluated as more effective at resolving conflict among staff members and in using conflict reduction techniques more often than men. Interestingly, an angry female was evaluated as more effective than an angry male in resolving conflictual situations, but both were most effective when they used compromising and conciliatory strategies, strategies most often employed by women. Because women display greater respect for the dignity of teachers in their schools than do men (Wiles & Grobman, 1955), it may be easier for them to manage conflict. Valuing the actors involved may go a long way toward resolving differences.

Not only are women more likely to use different conflict management styles than men, there is also evidence to suggest that the frequency and kind of conflict is not the same for males and females. In a study of elementary and secondary principals, Hughes and Robertson (1980) found that women elementary principals were more likely to have conflict with male central office administrators whereas men were more likely to have problems with parents. Women principals reported no major conflicts with teachers. Hughes and Robertson speculate that women were more likely than men to fight central administration because women had no ambition to become central office administrators. In other words, women didn't mind burning their career bridges. An equally plausible explanation, given what is known about women's emphasis on instructional leadership, is that the women elementary principals interpreted the actions of male central office administrators, most of whom have little experience in elementary school, as challenging their authority and expertise. One woman remarked:

> I was placed here to do a job. They will either let me do it or they had best replace me. I am a strong and positive person, but I'm also a fighter. Not afraid. Kids and this school come first, not my ambitions. Others are afraid of me but they respect me. Most men are scared blue of strong women. . . . I'm not asking for unreasonable requests, just the best interests of kids. . . . I am committed to schools and that means conflict. Conflict takes a lot out of you, but you can't avoid it. You've got to fight for better schools. (Hughes & Robertson, 1980, p. 13)

Conflict resolution or management is the least studied area of gender differences in administrative competencies. We know very little about how women and men administrators react to conflict. However, the little that has been studied as well as knowledge of female socialization have led to the speculation that women will tend to cool conflict out, rather than heat it up. Women, more than men, see conflict as a negative state. Thus ridding the school of conflict is more likely to occur when women are in charge. Others point to women's traditional roles as wife, mother, daughter—roles that call upon women to promote and maintain harmony within the family. And still others point to the literature on children's play, which shows that girls will quit a game rather than fight among themselves, whereas boys often spend the entire game haggling over rules and fighting to win. These female approaches have much to say about possible conflict reduction strategies used by female administrators.

WOMEN ADMINISTRATORS MANAGE DIFFERENTLY THAN DO MEN

This chapter has presented evidence that demonstrates that women and men approach the job of school administrator differently and, consequently, respond in ways that are often dissimilar. Women's ways of managing have seldom been included in formulations of theory, neither have researchers who generalized their results to women tempered their conclusions because of these differences.

I am not making the case that all women respond in one way and all men in another. What my research and the research of others demonstrate is that, as a group, women tend to have a different administrative style than do men and that effectiveness for a female may depend upon this altered approach. What the female administrative world and culture looks like in schools is discussed more fully in the next chapter.

REFERENCES

Adams, N. A. (1981). A study by class rank of high ability female education majors over a period of fifteen years. *Dissertation Abstracts International, 42*(8), 3562A.
Alderton, S. M., & Jurma, W. E. (1980). Genderless/gender-related task leader

communication and group satisfaction: A test of two hypotheses. *Southern Speech Communication Journal, 46*(1), 48-60.

Bachtel, D. C., & Molnar, J. J. (1981). Women as community decision makers. *Human Services in Rural Environment, 6*(2), 3-10.

Baird, J. E., & Bradley, P. H. (1979). Styles of management and communication: A comparative study of men and women. *Communication Monographs, 46*(2), 101-111.

Barnard, C. I. (1938). *The functions of the executive*. Cambridge, MA: Harvard University Press.

Bendelow, M. M. (1983). Managerial women's approaches to organizational conflict: A qualitative study. *Dissertation Abstracts International, 44*(9), 2620-A.

Benedetti, C. R. (1975). Similarities and differences in the leadership styles and personal characteristics of women in educational administration and women in business administration. *Dissertation Abstracts International, 36*(3), 1188A.

Berman, J. (1982, March). *The managerial behavior of female high school principals: Implications for training*. Paper presented at the annual meeting of the American Educational Research Association, New York.

Booth-Butterfield, M. (1984). She hears . . . he hears: What they hear and why. *Personnel Journal, 63*(5), 36-41.

Borisoff, D., & Merrill, L. (1985). *The power to communicate: Gender differences as barriers*. Prospect Heights, IL: Waveland Press.

Burns, T. (1954). The directions of activity and communication in a departmental executive group. *Human Relations, 7*(1), 73-97.

Charters, W. W. Jr., & Jovick, T. D. (1981). The gender of principals and principal/teacher relations in elementary schools. In P. A. Schmuck, W. W. Charters, Jr., & R. O. Carlson, (Eds.), *Educational policy and management: Sex differentials* (pp. 307-331). New York: Academic Press.

Cuban, L. (1976). *Urban school chiefs under fire*. Chicago: University of Chicago Press.

DeVito, A. J., Carlson, J. F., & Kraus, J. (1984). Values in relation to career orientation, gender, and each other. *Counseling and Values, 28*(4), 202-206.

Doughty, R. (1980). The black female administrator: Woman in a double bind. In S. K. Biklen & M. Brannigan (Eds.), *Women and educational leadership* (pp. 165-174). Lexington, MA: D. C. Heath.

Fairholm, G., & Fairholm, B. C. (1984). Sixteen power tactics principals can use to improve management effectiveness. *NASSP Bulletin, 68*(472), 68-75.

Fauth, G. C. (1984). Women in educational administration: A research profile. *Educational Forum, 49*(1), 65-79.

Fishel, A., & Pottker, J. (1977). Performance of women principals: A review of behavioral and attitudinal studies. In J. Pottker & A. Fishel (Eds.), *Sex bias in the schools* (pp. 289-299). Cranbury, NJ: Associated University Presses.

Frasher, J. M. & Frasher, R. S. (1979). Educational administration: A feminine profession. *Educational Administration Quarterly, 15*(2), 1-13.

Gilbertson, M. (1981). The influence of gender on the verbal interactions among principals and staff members: An exploratory study. In P. A. Schmuck, W. W. Charters, Jr., & R. O. Carlson (Eds.), *Educational policy and management: Sex differentials* (pp. 297-306). New York: Academic Press.

Goldman, B. H. (1981). Women, men and professional writing: Signature of power? In B. L. Forisha & G. H. Goldman (Eds.), *Outsiders on the Inside* (pp. 122-134). Englewood Cliffs, NJ: Prentice-Hall.

Gross, N., & Trask, A. E. (1964). *Men and women as elementary school principals* (Final Report No. 2). Cambridge, MA: Harvard University, Graduate School of Education.

Gross, N., & Trask, A. E. (1976). *The sex factor and the management of schools*. New York: John Wiley.

Hemphill, J. K., Griffiths, D. E., & Frederiksen, N. (1962). *Administrative performance and personality*. New York: Teachers College, Columbia University.

Henley, N. M. (1975). Power, sex, and nonverbal communication. In B. Thorne & N. Henley (Eds.), *Language and sex: Difference and dominance* (pp. 184-202). Rowley, MA: Newbury.

Henley, N. M. (1977). *Body politics: Power, sex, and non-verbal communication*. Englewod Cliffs, NJ: Prentice-Hall.

Hiatt, M. (1977). *The way women write*. New York: Teachers College, Columbia University.

Hines, V., & Grobman, H. (1956). The weaker sex is losing out. *School Board Journal, 132*, 100, 102.

Hoyle, J. (1969). Who shall be principal—a man or a woman? *National Elementary Principal, 48*(3), 23-24.

Hughes, L. W., & Robertson, T. A. (1980). Principals and the management of conflict. *Planning and Changing, 11*(1), 3-16.

Hughes, T. O. (1981). *Sex differences in writing: A contrast in cultures*. Unpublished manuscript, Western Michigan University, Kalamazoo.

Hyman, B. (1980). Responsive leadership: The woman manager's asset or liability? *Supervisory Management, 25*(8), 40-43.

Kahn, L. S. (1984). Group process and sex difference. *Psychology of Women Quarterly, 8*(3), 261-281.

Kanter, R. M. (1977). *Men and Women of the corporation*. New York: Basic Books.

Key, M. R. (1975). *Male/female language*. Metuchen, NJ: Scarecrow Press.

Kmetz, J. T., & Willower, D. J. (1982). Elementary school principals' work behavior. *Educational Administration Quarterly, 18*(4), 62-78.

Kotthoff, H. (1984). Conversational humor: Observations of sex specific behavior. *Women and Language, 8*(1/2), 14-15.

Kramer, C. (1974a). Folklinguistics: Wishy-washy mommy talk. *Psychology Today, 8*(1), 82-85.

Kramer, C. (1974b). Women's speech: Separate but unequal? *Quarterly Journal of Speech, 60*(1), 14-24.

Kramer, C. (1977). Perceptions of female and male speech. *Language and Speech, 20*, 151-161.

Lakoff, R. (1973). Language and woman's place. *Language and Society, 1*(2), 45-80.

Lakoff, R. (1975). *Language and woman's place*. New York: Harper & Row.

Leonard, R. (1981, April). *Managerial styles in academe: Do men and women differ?* Paper presented at the meeting of the Southern Speech Communication Association, Austin, TX.

Lester, L. W. (1984, August). Administrator burnout: A woman's perspective. *Association for Communication Administration Bulletin*, 41-45.

Martin, W. J. & Willower, D. J. (1981). The managerial behavior of high school principals. *Educational Administration Quarterly, 17*(1), 69-90.

Mickey, B. H. (1984). You can go home again, but it's not easy. *Journal of the National Association for Women Deans, Administrators, and Counselors, 47*(3), 3-7.

Mintzberg, H. (1973). *The nature of managerial work.* New York: Harper & Row.

Morsink, H. (1970). Leader behavior of men and women principals. *The Bulletin of the National Association of Secondary School Principals, 54,* 80-87.

Neuse, S. M. (1978). Professionalism and authority: Women in public service. *Public Administration Review, 38,* 436-441.

Palmer, D. D. (1983). Personal values and managerial decisions: Are there differences between women and men? *College Student Journal, 17*(2), 124-131.

Pearson, S. S. (1981). Rhetoric and organizational change: New applications of feminine style. In B. L. Forisha and B. H. Goldman (Eds.), *Outsiders on the inside* (pp. 54-74). Englewood Cliffs, NJ: Prentice-Hall.

Pitner, N. J. (1981). Hormones and harems: Are the activities of superintending different for a woman? In P. A. Schmuck, W. W. Charters, Jr., & R. O. Carlson (Eds.), *Educational Policy and Management* (pp. 273-295). New York: Academic Press.

Schaef, A. W. (1981). *Women's reality: An emerging female system in the white male society.* Minneapolis: Winston Press.

Scott, K. P. (1979, April). *Language and gender: Stereotypes revisited.* Paper presented at the annual meeting of the American Educational Research Association, San Francisco.

Scott, K. P. (1980). Perceptions of communication competence: What's good for the goose is not good for the gander. *Women's Studies International Quarterly, 3*(2-3), 199-208.

Shakeshaft, C. S. (1979). Dissertation research on women in educational administration: A synthesis of findings and paradigm for future research. *Dissertation Abstracts International, 40,* 6455a.

Shakeshaft, C. (1985). Strategies for overcoming the barriers to women in educational administration. In S. Klein (Ed.), *Handbook for achieving sex equity through education* (pp. 124-144). Johns Hopkins University Press.

Stewart, J. (1978). Understanding women in organizations: Toward a reconstruction of organizational theory. *Administrative Science Quarterly, 23*(2), 336-350.

Thorne, B. & Henley, N. (Eds.) (1975). *Language and sex: Difference and dominance.* Rowley, MA: Newbury.

Warshay, D. W. (1972). Sex differences in language style. In C. Safilios-Rothschild (Ed.), *Toward a Sociology of Women* (pp. 3-9). Lexington, MA: Xerox College Publishing.

Wiles, K., & Grobman, H. G. (1955). Principals as leaders. *Nation's Schools, 56*(10), 75-77.

Williams, R. H., & Willower, D. J. (1983, April). *Female school superintendents' perceptions of their work.* Paper presented at the annual meeting of the American Educational Research Association, Montreal, Canada.

Young, P. (1984). An examination of job satisfaction of female and male public school superintendents. *Planning and Changing, 15*(2), 114-124.

· 7 ·

The Female World of School Administration

The preceding chapters have demonstrated that women's lives in administration differ from men's. Although there are similarities in the backgrounds and experiences of male and female managers, it is also the case that they vary in important ways. The profiles of women administrators and their history in administration are not the same as the profiles and history of men in administration. Further, a legacy of discrimination and exclusion has shaped a world in which women's experiences and behaviors are often unlike those of men.

The world of women has important implications for theory and practice in a field. To be useful and inclusive, theory and practice needs to take into account the experiences of all the players. Unfortunately, the field of educational administration, not unlike most other fields and disciplines, has not seen the world from an inclusive perspective and thus presents only a partial picture. In this chapter, selected issues will be examined in an attempt to add the female perspective to theory in educational administration.

THE FEMALE WORLD OF SCHOOLS

Chapter 6 documented differences between female and male administrators in the ways they manage schools. What do these differences mean? A number of writers (Bernard, 1981; Ferguson, 1984; Gilligan, 1982; Lenz & Myerhoff, 1985; Lyons, 1983, 1985; Noddings, 1984) have written about a female culture and a female world. For instance, Jessie Bernard (1981, p. 3) writes that not only do women and men experience "the world differently but also that the world women experience is demonstrably different from the world men experience." Gilligan (1982, p. 164) elaborates:

> In the transition from adolescence to adulthood, the dilemma itself is the same for both sexes, a conflict between integrity and care. But approached from different perspectives, this dilemma generates the recognition of opposite truths. These different perspectives are reflected in two different moral ideologies, since separation is justified by an ethic of rights while attachment is supported by an ethic of care.

Thus men tend to follow a morality of justice whereas women tend to be guided by a morality of response and care. Lyons (1985) articulates these differences in Table 7.1. These worlds, although different, are not exclusive to each sex. However, women are more likely to deal from a perspective of response and care and men from a perspective of justice.

Studies of women administrators would tend to confirm the view that women occupy a world, in addition to the one in which white males live, that provides them with experiences and approaches to life that are different from those of men. The research on male and female administrators and the voices of the women administrators from interviews conducted, lead me to believe that both male and female administrators use a range of behaviors in their work, but that the patterns of use are different. Women administrators more often are guided by what Gilligan (1982, p. 100) describes as "an injunction to care, a responsibility to discern and alleviate the 'real and recognizable trouble' of this world," whereas male administrators are informed by "an injunction to respect the rights of others and thus to protect from interference the rights to life and self-fulfillment."

Lenz and Myerhoff (1985, p. 7) note this overlap in male and female cultures in their work.

> When we speak of masculine culture or feminine culture, we are using a metaphor, since those are not fully developed, entirely

TABLE 7.1
The Relationship of Conceptions of Self and Morality to Considerations Made in Real-Life Moral Choice: An Overview

A Morality of Justice

Individuals defined as SEPARATE/OBJECTIVE in RELATION to OTHERS: see others as one would like to be seen by them, in objectivity;

and tend to use a morality of *Justice* as *Fairness* that rests on an understanding of RELATIONSHIPS as RECIPROCITY between separate individuals, grounded in the duty and obligation of their roles;

moral problems are generally construed as issues, especially decisions, of conflicting claims between self and others (including society);

resolved by involing impartial rules, principles, or standards, considering:

(1) one's role-related obligations, duty, or commitments; or

(2) standards, rules, or principles for self, others, or society; including reciprocity, that is, fairness—how one should treat another considering how one would like to be treated if in their place;

and evaluated considering:

(1) how decisions are thought about and justified; or

(2) whether values, principles, or standards are (were) maintained, especially fairness.

A Morality of Response and Care

Individuals defined as CONNECTED in RELATION to OTHERS: see others in their own situations and contexts;

and tend to use a morality of *Care* that rests on an understanding of RELATIONSHIPS as RESPONSE to ANOTHER in their terms;

moral problems are generally construed as issues of relationships or of response, that is, how to respond to others in their particular terms;

resolved through the activity of care; considering:

(1) maintaining relationships and response, that is, the connections of interdependent individuals to one another, or

(2) promoting the welfare of others or preventing their harm; or relieving the burdens, hurt, or suffering (physical or psychological) of others;

and evaluated considering:

(1) what happened/will happen, or how things worked out; or

(2) whether relationships were/are maintained or restored.

SOURCE: Lyons (1983).

> separate systems. . . . Nevertheless, it is reasonable to speak of a distinctive sensibility, a style of life, set of values, as well as activities, relationships, and cognitive and emotional predilections that are present among women but absent when men and women are together or when men are together.

This female world exists in schools and is reflected in the ways women work in schools. Based on what is currently known of female work behavior in schools, this female world might be conceptualized in the following ways.

(1) Relationships with Others Are Central to All Actions of Women Administrators. Women spend more time with people, communicate more, care more about individual differences, are concerned more with teachers and marginal students, and motivate more. Not surprisingly, staffs of women administrators rate women higher, are more productive, and have higher morale. Students in schools with women principals also have higher morale and are more involved in student affairs. Further, parents are more favorable toward schools and districts run by women and thus are more involved in school life. This focus on relationships and connections echoes Gilligan's (1982) ethic of care.

(2) Teaching and Learning Are the Major Foci of Women Administrators. Women administrators are more instrumental in instructional learning than men and they exhibit greater knowledge of teaching methods and techniques. Women administrators not only emphasize achievement, they coordinate instructional programs and evaluate student progress. In these schools and districts, women administrators know their teachers and they know the academic progress of their students. Women are more likely to help new teachers and to supervise all teachers directly. Women also create a school climate more conducive to learning, one that is more orderly, safer, and quieter. Not surprisingly, academic achievement is higher in schools and districts in which women are administrators.

(3) Building Community Is an Essential Part of a Woman Administrator's Style. From speech patterns to decision-making styles, women exhibit a more democratic, participatory style that encourages inclusiveness rather than exclusiveness in schools. Women involve themselves more with staff and students, ask for and get higher participation, and maintain more closely knit organizations. Staffs of women principals have higher job satisfaction and are more engaged in their work than those of male administrators. These staffs are also more aware of and committed to the goals of learning, and the members of the staffs have more shared professional goals. These are schools and districts in which teachers receive a great deal of support from their female administrators. They are also districts and schools where achievement is emphasized. Selma Greenberg (1985, p. 4) describes this female school

world: "Whatever its failures, it is more coöperative than competitive, it is more experiential than abstract, it takes a boad view of the curriculum and has always addressed 'the whole child.'"

(4) Marginality Overlays the Daily Worklife of Women Administrators. Token status and sexist attitudes toward women combine to create a world in which the woman administrator is always on display and always vulnerable to attack. Whether the assault actually occurs is less important than the knowledge that it is always possible. Women perceive their token status and realize that their actions reflect on all women. Jessie Bernard, in *The Female World* (1981, p. 31), writes of this undercurrent of danger for women when she says:

> I take the misogyny of the male world as a given, as part of the environment of the female world. It has to be recognized and dealt with.

This misogyny of the male world makes women's lives in administration different from men's.

(5) The Line Separating the Public World from the Private Is Blurred. Women are more likely than men to behave similarly whether in a public sphere or a private one. Men, on the other hand, most often have two very different ways of behaving depending upon whether they are in the privacy of their homes or in the public space of work. This lack of separation between the two worlds for women results in behavior that men often label inappropriate.

ADMINISTRATION AND THE FEMALE WORLD

What if the study of school administration took into account this female world? What would theory and practice look like? It's clear from an examination of the research and theory in educational administration that the female world of administrators has not been incorporated into the body of work in the field. Neither are women's experiences carried into the practice literature. Prescriptions for practice in educational administration are primarily found in textbooks, in books and journal articles by practitioners, and in the conversations or lore shared within the field. A number of studies of the journals and textbooks of the field (both theory and practice oriented) have documented that women are not a subject of these documents (Nagle, Gardner, Levine, & Wolf, 1982; Schmuck, Butman, & Person, 1982; Tietze, Shakeshaft, & Davis, 1981).

If absence is the watchword in the traditional educational administration literature, imitation is the theme in books and articles for women managers, many of which have been described as survival manuals for women in bureaucracies. Books such as *Games Mother Never Taught You* (Harragan, 1977) and *The Managerial Woman* (Hennig & Jardim, 1977) "take existing institutional arrangements for granted and seek strategies to integrate women into these arrangements (Ferguson, 1984, p. 183). In these approaches, males have been studied and then women have been advised to imitate them. Women have been told to "act like a man," "not to cry," and "dress for success." What these books fail to examine are the ways in which acting like a man may not be the best strategy for a woman and, worse, may interfere with the goals of schooling.

For instance, the female world is very similar to the world of effective schools. Traditional female approaches to schooling look like the prescriptions for administrative behavior in effective schools. In a recent synthesis of studies on effective leadership behavior (Sweeney), six themes emerge as behaviors consistently associated with well-managed schools in which student achievement is high. Principals of such schools, according to the research:

1. Emphasize achievement. They give high priority to activities, instruction, and materials that foster academic success. Effective principals are visible and involved in what goes on in the school and its classrooms. They convey to teachers their commitment to achievement.

2. Set instructional strategies. They take part in instructional decision making and accept responsibility for decisions about methods, materials, and evaluation procedures. They develop plans for solving students' learning problems.

3. Provide an orderly atmosphere. They do what is necessary to ensure that the school's climate is conducive to learning: it is quiet, pleasant, and well-maintained.

4. Frequently evaluate student progress. They monitor student achievement on a regular basis. Principals set expectations for the

> entire school and check to make sure those expectations are being met. They know how well their students are performing as compared to students in other schools.
>
> 5. Coordinate instructional programs. They interrelate course content, sequences of objectives, and materials in all grades. They see that what goes on in the classroom has bearing on the overall goals and program of the school.
>
> 6. Support teachers. Effective principals communicate with teachers about goals and procedures. They support teachers' attendance at professional meetings and workshops, and provide inservice that promotes improved teaching. (Sweeney, 1982, p. 349)

Similarly, Rutherford in a five-year study of school principals found that effective principals:

> 1) have clear, informed visions of what they want their schools to become—visions that focus on students and their needs; 2) translate these visions into goals for their schools and expectations for the teachers, students, and administrators; 3) establish school climates that support progress toward these goals and expectations; 4) continuously monitor progress; and 5) intervene in a supportive or corrective manner, when this seems necessary. (1985, p. 32)

It is interesting to compare these two descriptions of effective administators with the portrait of the female administrative world. The similarities are striking and the implications of a female world for effective schooling are dramatic. It appears that, for a number of reasons, women possess characteristics that are conducive to good schooling. Women enter teaching with clear educational goals, supported by a value system that stresses service, caring, and relationships. Women are focused on instructional and educational issues and have demonstrated that, when in charge, they are likely to build a school community that stresses achievement within a supportive atmosphere. Women's communication and decision-making styles stress cooperation and help to facilitate a translation of their educational visions into actions. Women monitor and intervene more than men, they evaluate student progress more often, and they manage more orderly schools. Women demonstrate, more often than men, the kinds of behavior that promote achievement and learning as well as high morale and commitment by staffs. Analyzing female approaches to administration might help to isolate particular strategies and behaviors that promote effective schooling that can be used by all administrators. Perhaps Bach (1976, p. 465) summarizes much of what is good for schools about women's culture and women's styles when she says:

> The ideal principal must now cultivate all the virtues that have always been expected of the ideal woman. Women have finally lucked out by having several thousand years to train for jobs where muscles are out and persuasion is in!

Thus to counsel women to act like men may not be in the best interests of either women or schooling.

Although we don't really know what we would see if we reshaped the school world around female culture and experience, we do have enough information about the female world to allow us to speculate on some issues of practice. The following section addresses practice issues with the perspective of gender in mind in an attempt to begin to think about the ways gender may be an important variable for understanding effective administrative practices. Imbedded in this discussion is the notion that these issues must be confronted by the entire field: Researchers need to redirect their inquiries not only to include women but also to see the world through female eyes, and administrative training programs must incorporate this literature into their courses so that both men and women can begin to understand how gender affects their administrative style.

Taking the world of women into account in research and practice means a complete reshaping of the field. What, who, and how we study organizations will change. If we were to include the perspective of women, administrative training programs would need to be completely restructured—the content of every course would be forced to change dramatically. The following issues are presented only as ways we might think about gender and administration, offering some preliminary questions to begin to move the field toward a reconceptualization of theory and practice that includes both males and females.

Supervision

Little has been written on the impact of gender on successful supervision. This issue seems particularly salient given the sex structuring in schools, which results in an organization in which males most often supervise females. Research tells us that the sex of participants affects what is communicated and how it is communicated. The same words spoken by a male supervisor have different meanings to male and female teachers. Conversely, an interaction between a female principal and a male teacher is not the same as an exchange between a female principal and a female teacher. What impact might our understanding of gender issues have on supervision?

We know that men and women communicate differently and that they listen for different information. It may be that in a supervisory conference in which a principal is discussing an instructional issue with the teacher, the women participant is listening for the feeling and the man for the facts. It may also be, given what we know of the values that males and females carry into their jobs in schools, that the woman is focused upon an instructional issue or a matter concerning the child, whereas the man has chosen to discuss an administrative problem.

Further, research tells us that there may be discomfort in communicating with a member of the other sex. Certainly, we know that male teachers exhibit more hostility in dealing with female administrators than do female teachers. We also know that women administrators have to work to get male teachers to "hear" them. Whether in job interviews or in determining job performance, women are initially evaluated less favorably than equally competent men. Knowing that women are rated as less competent or less effective than men is important for developing supervisory styles (Frasher & Frasher, 1980).

Although women are often seen in a more negative light, this view is seldom directly communicated to them. Studies tell us that male administrators are less likely to be candid with a female teacher than are female administrators. When a male subordinate makes a mistake, his supervisor tends to level with him, "Telling it like it is." When a female errs, she often isn't informed. Instead, the mistake is corrected by others. The results are twofold. For the male, learning takes place instantly. He gets criticism and the chance to change his behavior. He learns to deal with negative opinions of his work and has the option of improving. Females often never hear anything but praise, even if their performance is known to be less than ideal. This results in the woman being denied the opportunity for immediate feedback, which would allow her to improve her performance. It also results in a woman's misconception of her abilities. If all she hears is that she is doing a good job, it comes as a shock to her when she is fired, demoted, or not promoted. Illustrative is a sex discrimination case in California. A woman supervisor had been demoted because of poor performance and it was clear from the record and from the woman's own accounts that she had not been an effective administrator. And yet, all of her evaluations rated her in the highest category possible. Further, her supervisor—the assistant superintendent—revealed that he had never communicated his displeasure but rather had "fixed her mistakes" without her knowledge. When she was demoted, she cried sex discrimination because she had no feedback that would have given her another picture. Why had no one honestly discussed her performance with her?

Interviews with women administrators and their supervisors indicate that her case is not unusual. Women do not get corrective feedback as often as men. In interviews with male superintendents and principals in which I asked them why they didn't confront women, all expressed that one reason was their fear of women's tears. The threat of crying kept supervisors from giving important corrective feedback that would have allowed women to improve their performance as educators.

Does this mean that we should advise women not to cry? I think not. In reality, women administrators seldom give way to tears. Because it is the threat of crying that deters feedback, we need to demystify this emotion by teaching people mechanisms for coping with tears in the same way that we have instructed them in dealing with the traditional male response of anger.

Authority

There are a number of ways that males and females have been advised to establish their authority as leaders, but very little has been done to determine whether these approaches work for women. Are the issues surrounding authority the same for a male and a female? Do men carry with them, by the nature of their sex, legitimate authority—authority that women must earn in other ways? Is authority the same for a female supervising a female staff as for a female supervising a male staff? How does a woman become identified as "in charge" without also being identified in negative or "unfeminine" ways? These are issues that women administrators often discuss and that are not covered in the sections on authority in the traditional texts in administration.

In trying to command or maintain authority, women must take into account not only the people with whom they work but also how those people view women. Many women note that ways of establishing authority that work for men don't necessarily work for them. Contrary to the notion that being like a man will automatically signify authority, many women voice concern over the effectiveness of such strategies. Some women report that they try to look less authoritarian, less in charge, and less threatening in an effort to be effective. Many comment that "the less I threaten the men I work with, the more I am able to accomplish." As a result, these women administratrators often downplay their power, intellect, and skill. Through language and appearance, they make themselves more tentative and less threatening. These strategies appear to work. The success these women report is supported by studies that confirm that women with male subordinates were more influential when they used a consideration style as opposed to a dominant one, whereas with woman subordinates both styles worked. Similarly, studies indicate that men rate women who appear less threatening higher than women who are seen as more competent.

Not surprisingly, women report using strategies that subtly signal authority. For instance, a number of women have confided that they completed doctoral work so that they could carry with them the aura of legitimate authority, transmitted by the title, "Dr." These women want to be called Dr. not only because it confers legitimacy, but also because they are seeking ways to shed the use of "Mrs." and "Miss," titles that diminish them. "Ms." has been found to be a more powerful title than either Mrs. or Miss as it has been shown to establish authority more quickly and to elicit the image of a person in charge more often than Mrs. or Miss does (Anderson, Finn, & Leider, 1981).

Climate

The climate in which women work may have an impact on the strategies they choose to use in managing. The more male dominated an organization, the more women are conscious of their own behavior and the more they calculate each move. Being a token means that women are always on stage, a condition that adds stress to already stressful jobs. How can we diagnose the climate of a school if we fail to include in that description the ways that a particular group of people—that is, women—are treated? Climate descriptions need to incorporate the day-to-day lives of women that men seldom experience—sexual harrassment, subtle forms of discrimination, and lowered expectations.

Motivation

Studies of motivation have demonstrated that women educators are motivated differently than are men. Women also define career in ways that are foreign to men (Biklen, 1985). The implications of this research for administrators attempting to motivate staffs are crucial to the formulation of a restructuring of the profession that has been called for in recent reform reports. Women enter education to teach, to be close to children, to be able to make a difference. Offers of money or career ladders, which take women away from the instructional decisions of the school, may not be effective ways of motivating them. Further, continuing to structure school so that administrative jobs become more and more dissociated from the task of learning almost ensures that women will opt out of administration. Intriligator points out that women seek leadership roles in schools that don't take them away from teaching.

> Women union leaders reported that they became a union leader in order to both be in the company of adults and to do important things, while at the same time maintaining their satisficing professional role as teacher. (1983, p. 11)

Structure of Schools

The structure of schooling is itself antithetical to the ways women work best. Separating teaching from administration so that the power for change is in the administrator's hands is an organizational format that women did not choose. Studies of female-defined schools indicate that they are child centered, small, use shared decision making, and are nonhierarchical (Greenberg, 1985; Smith, 1979). In the initial organization of schools, education didn't have to follow the lead of industry and separate teaching from the decision-making process. We could have selected another metaphor of organization (Hanson, 1984). Administrative paperwork and tasks could have been delegated to secretaries or clerks, and the definition of administrator might have remained as instructional leader. However, over the years, instructional leadership has been more and more replaced by a management metaphor. Some even believe that a good school administrator needs never to have been a teacher or, in fact, needs to know nothing of education as schools are really big business. Interestingly, few women educators hold this view. A female-defined organizational structure probably would not have resulted in such overspecialization, in extreme forms of hierarchy, or in administrators being mere managers.

Personnel Selection

The issues of personnel selection need to be examined in light of both gender differences and discriminatory practices. Those who hire must become aware of the subtle and not so subtle biases that we all hold toward women. It is crucial that we examine interview and selection procedures for the presence of bias as well as to determine ways of overcoming these biases so that the best person is hired. Until we do that, women should to be instructed in the most effective ways to confront bias in personnel selection as well as to be given the context in which to understand discriminatory practices directed toward them so that they do not internalize rejection and label it their failure.

Power

Power means different things to men and women. A number of studies provide evidence that women use power to empower others. This sharing of power is based on the notion that power is not finite but rather that it expands as it is shared. Uses of power in this way need to be further explored and their impact upon schools should be investigated.

Similarly, the team concept for women incorporates this notion of community. Women define a team player as someone who cooperates toward the achievement of group goals. Women see the "support of group action and the achievement of group satisfaction" as the primary descriptors of a team player (Gips, Navin, Branch, & Nutter, 1984, p. 7). Men, on the other hand, more often define a team player as one who has a job to do and who is responsible for one piece of the action. Women more often stress cooperation and collaboration whereas men tend to stress autonomy and individuality. Harragan (1982, pp. 17-18) offers a contrast between a female and a male team concept:

> If you ask a group of women what a team is, they will usually say it means: "Everybody should cooperate to get the job done," "Everybody pitches in, doing whatever they can to help others," . . . Everyone is responsible for the team result, thus, you have to cover for somebody who slacks off." . . . If you ask a ten year old boy what a team is, he will often respond in baseball terminology. "There's a pitcher, a catcher, a first baseman, second baseman, third baseman, fielders, and so on." Notice, there is nothing vague about that description, no generalized vagaries about "a bunch of guys supporting one another." By the time they are ten, little boys know—and they don't even know they know, but they do—that a team is a very rigid structure and has a prescribed function, that each player covers his own position and nobody elses.

These differences can result in misunderstandings between men and women about the definition of a good team player. A good team player for a male might be considered a lazy deadweight by a female, whereas a female's concept of team may cause her to be judged as an interfering meddler by a male.

The collaborative approach to decision making that shares power may cause women to be initially evaluated as weak or ineffective. Women who manage from a collaborative framework do so in a system that stresses the value of competitive individualism and personal achievement at the expense of community goals. Thus women often report that they first establish themselves and then introduce participatory styles. Those women who initiate collaborative approaches immediately generally prepare their staffs for these approaches and acknowledge that, at first, they were mistaken for weak administrators. Nevertheless, the research offers overwhelming evidence that women's collaborative style works best and over the long haul is instrumental in women being rated as effective leaders.

Community Relations

Because of these collaborative strategies, women seem to have more positive interactions with community members. Just as women administrators differ from men, so, too, do women school board members approach their jobs with a different perspective than their male colleagues. Women board members not only tend to "give priority to the content and quality of the education program" (Marshall & Heller, 1983, p. 31), they perceive their roles more politically than men, answering to a constituency." Men board members leave the educational decisions to the administrators, but gauge a superintendent's effectiveness by how efficient she or he is administratively. Women, on the other hand, emphasize superintendent and board evaluations focused on educational content. These gender differences have ramifications for a superintendent's interactions with her or his board.

WOMEN AND EDUCATIONAL ADMINISTRATION

The implications of the research on women administrators for training programs, for practice, and for theory and research in educational administration are wideranging. If the field were to heed women's experiences, we might restructure training programs and rewrite the textbooks. Theory and research would need to be reconceptualized to take women into account. Only when this is done will we be able to understand human behavior in organizations. Until then, we are writing a history and practice of males in school administration. As scholarship, this is shoddy and deficient. As practice, it is useful to only some practitioners. The most immediate action that needs to be taken is to develop a research agenda that allows us to discover the factors that need to be taken into consideration if we are to respond to our women students.

Specifically, the following recommendations are made to those involved in training programs in administration.

1. Courses should be expanded to include women's experiences in administration. Where materials are unavailable to address these, they should be developed. UCEA, ASCD, AASA and other involved organizations should be requested to prepare curricular aids that incorporate the female world.

2. Case studies of women administrators should be developed and used in classes.

3. Women speakers should be brought to the classroom and to the campus to discuss the issues relevant to female students.

4. Where possible, women students should intern with women administrators.

5. Research on the styles of women administrators should be supported and encouraged.

6. Women should be added to faculties in educational administration.

7. Workshops sponsored by UCEA might be held for administration professors in an effort to help incorporate research on women into course materials.

Most importantly, research must be undertaken that reflects both the presence of females and the female world. Only then will we be able to determine whether or not there are differences and, if so, whether they have any real meaning.

REFERENCES

Anderson, L. R., Finn, M., & Leider, S. (1981). Leadership style and leader title. *Psychology of Women Quarterly, 5*(5), (Supp.), 661-669.

Bach, L. (1976). Of women, school administration and discipline. *Phi Delta Kappan, 57*(7), 463-466.

Bernard, J. (1981). *The female world.* New York: Free Press.

Biklen, S. K. (1985, October). *Can elementary schoolteaching be a career? A search for new ways of understanding women's work.* Paper presented at the annual meeting of the American Educational Research Special Interest Group: Research on Women in Education, Boston.

Ferguson, K. E. (1984). *The feminist case against bureaucracy.* Philadelphia: Temple University Press.

Frasher, J. M., & Frasher, R. S. (1980). Sex bias in the evaluation of administrators. *Journal of Educational Administration, 18*(2), 245-253.

Gilligan, C. (1982). *In a different voice.* Cambridge, MA: Harvard University Press.

Gips, C. J., Navin, S., Branch, D., & Nutter, N. (1984, October). *Can women bat clean-up, or must they simply do the cleaning? A look at women as organizational team players.* (ERIC Document Reproduction Service No. ED 251 975)

Greenberg, S. (1985, October). *So you want to talk theory?* Paper presented at the annual meeting of the American Educational Research Association Special Interest Group: Research on Women in Education, Boston.

Hanson, M. (1984). Exploration of mixed metaphors in educational administration research. *Issues in Education 2*(3), 167-185.

Harragan, B. L. (1982). Women and men at work: Jockeying for position, in J. Farley (Ed.), *The woman in management: Career and family issues.* Ithaca: IUR Press.
Hennig, M., & Jardim, A. (1977). *The managerial woman.* Garden City, NY: Anchor/Doubleday.
Intriligator, B. A. (1983, April). *In quest of a gender-inclusive theory of leadership: Contributions from research on women leaders in school unions.* Paper presented at the annual meeting of the American Educational Research Association, Montreal, Canada.
Lenz, E., & Myerhoff, B. (1985). *The feminization of America.* Los Angeles: Jeremy P. Tarcher.
Lyons, N. (1983). Two perspectives: On self, relationships and morality. *Harvard Educational Review, 53*(2), 125-145.
Lyons, N. (1985, October). *Overview: Perspectives on what makes something a moral problem.* Paper presented at the annual meeting of the American Educational Research Association Special Interest Group: Research on Women in Education, Boston.
Marshall, S. A., & Heller, M. (1983, August). A female leadership style could revolutionize school government. *The American School Board Journal,* 31-32.
Nagle, L., Gardner, D. W., Levine, M., & Wolf, S. (1982, March). *Sexist bias in instructional supervision textbooks.* Paper presented at the annual meeting of the American Educational Research Association, New York.
Noddings, N. (1984). *Caring.* Berkeley: University of California Press.
Rutherford, W. L (1985). School principals as effective leaders. *Phi Delta Kappan, 67*(1), 31-34.
Schmuck, P. A., Butman, L., & Person, L. R. (1982, March). *Analyzing sex bias in Planning and Changing.* Paper presented at the annual meeting of the American Educational Research Association, New York.
Smith, J. K. (1979). *Ella Flagg Young: Portrait of a leader.* Ames: Educational Studies Press and the Iowa State University Research Foundation.
Sweeney, J. (1982). Research synthesis on effective school leadership. *Educational Leadership, 39*(5), 346-352.
Tietze, I. N., Shakeshaft, C., & Davis, B. N. (1981, April). *Sexism in texts in educational administration.* Paper presented at the annual meeting of the American Educational Research Association, Los Angeles.

APPENDIX

Strategies for Increasing Women's Access to Administrative Positions

The following table lists the strategies that have been used to demolish the barriers to women who wish to become school administrators. Where documentation of success is available, it is listed. Specific examples of programs that have used these strategies are also included.

Strategy	*Barrier(s) Targeted*	*Documented Outcomes*	*Examples of Use*
Consciousness-raising and recruitment of women into preparation programs	Lack of support, encouragement, counseling Socialization and sex-role stereotyping Lack of preparation	WISA: Increased enrollment of women in certification courses from 20 to 80%	WISA, ICES, FLAME, SEEL: Talks to educational groups, professional organizations WISA: Field-based courses taught whereby professors traveled to rural areas to recruit; statewide recruitment and selection FLAME: Recruited applicants from local educational agencies SEEL: Counseled students St. Paul recruitment model: Recruited 35 women into training program
Financial assistance	Lack of finances	FLAME: Interns completed training that would have otherwise been impossible without financial assistance	FLAME: Interns were paid a monthly stipend while taking leave of absence to return to graduate school full time ICES: Scholarships were given to women to attend university summer session and ICES workshops
General administration courses and workshops	Lack of preparation/experience	FLAME: Some interns became knowledgeable in previously male-dominated areas ICES: Interns kept high grade point average and impressed administration faculty WISA: Evaluated by participants as important activity	FLAME: Interns enrolled in full-time doctoral programs ICES: Interns took summer administration courses, workshops on conflict management, business management, and politics of education The Next Move: Leadership and management clinic for women in higher education WISA: Workshops on conflict management, study of power and leadership, time management, and grant writing

(continued)

APPENDIX Continued

Strategy	*Barrier(s) Targeted*	*Documented Outcomes*	*Examples of Use*
Increase number of women professors of educational administration	Too few role models	FLAME: Three women professors of educational administration hired	FLAME: Three women professors of educational administration hired
	Lack of sponsorship	WISA: Courses team-taught by professors and women administrators	WISA: Courses team-taught by professors and female administrators
Courses and workshops concerned with specific barriers to women in administration	Poor self-image/lack of self-confidence	AWARE: Decreased external barriers	AWARE: Workshops at six project sites and at conferences
	Lack of support, encouragement, counseling	Florida State University: Formal evaluation indicates changes in goals, values	Florida State University: Workshops for women to encourage entrance into nontraditional careers
	Socialization and sex-role stereotyping	Hofstra University: Formal evaluation indicates changes in self-confidence, goals, and jobs	Hofstra University: Course for women within administrative certification program
	Too few role models		ICES: Workshops on educational equity
	Lack of sponsorship		SEEL: Yearly conferences for women in administration
	Sex discrimination	Social literacy training: Evaluation indicates that those who received training were more likely than those who did not to apply for administrative positions	Social literacy training: Training to overcome internal factors that inhibit entrance into administrative careers
		The Next Move: Participants indicated usefulness of program	The Next Move: Seminars for women
			St. Paul recruitment model: 25-hour training program
			WILL: Conferences and workshops for women
		WISA: Evaluated by participants as most helpful training activities	WISA: Activities including understanding of assertiveness training, sex-role stereotyping, and socialization
Curriculum materials	Poor self-image/lack of self-confidence		DICEL: Videotape/modules
	Lack of support, encouragement,		ICES: Four videotapes
			SEEL: Book, slide-tape, newsletters

	counseling Socialization and sex-role stereotyping Lack of preparation Too few role models Lack of network Sex discrimination		UCEA: Six modules WILL: Modules WISA: Hiring procedures manual
Internship	Lack of experience	FLAME: Evaluated by participants as one of the most rewarding activities; most interns were offered jobs at the conclusion of the field experience	FLAME: 12 women in executive-level internships in noneducational and educational settings ICES: 13 women in 10-month internships WISA: 12 interns in seven school districts
Support systems	Lack of support, encouragement, counseling Family and home responsibilities Lack of sponsorship	FLAME: Majority of interns had support of family	FLAME: Families of interns were invited to retreat workshop so they could understand the program and anticipate problems; family counseling made available; advisory groups of educators acted as sponsors WILL: Human Resources Center established to provide support system ICES: Each intern identified a support team in her district SEEL: Oregon Women in Educational Administration was formed as a support group
Networking	Too few role models Lack of networking	AWARE: Networks increased	SEEL: } UCEA: } Directories of women in administration SEEL: Oregon Women in Educational Administration; link with national organization AWARE: } FLAME: } HOSFTRA: } Formal network systems WISA: } FLAME: } Interns traveled to gain visibility

(continued)

APPENDIX Continued

Strategy	*Barrier(s) Targeted*	*Documented Outcomes*	*Examples of Use*
Political clout	Socialization/sex-role stereotyping Sex discrimination		SEEL: Oregon Women in Educational Administration
Legal remedies and affirmative action programs	Sex discrimination	Legal remedies: Little documentation on the number of successful and unsuccessful instances of litigation Affirmative action programs: Effectiveness of affirmative action programs has not been systematically studied	*Szewiola and Jones v. Los Angeles Unified School District* Oregon: New teaching standards require familiarity with EEO concepts and laws
Consciousness-raising and technical assistance to those who have impact on hiring policies and practices	Sex discrimination Socialization/sex-role stereotyping Lack of sponsorship Lack of network		WISA: Developed hiring procedures manual for use by school boards; held classes for men and women UCEA: Developed modules for professors of educational administration and policymakers in K-12 and higher education
		FLAME: Those superintendents who participated were most often supportive of interns SEEL: Internal sponsorship had high attendance; presentations to male groups less successful	FLAME: School superintendents were asked to participate in workshops and seminars SEEL: Presentations made to male groups
		Judgment analysis: Provides nonsexist evaluation	Judgment analysis: Technique used to provide nondiscriminatory rating performance
Creating jobs	Sex discrimination	Two FLAME interns created jobs for themselves	FLAME: Interns took courses in grant writing and submitted actual proposals

Index

About the Author

Charol Shakeshaft is Associate Professor and Director of the doctoral program in the Department of Administration and Policy Studies at Hofstra University. For the past eight years, she has coordinated a training program for women in educational administration, the only one of its kind in the United States. She researches and writes on the issues of gender and organizations, and on bias in educational research and theory. Her work has appeared in various books and journals including the *Educational Administration Quarterly, Phi Delta Kappan, Educational Researcher,* and *Issues in Education.*